TUNGKHUNGIA BURANJI

OR

A HISTORY OF ASSAM

1681-1826 A.D.

TUNGKHUNGIA BURANJI

OR,

A HISTORY OF ASSAM,

1681-1826 A.D.;

AN OLD ASSAMESE CHRONICLE OF THE TUNGKHUNGIA DYNASTY OF AHOM SOVEREIGNS

WITH MARGINALIA, GENEALOGICAL TABLES, BIBLIOGRAPHY, GLOSSARY, AND INDEX

COMPILER, EDITOR, TRANSLATOR

S. K. BHUYAN

GYAN

Published by

Gyan Publishing House
5, Ansari Road
Daryaganj, New Delhi-110002
Phone: 011-47034999, 9811692060
E-mail: books@gyanbooks.com

Distribution Network
gyanbooks.com
India, USA, Canada, UK, Australia

ISBN: 978-93-6920-073-3 (HB)
First Published, 1933

2nd Impression 2025

Printed at: Gyan Press, Delhi.

TUNGKHUNGIA BURANJI OR, A HISTORY OF ASSAM, 1681-1826 A.D.
Compiler, Editor, Translator: S. K. BHUYAN

TUNGKHUNGIA BURANJI

OR

A HISTORY OF ASSAM,

1681–1826 A.D.

MAHARAJA SIVA SINGHA,
King of Assam,
1714–1744 A.D.

শ্ৰীশ্ৰী মহাশিৱসিংহ মহাৰাজা

MAHARANI AMVIKA DEVI,
Queen Regnant of Assam,
1732–1739 A.D.

শ্ৰীশ্ৰীমতি অম্বিকাদেবী

roduced from an old painting
Hasti-vidyarnava D H A S.

TUNGKHUNGIA BURANJI

OR

A HISTORY OF ASSAM,

1681–1826 A.D.

An Old Assamese Chronicle of the
Tungkhungia Dynasty of Ahom Sovereigns

With Marginalia, Genealogical Tables, Bibliography, Glossary, and Index

Compiled, edited, and translated by

S. K. BHUYAN, M.A., B.L.

Professor, Cotton College, Gauhati, and Honorary Assistant Director of Historical and Antiquarian Studies, Assam

Humphrey Milford

OXFORD UNIVERSITY PRESS

LONDON BOMBAY CALCUTTA MADRAS

1933

1.

PUBLISHED BY THE OXFORD UNIVERSITY PRESS,
FOR THE GOVERNMENT OF ASSAM IN THE
DEPARTMENT OF HISTORICAL AND
ANTIQUARIAN STUDIES, ASSAM

PRINTED BY P. KNIGHT, AT THE BAPTIST MISSION PRESS,
41, LOWER CIRCULAR ROAD, CALCUTTA

नत्वा श्रीकृष्णपादाब्जौ सन्मनो मधुलेहकौ ।
लिख्यते शक्रवंश्यानां नृपाणाञ्जन्मकर्म्मणी ॥
विचित्रकर्म्मणां तेषां नृपाणां कर्म्मकीर्त्तने ।
नात्र हास्यास्पदं विज्ञा यतोऽनेकत्र संस्थितिः ।
एकत्रीकरणे तेषां शक्तिः केषां न कुण्ठिता ॥

After due salutation at the lotus-feet of Srikrishna, which are drunk by the hearts of the righteous like so many honey-sucking bees, the origin and deeds of the Kings sprung from the line of Indra are here described. Oh learned ones! In the recital of the history of those Kings who are credited with varied and brilliant achievements one is not to be an object of laughter (if mistakes and discrepancies creep in), as the accounts exist in diverse places, and in their unification whose powers are not strained?

—*Sanskrit preamble to an old Buranji.*

PREFACE.

The contents of the present book *Tungkhungia Buranji* fall distinctly into three classes :

First, the English translation of the Assamese chronicle of Srinath Duara Barbarua, the compilation of which was commenced on March 6, 1804, during the fifth year of the author's Barbaruaship. He gives a detailed account of the reigns of Rajeswar Singha, Lakshmi Singha, Gaurinath Singha and the first eleven years of the reign of Kamaleswar Singha, with a prefatory synopsis mentioning the dates of the Tungkhungia rulers from Gadadhar Singha to Gaurinath Singha. The Tungkhungia sovereigns ruled in Assam for 145 years, 1681–1826. Srinath's chronicle thus represents only the events of 55 years, 1751 to 1806. He calls his book "The Chronicle of Tungkhungia Kings"; but at best it is a fragmentary chronicle as the major portion of the Tungkhungia period is unrepresented in it. As a contemporary source-book the Barbarua's chronicle is extremely valuable as the author was a member of the distinguished Rangachila Duara family many of whom held the offices of Barbarua and Barphukan. The author had served the Ahom Government in several capacities, as a military commander, as chief justice and ultimately as the highest judicial and executive authority of the state till his dismissal in 1817 by his nephew Badanchandra Barphukan. The editor's aim has been to present the Barbarua's chronicle in as complete a form as possible by incorporating accounts of the preliminary and supplementary periods left out by the author. The Barbarua's chronicle corresponds to paragraph 1, the first 27 lines of paragraph 2, and paragraphs 83 to 342 of this book.

Second, the English translation of the history of the reigns of the first Tungkhungia King Gadadhar Singha and of his successors Rudra Singha, Siva Singha, and Pramatta Singha, 1681–1751, as well as the history of the eleven years of anarchy and misrule, 1670–1681, leading to the establishment of the Tungkhungia dynasty on the throne of Assam. This has been compiled by the editor from numerous contemporary Buranjis in the language and manner of the old chronicles. The editor has not framed any new sentence; he has simply picked up sentences or passages from the older chronicles and inserted them in due place in the evolution of a monarch's reign. No information acquired from sources other than old chronicles has been incorporated in this section. The editor's object has been to compile the history of the earlier period of the Tungkhungia supremacy in a style naturally fitting in with Srinath Barbarua's chronicle which follows. This new portion corresponds to the later 36 lines of paragraph 2, and paragraphs 3 to 82. The Assamese version of the *Tungkhungia Buranji*, which was published by the Department of Historical and Antiquarian Studies in December 1932, contains the first and second classes of contents described above.

Third, the Tungkhungia dynasty came to an end in 1826 when Assam was occupied by the British, and Srinath Barbarua's chronicle ends with the events of November 1806 amidst comparative peace and stability. The intervening twenty years, 1806 to 1826, witnessed momentous changes. The Burmese came, saw and conquered Assam; but being defeated in their wars with the British they handed over the province to the control and authority of the English East India Company. The English version of the *Tungkhungia Buranji* would be read by people who are not expected to have by their side other sources of information; and in order to complete the history of the Tungkhungia period the editor has compiled the history of the twenty years, 1806–1826, from numerous sources, published and unpublished. I have tried my best to make this new portion conform to the style of old chronicles, but as Assamese prose chronicles dealing with this period are absolutely non-existent I have found it difficult to consistently adhere to this ideal. My sources of information have been Assamese metrical chronicles, Ahom chronicles, records of the East India Company, ballads, coins, inscriptions, and published accounts. The critical outlook has been left severely alone, and has been given some scope in the Introduction. The supplementary portion compiled by me corresponds to paragraphs 343 to 377.

The object of the whole book has been to present to the world a history of Assam of the Tungkhungia period "as told by its own historians". Histories compiled on scientific and constructive lines have their own value as criticisms of facts; but the history of an Indian province written in a secluded place by contemporary eye-witnesses and actors is equally important as preserving in an unsophisticated form the outlooks, the political and social sympathies of the people, the germs of decay inherent in an oriental monarchy, and the lost opportunities of rehabilitation. The history of the 145 years of Ahom supremacy, as preserved in this book, gives us an accurate glimpse into the causes which led to the extinction of a great ruling power which exercised its supremacy for 600 years, and its ultimate incorporation as a distinct unit of the British Empire. Protracted internecine feuds and convulsions, which excited the wanton aggressiveness of the rapacious neighbours, are the circumstances which operated in many parts of India culminating in the downfall of Indian dynasties and the consequent expansion of British power in India. What happened in Assam happened almost all over India. Other provinces in India do not possess such elaborate, realistic contemporary records; and hence the dissolution of an Indian dynasty can be studied with great interest and advantage in the present chronicle *Tungkhungia Buranji*.

The limitations of the first translator of an old classic can be easily realised. He grapples with archaic expressions, names of offices, institutions and commodities which are now extinct, and ways of thinking and saying things which are no longer prevalent. His difficulties become more arduous if he has, besides, to translate from an old manuscript where the contents are not systematically arranged and the expressions tend to coalesce into one another due to the absence of punctuation marks. I have translated the original as literally as possible, aiming at the same time to give a translation that will be understood by any reader uninitiated in the Assamese way of thinking. Expressions deserving fuller explanation have been relegated to the Glossary, which thus compresses a mass of information on the political, social and religious system of the Assamese people. A Bibliography and four Genealogical Tables have been added to help readers who might be inclined to continue further their study of Assam history. The Index has been compiled on exhaustive lines. The paragraph numberings in the English version correspond to those of the Assamese text which will facilitate references and comparisons. We have inserted paragraph numbers as references in the Glossary and the Index.

The manuscript of Srinath Barbarua's chronicle is enclosed in a beautifully painted wooden box. The folios of the manuscript are made as usual of *Sachipat* or slices of the bark of aloes wood, *Aquilaria agallocha*. The other chronicles laid under contribution for the preliminary chapters are also made of the same *Sachipat*. The pictures of King Siva Singha and his consort Maharani Amvika Devi, inserted as frontispiece to this volume, have been reproduced from a contemporary painting, being one of the numerous illustrations forming part of the famous treatise on elephants entitled *Hasti-vidyarnava*, compiled by Sukumar Barkath under the orders of that royal pair in 1734 A.D. For further enlightenment on the subject of the *Tungkhungia Buranji* the reader is referred to the critical Introduction in the Assamese version of the book, pp. ix to xxvii, where the matter has been elaborately discussed under heads, Manuscript, Author, Date, Tungkhungia Dynasty, Historical Value and Literary Features.

It should be noted that the dates have been mentioned in paragraphs 1–342 according to the *Saka* era which has been prevalent in Assam from very ancient times. In the supplementary portion, paragraphs 343 to 377, the Christian era has been systematically used. The *Saka* year can be easily converted into the Christian year by adding 78 to the former if the dates fall within the first of Baisakha to the fifteenth of Poush; and 79 in other cases of dates from the sixteenth of Poush to the last day of Chaitra.

I acknowledge with thanks my indebtedness to Mr. A. H. W. Bentinck, C.I.E., I.C.S., M.A., Honorary Provincial Director of the Department of Historical and Antiquarian Studies, Assam, for providing funds for the publication of this volume; to Srijut Hiteswar Barbarua for supplying information which has been helpful in preparing the genealogical tables of the Tungkhungia dynasty; to Mr. P. Knight, Superintendent of the Baptist Mission Press, Calcutta, for his unfailing courtesy and personal interest in the printing of the book; to Srijuts Basudev Misra, B.A., and Madhabchandra Barooah, for assistance in the compilation of the Index and transcription of the prefatory and supplementary matter. The thanks of all students of history are due to the Government of Assam for their attempt to promote investigations into the history and antiquities of the Province as evinced by their establishment and continued maintenance of a distinct Department for that purpose.

S. K. BHUYAN,
Honorary Assistant Director of Historical and Antiquarian Studies, Assam.

Cotton College,
Gauhati, Assam.
September 1, 1933.

CONTENTS.

TUNGKHUNGIA BURANJI

APPENDICES

INTRODUCTION.

Assamese Buranjis.

The *Tungkhungia Buranji* is one of the numerous Assamese chronicles or Buranjis which were preserved in olden times in all families of distinction. The Buranjis were to the Assamese what the *Bakhars* were to the Mahrattas, the *Twarikhis* to the Moguls and the Persians, the *Yazawins* or *Rajawins* to the Burmese and the *P'ongsawadans* to the Siamese. The term *Buranji*, originally a word of Ahom or Shan origin, has been naturalised in Assamese, being applied to all chronicles or histories. The Ahoms maintained regular chronicles of their rule up to its termination and even later. They were compiled by duly appointed officers who were granted free access to the deliberations of the court and the archives of the state. They were also compiled by private scholars with the help of other existing chronicles and materials collected by them. The Buranjis are a direct product of the universal custom in vogue among the Tai race, the Shans, the Burmans, the Siamese and the Chinese of reducing all important things to writing, and they are profuse and varied. Assamese historical literature is the legacy which the people of the Brahmaputra Valley have received from their contact with the Ahom invaders and settlers. The Buranjis were first compiled in the Ahom language and later on in Assamese as well; and their use was universal as they offered all precedents on which the Ahom government was conducted, the laws administered, pedigrees ascertained and titles conferred. The Buranjis are valuable studies inasmuch as they have conserved the customs, the traits, the hopes and aspirations of the people. They are also perfect specimens of racy Assamese prose and their value is enhanced by the fact that very few countries in India had such a developed prose literature as Assamese. The universal absence of historical literature among the numerous peoples and races of India and their existence in Assam have led Sir George Abraham Grierson to write,—"The Assamese are justly proud of their national literature. In no department have they been more successful than in a branch of study in which India, as a whole, is curiously deficient. The historical works, or *Buranjis*, as they are styled by the Assamese, are numerous and voluminous. According to the custom of the country, a knowledge of the *Buranjis* was an indispensable qualification to an Assamese gentleman".[1]

The Assamese Buranjis are supplementary in their character. No two Buranjis contain the same set of facts. One Buranji dismisses

---

[1] *Linguistic Survey of India*, Vol. I, Part I, Introductory, p. 156.

the invasion of Mir Jumla in two folios while another expands the theme in twenty folios. It is surprising that such a large number of Buranjis have been found to exist in Assam at the present time when we recollect the convulsions and revolutions through which the country has passed, namely, the insurrections of the Moamarias, the depredations of the Burmese, combined with the havocs made by fires, earthquakes and floods. In our belief the Buranjis constitute the most effective weapon in strengthening the solidarity of the Assamese people as a distinct racial and cultural entity.

The present-day Assamese type, specially among the educated section of the people, is a lamentable anomaly as far as cultural affinities are concerned. His sympathies and predilections are extensive and numerous and are more inclined towards divergence from the original racial standard than towards conformity to it. The world is drifting towards a kind of utopian internationalism which tends towards the abolition of racial individuality which is pooh-poohed and derided under the name "provincialism". But the strength of all ideals of world-nationalism lies in the variety and distinctiveness of the contributory streams of nationalities. The Assamese as a distinct race, with an individual background of history and civilization, will be an asset of greater potentiality in the parliament of nations than their atrophied existence as a mere replica of Nation B or Nation C.

The Buranjis were compiled during, and deal with the events of, the centuries before the avalanche of changes had swept over India; the Buranjis have conserved the original outlooks, feelings, political thoughts, social and religious sympathies of the Assamese people when they were a distinct race uninfluenced by any exterior circumstance or surrounding, and unthreatened by the grim spectre of denationalisation.

The historical instinct of the Assamese people led them to take interest in other countries besides their own. We have regular chronicles in Assamese dealing with the Muhammadan rulers of Delhi, the Afghan Sultans and the Mogul Emperors, all written during the seventeenth century when the Assam-Mogul relations were brought to their highest tension. In the pages of Assamese chronicles we have numerous references to the contemporary events of Mogul history besides numerous epistles exchanged between the Ahom kings and the Emperors of Delhi or their subordinate governors, ministers and commanders.[1]

---

[1] The *Padshah-Buranji* dealing with the Muhammadan rulers of Delhi written in the seventeenth century has been edited from several versions by Prof. S. K. Bhuyan. It is being published by the Kamarupa Anusandhan Samiti, Gauhati, Assam. A complete English translation of the *Padshah-Buranji* by Prof. Bhuyan has been published as a serial in *Islamic Culture*, Hyderabad, Deccan, from its issue of January, 1933.

Ascendency of the House of Tungkhung

The present book *Tungkhungia Buranji* is a chronicle of the last dynasty of the Ahom sovereigns of Assam. The Ahoms ruled in Assam from A.D. 1228 to 1826, till it passed into the hands of the British by the Treaty of Yandaboo. The Tungkhungia dynasty wielded the Ahom sceptre for the last 145 years, from 1681 to 1826. The dynasty has derived its name from the village Tungkhung or Tingkhang in Upper Assam where they had their ancestral residence. King Suhungmung, 1497–1539, established his sons at different places, and the different Ahom royal houses, Dihingia, Charingia, Tipamia, Namrupia, Parvatia and Tungkhungia, sprang from these princely establishments. Suteng, son of Suhungmung, was the first prince to settle at Tungkhung. He had a son named Saranga Gohain. In January 1675, an intriguous noble named Debera Barbarua set up Saranga Gohain's son Gobar Gohain on the Ahom throne, but he reigned only for twenty days, after which he was dethroned by the saner section of the Ahom aristocrats, who were determined to put an end to the unscrupulous designs of Debera. Gobar was followed by Sujinpha Dihingia Raja in 1675, Sudaipha Parvatia Raja in 1677 and Sulikpha Samaguria Raja in 1679. These three monarchs were, like their predecessors, mere puppets in the hands of the ministers.

During the reign of Sudaipha Parvatia Raja, the ambitious Ahom viceroy of Gauhati, Laluksola Barphukan, surrendered the territory under his charge to Nawab Mansur Khan, a deputy of Sultan Azamtara, Governor of Bengal. The Barphukan then proceeded up to the Ahom capital in Upper Assam, deposed Sudaipha and placed Sulikpha, a stripling of fourteen years on the throne, and assumed virtual sovereign powers. He organised an extensive campaign of disqualifying all possible rivals to the throne by maiming or mutilating their limbs. Gobar Raja's son Gadapani eluded the vigilance of Laluksola Barphukan's emissaries. They seized the person of Gadapani's wife Jaymati Kuanri and attempted to extract information from her about her husband's movements. The princess refused to offer any clue whatsoever which might lead to the discovery of her husband's whereabouts. The severest tortures were inflicted upon the inexorable princess but she prepared to die in the hands of the royal executioners rather than become an instrument of her husband's destruction. The high-handed actions of Laluk Barphukan and the domination of the Moguls over Western Assam opened the eyes of the hereditary ministers and nobles. They searched for prince Gadapani as he was looked upon as the only man who could effectively combat the intrigues and designs of self-seeking potentates and recover Western Assam from the hands of the foreigners. They assembled at Kaliabar where they declared prince Gadapani as king. The monarch designate proceeded up to the capital Gargaon where he was formally installed on the throne under the name Gadadhar Singha. Sulikpha was deported to the impenetrable wilds of Namrup where he was subsequently killed. Gadadhar Singha was the founder of the Tungkhungia dynasty, and the princes of this line exercised the reins of government till the termination of Ahom rule in 1826.

Earlier Ahom History

The Ahoms, a branch of the Shan race, crossed the Patkai range to the south-east of Assam in the early years of the thirteenth century A.D. under the leadership of Sukapha, who was compelled to leave his ancestral kingdom of Nara as he had no prospect of sovereignty there. Sukapha's followers hardly came up to a thousand and they had left behind their women folk as being incapable of undergoing the strenuous hardships of hill-climbers and adventurers. The Ahoms were thus compelled to increase their numerical strength by incorporating non-Ahoms into their fold accompanied by inter-marriage with the original settlers of the land.

By right of joint conquest the enjoyment of the soil was vested in the leader Sukapha, and his commanders and camp-followers who had shared with him the fatigues of the adventurous march. All subsequent appointments in the Ahom administration were made on this understanding. Sukapha's descendants enjoyed a hereditary title to the throne; those of his commanders and camp-followers to the principal offices of the state; and this principle was followed throughout the entire period of Ahom rule in Assam. Only the descendants of Sukapha's Buragohain and Bargohain could be appointed to these respective posts; and the Barbarua and the Barphukan must always be selected from the four leading families who had accompanied Sukapha, viz., Lahan, Duara, Dihingia and Sandikai. Any appointment from outside these families was viewed with disfavour by the nobiliary of the land. The language and religion of the Ahoms were distinct from those of the conquered races, but gradually the Ahom rulers accepted the Assamese language and the Hindu religion, and the change was perceptible from the reign of Pratap Singha, 1603–1641.

From the thirteenth to the sixteenth centuries the Ahoms were mainly busy in consolidating their power and in adjusting the relationship with the neighbouring principalities, Kamata which was subsequently transformed into the well-known Cooch Behar kingdom, Cachar, Jayantia, Darrang, Chutia and Kamrup. The principality of Kamrup, a part of a much greater kingdom of the same name, was contiguous to the Mogul territories, and thus as a bone of contention it became the theatre of many a long-drawn contest between the forces of the Moguls and the Ahoms. The history of the Ahoms of the seventeenth century was the history of the Assam-Mogul conflicts. Cooch Behar intervened now and then but its hold over Kamrup was abortive and easily resistible.

The veteran general Nawab Mir Jumla, the uncrowned king of Golkonda and the Carnatic, the right hand of Aurangzeb in the War of Succession, entered the borders of Assam in January 1662, marched through the entire length of the country and occupied the Ahom capital Gargaon. The Treaty of Ghilajari enacted in January 1663 between the Ahom King Jayadhwaj Singha and the Mogul general Mir Jumla transferred Kamrup to the Moguls and imposed a heavy war-indemnity upon the Ahoms. Jayadhwaj Singha's successor Chakradhwaj Singha launched elaborate preparations to re-establish the lost prestige of his country. The courageous personality of the Ahom king was imbibed by his generals and his soldiers. Kamrup was wrested back from the Moguls in August 1667. The Assamese general was Lachit Barphukan, son of Momai-Tamuli Barbarua, who was the leading figure in the Assam-Mogul conflicts of the first half of the century. Chakradhwaj died in the lap of victory, and his successor Udayaditya Singha continued his predecessor's policy with equal tact and vigour. Aurangzeb despatched a fresh army under Raja Ram Singha of Amber. The Ahoms concentrated all their resources at Gauhati, the capital of Kamrup. The Mogul army was lured into the war-zone of Gauhati, fortified on all sides by natural hills and artificial ramparts with the mighty Brahmaputra flowing in between. In the battle of Saraighat, fought in the vicinity of Gauhati in March 1671, a crushing defeat was inflicted on the Mogul army and Ram Singha retired to the frontier Mogul garrison at Rangamati where he waited till 1676 for another opportunity to invade Assam.

The eventual renewal of hostilities with the Moguls was foreshadowed by the Ahoms, and all their best generals and nobles were deputed to Gauhati to remain in vigilant preparedness. The Ahom capital Gargaon was manned by inferior talents and arms who took advantage of the absence of the able leaders and exploited the opportunity for self-aggrandisement. Machinations and intrigues became the order of the day. Kings became mere puppets; they were appointed, dismissed and killed as suited the convenience of the king-making ministers. Chaos and anarchy ruled the land and some of the Saraighat veterans even were tainted by the widespread demoralization. The Moguls were in occupation of Gauhati; discordance and rivalry were rampant in the Ahom camp; and the next inevitable consequence would be the reduction of the entire kingdom to the vassalage of the Moguls. There were traitors and patriots in the fold; the former had played their rôle and brought their country to the verge of destruction. It was now the turn of the patriots to do what they could. They assembled at Kaliabar and deliberated on the affairs of the state. "Our only remedy is a strong-minded prince" was their deliberate and unanimous decision, and the selection naturally fell on prince Gadapani, who had already gained reputation in the land for his vigilance, fortitude and adroitness.

Tungkhungia Period

Gadadhar Singha ruled the country for fifteen years, 1681 to 1696 A.D. With an iron hand he put an end to the intrigues and machinations of the preceding period. Western Assam was wrested back from the Moguls in July 1682, and the boundaries of Assam were restored to their original limit. The river Manaha became as of old the western limit of Assam. Peace and order were established and the people began to live with confidence and security. Gadadhar Singha was a man of extraordinarily vigorous constitution and his dietetic vagaries have become traditional in the land. He viewed with disfavour the growing influence of the Vaisnava monks; he confiscated their property and put several of them to torture and death.

King Gadadhar Singha was succeeded by his son Rudra Singha, 1696–1714. The son was more statesmanlike than his father. He formulated a definite policy of his administration and exerted his utmost powers to carry it out as far as time and circumstances would permit. He aimed at elevating his kingdom to the rank of a first-rate power in India. He began by reforming the internal administration of the land with a view to secure the highest degree of efficiency. With the resources of a fully developed state at his command he proposed to unfurl the flag of victory in the neighbouring Mogul territories, and if possible to seize the throne of Delhi. He restored the Vaisnava abbots to their original homes, encouraged arts, literature and music, and remodelled the state army on the most up-to-date lines. The neighbouring territories of Jayantia and Cachar were subdued and their chiefs made promises to help the Ahom King with men and provision when such aid would be solicited. The vassal chieftains on the Assam frontier were bound by treaty terms to render timely assistance to their liege-lord. Rudra Singha deputed agents in the garb of itinerant hermits to different places of India to study the customs of these places and collect informations regarding their resources and strength. When the preparations were completed the King left the capital and marched to Gauhati where his army was joined by those of his allies and the vassal chieftains. The King deputed messengers to the Rajas of different parts of India asking them not to offer him any resistance in his expedition. The messengers came back with a reply from the Rajas that they would render all possible co-operation to the powerful Swargamaharaja of Assam if he attempted to occupy the throne of Delhi as the indignities hurled at them by the Mogul Badshahs were becoming more and more intolerable. Rudra Singha mobilised at Gauhati an army of 4,00,000 and he planned to enter into Mogul territories in November 1714. When preparations were on foot for the march of the expedition Rudra Singha suddenly died at Gauhati in September 1714. If the greatness of a man is to be judged by the greatness of his designs and his conscious and rigorous efforts to uplift his country, apart from any success which finally meet his endeavours Rudra Singha can be called Rudra Singha the Great. It will be easy to imagine the impression that would have been made by the dash and gallantry of the primitive mountaineers who constituted the backbone of Rudra Singha's legions upon the ease-loving and discontented hosts of the Timurid generals. Emperor Aurangzeb had died seven years before; and Delhi, now reduced to a theatre of contest between rival powers, excited the cupidity of trans-border invaders.

Siva Singha succeeded Rudra Singha, 1714–1744. The new monarch unfortunately lacked the courage and foresight of his great father. He accepted initiation into Saktaism from the hand of Krishnaram Bhattacharyya of Nadiya. The monarch newly initiated into the mysteries of Tantric worship devoted more time to religious practices than his royal preoccupations permitted. The astrologers found out by calculating the stars that the dethronement of the monarch would be an inevitable feature of his reign. He therefore surrendered his sceptre to his consorts Phuleswari Devi, Ambika Devi and Sarveswari Devi in succession. Phuleswari Devi with the characteristic fanaticism of a neophyte insulted a number of Vaisnava monks by rubbing on their forehead the blood of goats sacrificed in the worship of Durga. The Mahanta of Moamara who had a very large number of disciples and whose wealth and influence were the talk of the day was among the insulted monks. He and his disciples began thenceforth to plan schemes of revenge.

Siva Singha was succeeded by his brother Pramatta Singha, 1744–1751. He was a sober monarch and governed his country with discretion and benevolence.

After the death of Pramatta Singha his brother Mohanmala Gohaindeo was entitled to the throne according to the death-bed injunction of King Rudra Singha. Kirtichandra Barbarua, the most powerful potentate of the time, set aside the claims of Mohanmala and placed his younger brother Rajeswar Singha on the throne who reigned from 1751 to 1769. Rajeswar Singha proved a capable monarch and the kingdom attained in his time the acme of peace and prosperity. There was no disturbance, no war and no cause of annoyance in his reign of any significant character. Jai Singha, Raja of Manipur, solicited the aid of the Ahom monarch to expel the Burmese usurpers from Manipur. Rajeswar Singha despatched a vast army against the Burmans and was in turn offered the hands of Jai Singha's daughter Kuranganayani. Kirtichandra by his acts of imperiousness and hauteur irritated the other nobles and a murderous attempt was made on his life. The Barbarua destroyed all chronicles which were supposed to contain calumniating references to his descent. He irritated the Moamara Mahanta on several occasions, but the Mahanta refrained from any act of violence out of consideration for the benignant monarch.

Rajeswar Singha was succeeded by his brother Lakshmi Singha, 1769–1780. His succession to the throne, though it was in conformity with the will of Rudra Singha, was not a popular one, as he was blackish in hue which originated suspicion about his legitimacy. Kirtichandra acting with his customary high-handedness banished Rajeswar Singha's sons and wives to Namrup, and gave fresh provocation to the Moamara Mahanta by attributing to him illicit behaviour with the exiled consorts of Rajeswar Singha during their halt near the Mahanta's monastery to receive supplies of food-provisions. He further inflicted undeserving punishment on a leading disciple of the Moamara Mahanta, Ragha Moran. The Mahanta and his disciples who were long waiting for an opportunity to strike now raised the standard of revolt, marched against Rangpur, occupied the capital and seized the person of the King and his principal nobles in their retreat near the Sonari river. Nahar Khora's son Ramakanta became Raja and Ragha Barbarua became the *de facto* ruler. Kirtichandra Barbarua, the Buragohain and the Bargohain were executed by the rebels. Ragha Barbarua admitted into his harem the ex-queen Kuranganayani and a numerous bevy of Ahom damsels. He summoned all the Vaisnava monks and compelled them to accept initiation from the Moamara Mahanta. The royalists were now roused to action, they intrigued with Kuranganayani and killed Ragha in April 1770 followed by massacre of the leading Moran rebels. Lakshmi Singha was restored to his lost throne. He suppressed the Moamaria insurrection with a firm and determined hand, and during the remaining ten years of his reign there was no effective recrudescence of the Moamaria discontent. But the succession of the sons of Rudra Singha to the throne one after the other left in the country a large number of disgruntled and disappointed princes who were the sons and grandsons of the reigning monarchs. Besides, the Moamaria success exposed the vulnerability of the Ahom crown. The princes attempted, though severally, to seize the throne, but their ill-planned and impetuous efforts were easily detected and suppressed.

Lakshmi Singha was succeeded by his son Gaurinath Singha, 1780–1795. He was the only son of his father and shared all the effects of a bad training. He was a libertine ; and his cruelties and whims were disgusting to all except his time-serving myrmidons. The Moamarias, long held in check, rose again with redoubled fury. Rangpur was occupied by the rebels for a few days but it was recovered through the timely measures of Ghanashyam Buragohain. Ghanashyam died in 1782 and was succeeded by his son Purnananda, who remained in power till the advent of the Burmese in 1817. The Moamaria insurgents now concentrated their attacks in the north bank, and the Ahom commanders sent against them attained but little success. The Moamarias if subdued in one place again appeared at another and the royalist army could not encounter the guerilla methods of the enemy. Gaurinath fled down to Gauhati and the Buragohain shifted the headquarters to Jorhat. The Manipuri Raja Jai Singha came in person to fight against the rebels but his participation was equally futile and ineffective. In the meantime freebooters from Bengal taking advantage of the internal disruption had entered into Assam and harassed and plundered the defenceless inhabitants. King Gaurinath Singha requested Lord Cornwallis, Governor-General of India, to expel the Burkendaz pillagers from the land and help him in re-occupying the capital. Captain Welsh with a contingent of sepoys reached Gauhati in November 1792, escorted Gaurinath to Upper Assam, subdued the rebels and re-occupied Rangpur. Gaurinath was placed on his ancestral throne, and Captain Welsh returned to Calcutta in July 1794 after having enacted a treaty for the promotion of commercial intercourse between Assam and the East India Company.

Gaurinath Singha was succeeded by Kamaleswar Singha, a descendant of Lechai Namrupia Raja, brother of Rudra Singha. The zone of rebellion was now shifted to Kamrup, Nowgong and North Lakshimpur; but the insurrections at these three different places were subdued through the timely measures of Purnananda Buragohain. Ahom subjects had sought refuge in the outlying districts of Cachar, Jayantia, Bhutan and Bengal. The Buragohain deputed embassies to these states demanding the repatriation of the Assamese fugitives. The Singphous and Khamtis near Sadiya had frequently entered into the jurisdiction of Assam and carried off a large number of Assamese subjects as captives. An expedition was sent to Sadiya in November 1806. The old chronicle of Srinath Barbarua ends here abruptly and what follows next has been compiled by the translator from published and unpublished sources to bring down the history to the termination of Ahom rule in 1826.

Kamaleswar Singha was succeeded by his brother Chandrakanta Singha, 1811–1818. Chandrakanta was only fourteen years old when he assumed sovereign power. Purnananda Buragohain was all in all but his unlimited powers were viewed with jealousy and suspicion by Chandrakanta's favourites and sycophants of whom Satram Bhutar Putek was the most powerful. Satram organised a conspiracy to kill the Buragohain. The name of Badanchandra Barphukan, the Ahom viceroy of Gauhati, was found among the papers in possession of Satram and his accomplices. Purnananda deputed emissaries to arrest Badanchandra but the wily Barphukan having received previous intelligence of this design fled from Gauhati, proceeded to Calcutta and then to Ava. The Burmese monarch King Bodawpaya granted him an army to enable him to wreak vengeance upon his enemies in Assam. The Barphukan made his appearance on the frontier of Assam with his Burmese hordes in March 1817. The Buragohain died accidentally of fever and his son and successor Ruchinath Buragohain could not offer an effective resistance to the Burmans. Through the instrumentality of Badanchandra, Chandrakanta entered into peace terms with the Burmans and they retired to their country with presents from the Ahom sovereign. At the instigation of Dhani Barbarua, Nirbhaynarayan Bargohain and Numali Rajmao, Badanchandra was murdered one morning by Rupsing Subedar and Rahman Khan Jamadar.

Chandrakanta was suspected as being instrumental in bringing the Burmans to Assam by deputing Badanchandra to Burma. Ruchinath took up the cause of Purandar Singha, a descendant of Ratneswar Gohain, son of Rajeswar Singha. Ruchinath and his party marched up to Rangpur, deposed Chandrakanta and placed Purandar Singha on the throne.

The king of Burma regarded the murder of Badanchandra and the deposal of Chandrakanta as an affront offered to himself and he deputed a fresh army to punish the enemies of Chandrakanta. The battle of Phulpanichiga fought between the Burmese army and the adherents of Purandar Singha resulted in the victory of the invaders. Purandar Singha fled down to Bengal and Chandrakanta was placed once more on the throne after which the Burmans left Assam having perpetrated atrocities upon all those suspected to have sympathy for Purandar.

Having recovered his throne Chandrakanta made preparations for effectively counteracting future Burmese designs in Assam. This was reported to the Burmese monarch who now despatched an army to punish Chandrakanta. The Ahom monarch fled to Gauhati and the Burmans placed Jogeswar Singha on the throne. The Burmese commander-in-chief was the virtual ruler of Assam and Jogeswar's elevation to the throne was only a make-believe to pacify the Assamese people. In the meantime the Burmese had come into collision with the British in Manipur, Cachar and Jayantia accompanied by sporadic fightings. The British, aiming at dislodging the Burmans from the commanding position they occupied up the river Brahmaputra, ordered the marching of troops from Goalpara towards Gauhati. The Burman resistance to the British army during the ten months of their conflicts, March 1824 to January 1825, was of no avail. Rangpur, the Assamese capital, was occupied by the British, and promises were extracted from the Burman commanders that they would no longer interfere with the affairs of Assam. By the Treaty of Yandaboo enacted on February 24, 1826, Assam finally passed into the hands of the British; and with it the supremacy of the Tungkhungia dynasty came to an end.

A Survey of the Period

We shall now refer to the pivotal landmarks round which revolved the main trend of the events of the Tungkhungia period. Laluksola Barphukan's bloodless surrender of Western Assam to the Mogul Fauzadar Nawab Mansur Khan for a consideration of four lakhs of rupees and a flimsy promise by Sultan Azamtara to make the Barphukan king of Eastern Assam, followed by the

Barphukan's assumption of sovereign power and the elaborate campaign to disqualify all possible rivals to the throne, culminating in the martyrdom of Princess Jaymati, compelled the ministers and nobles to search for a capable prince who would readily suppress such acts of high-handed usurpation and save the country from the yoke of foreign domination. Gadadhar Singha's recovery of Western Assam terminated the long-drawn hostilities between the Moguls and the Ahoms. The monarch's attempt to dissolve the Vaishnava monasteries evinced his Sakta proclivities, and alienated the sympathy of the ancient hierarchy of Vaishnava leaders who had a very vast and powerful following in the country. In Rudra Singha's scheme to conquer Bengal and if possible the rest of Mogul India, was reached the high-water-mark of nationalistic idealism, which vanished with the last breath of that illustrious monarch.

Siva Singha's initiation into Sakta Hinduism threw the Vaishnava monks into the background, and Phuleswari's attempt to humiliate the peace-loving Vaishnava pontiffs deepened their apathy, if not their antipathy, towards the Ahom crown. The hope of political preferments did not infrequently inspire the adoption of the new creed among the leading officials and nobles. The monarchs became ardent devotees of the elaborate rituals and ceremonies connected with the new faith, and the orthodox Ahom priests viewed this change as the beginning of the end of Ahom supremacy. Adherence to common interests and objects among a people having divergent religious sympathies became a thing of the past. Kirtichandra Barbarua's exclusion of Mohanmala Gohaindeo from his lawful succession to the throne was an extremely unpopular measure as the prince was the people's pet and the ministers' darling. Kirtichandra's support of Lakshmi Singha in his candidature for the throne to the exclusion of the sons of the preceding monarch Rajeswar Singha was an impolitic act as Lakshmi Singha's legitimacy was seriously in question owing to his dark complexion. Kirtichandra's overbearing temper, partially kept in check by the strong hand of Rajeswar Singha, now burst forth into full play during the reign of Lakshmi Singha, Kirtichandra's nominee on the throne. The Barbarua inflicted unwarranted insults on the Moamara Mahanta and one of his chief disciples, which precipitated the insurrection of the Morans long seething underground. The rebels occupied the capital and exercised all the powers of sovereignty. They would have been able to perpetuate their government if they had conducted it on sober and systematic lines rigorously resisting the temptations of the moment. The daring intelligence and pluck of the Manipuri princess Kuranganayani effected Lakshmi Singha's restoration to the throne.

Gaurinath Singha ordered the ruthless massacre of the Moamarias among whom were counted the redoubtable stalwarts of the land. The insurrection was not confined to the disciples of the Moamara Mahanta; many leading potentates had joined the standard of the mutineers or entertained secret sympathy with their cause. The forces of disruption moved on apace and the gauntlet was taken up by the survivors including amiable matrons and virgins. The appointment of Purnananda Buragohain to the office of the Prime Minister in 1782 brought to the side of the royalists a capable, far-sighted and sagacious statesman-warrior. But it was impossible for him in the beginning to counteract the elements of disorder brought into existence by the rapacity and indiscretion of the nobles of the preceding regime. The King fled to Gauhati from where he moved from place to place in Nowgong where he was received with indifferent courtesy.

The intervention of the Honourable East India Company was instrumental in restoring Gaurinath Singha to his ancestral throne, and it laid the foundation of the commercial relations between Assam and the Company's traders. The establishment of commercial intercourse with Assam was long solicited by the European merchants of Bengal, but it could not be placed on a sound and secure footing owing to the reluctance of the Assamese to admit foreigners into their land. Assam was now discovered to the British and *vice versa* to their prolonged and mutual benefit. Assamese troops were trained on the lines of the Company's army, and the Ahom government purchased ordnances and ammunitions from the British factories at Calcutta.

There was considerable peace during the reign of Gaurinath Singha's successor Kamaleswar Singha and the latter's brother Chandrakanta Singha. Purnananda Buragohain's selection of Satram, the son of a poultry-keeper, to be the companion of the boy-king Chandrakanta, was a blunder of the highest magnitude. Satram uninspired by considerations of gratefulness towards his benefactor poisoned the ears of the young king against the veteran patriot and statesman Purnananda Buragohain. The result was a conspiracy to murder the Premier followed by the despatch of emissaries to arrest Badanchandra Barphukan. The Barphukan's flight to Calcutta and then to Burma introduced the Burmans to the paths and defiles, the wealth and resources of the Brahmaputra Valley which were vigilantly guarded for centuries from the observations of foreigners and aliens. Assam, already weakened by internal jealousies and dissensions, became an easy prey to the first touch of the Burmese spear.

Extent and Limits of Assam

After the recovery of Western Assam from the Moguls in July, 1682, during the reign of Gadadhar Singha, the boundaries of Assam remained fixed and unaltered till the occupation of the country by the British. The Assam of those days was practically equal to the Brahmaputra Valley or Assam Proper of the present day, *minus* the district of Goalpara. It was bounded on the north by the

Bhutan hills, on the west by the Manaha river and the Habraghat Pargana, on the south by the Naga, Khasi, Mikir and Garo hills, and on the east by the Mismi, Singphou and Khamti ranges. The total population of Ahom Assam during the reign of Rajeswar Singha before the depredations of the Moamarias and the Burmese was computed at 24,00,000. During these disturbances many were killed, many took shelter in the districts of the Surma Valley and of Bengal, many were carried off as captives by the Singphous and the Khamtis and many more by the Burmese conquerors. It is generally believed that between the death of Rajeswar Singha in 1769 and the occupation of the country by the British in 1825 Assam lost half its population by the above processes. The population has been on the increase since 1825 and the total strength of the Assamese-speaking people at the present time is 1,994,564 and the total population of the Assam Valley is 4,855,711, according to the Census of 1931.

Dr. John Peter Wade, who came to Assam in 1792 as Assistant Surgeon to Captain Welsh's detachment, has penned the following lines about the extent and limits of Assam in his *Geographical Sketch of Assam*, compiled between 1796 and 1802, and the only manuscript copy of which is preserved in the India Office Library, London.—

"The kingdom of Assam is seven hundred miles in length and from sixty to eighty in breadth. In a few places however of Upper Assam where the mountainous confines recede furthest the breadth greatly exceeds this proportion; and it will be within a very moderate calculation to consider the surface as containing about sixty thousand square miles; and extent much superior to that of England which is stated at forty-nine thousand, four hundred and fifty. From this computation may be deducted the numerous rivers, which everywhere intersect the country. I shall not offer a vague conjecture on the sum of this deduction; but it will not be exaggeration to say that the remainder exhibits a highly fertile soil throughout; for even the great number of hills which are interspersed in every part of Assam are susceptible of cultivation, and increase considerably the superfices of the country fit for culture. From this computation of square miles, are excluded all the dependencies and conquered countries in or beyond the mountainous limits which surround Assam in every direction; as well as several provinces of Eastern Bengal, which formerly acknowledged their subjection to the Assamese Government.

"Assam is a valley. It extends between the parallels of 25–45 and 27–30 degrees of North Latitude and from 90–95 to between 98 or 99 degrees of East Longitude. This extent to the Eastward beyond the capital Gargaon is of course conjectural; for it was not my fortune to meet with a single Native who has travelled to the utmost limit of Assam in that quarter. The kingdom is separated by the great stream of the Brahmaputra into three grand divisions called Uttarkol or Uttarpar, Dakhinkol or Dakhinpar and the Majuli or great island. The first denotes the provinces lying on the northside of Brahmaputra, the second those on the south. The Majuli is a large island in the middle. It is also divided into Upper and Lower Assam; the first includes the country above Kaliabar, where the river diverges into two considerable streams as far as the mountainous confines to the north and south. This division included the whole of Assam at an earlier period; but the lower provinces to the westward having been afterwards annexed by conquest to the dominions of the Swargadeo, became a separate Government under an officer entitled Burra-Phukan with the powers of a viceroy. The distinction of Uttarkol and Dakhinkol were previous to the period in question, applicable only to Upper Assam; and the more learned among the natives affect to confine those appellations even now to the Eastern provinces only."

THE AHOM SYSTEM OF ADMINISTRATION

Some knowledge of the essential features of the Ahom administration is necessary to read this book with advantage. The Ahom government was a monarchical oligrachy. The king, or Swargadeo, as he was called, was the supreme head of the state; and all honours, titles, offices, decisions, and war-measures, emanated from him. But he had to act according to the advice of the three hereditary councillors of state, the Buragohain, the Bargohain and the Barpatragohain. The duty of selecting a king from among the members of the existing princely families was vested in these three nobles, and if united they could dethrone or execute a monarch. A powerful sovereign could override the decisions of the three Gohains, and similarly an astute Gohain could impose his will upon his two colleagues and the vast body of Phukans and Baruas. The Barbarua was the head of the executive and the judiciary, but he could not act independently of the three Gohains. Any matter placed before the king by the Barbarua would be considered in the presence of the three Gohains, and if it was one of great moment the Phukans and Baruas would also be summoned to express their opinion.

The Barphukan lived at Gauhati as the king's deputy and administered the territory from Kaliabar to the frontier of Mogul India. He conducted the diplomatic negotiations with Bengal and Bhutan and the chieftains on the Assam frontier. The states of Jayantia, Cachar, Manipur, and Khyrim were in friendly alliance with the Ahom government, though some degree of subordination was accepted by the first two through the usages of centuries. The province of Darrang enjoyed complete autonomy in its internal affairs, as well as the other vassal states,—Rani, Beltola, Luki, Barduar, Bholagaon, Mairapur, Pantan, Bangaon, Bagaduar, Dumaria, Neli, Gobha, Sahari, Dandua, Barepujia, Topakuchia, Khaighoria, Panbari, Sora, Mayang, Dhing, Tetelia, Salmara, Garakhia, Baghara and Bhurbandha. The frontiers of the kingdom were protected from the inroads of the hill people by several wardens, the Sadiya-khowa

Gohain, the Marangi-khowa Gohain, the Solal Gohain, the Jagiyalia Gohain and the Kajalimukhia Gohain, and they were always selected from the families of the three Gohains at the metropolis. The frontier tribesmen were allowed regular blackmail either in the shape of money, articles or servitors.

The representation of the different Ahom families or *faids* was an important factor in the grant of appointments. The king had to be selected from the royal families, Dihingia, Charingia, Tungkhungia, Namrupia, Samaguria and Parvatia. The members of the different princely dynasties sprang from their common ancestor Sukapha, and their settlement in different places occasioned by the expansion of their numbers led to the existence of the different *faids*. This was also the case with the different branches of the Buragohain and Bargohain families. The Buragohain clans were Tepartalia, Kuoigayan, Bahgaria, Langkakia, Moran-gharia and Railungia; and those of the Bargohain were Guimela, Parvatia, Pilinga, Mechagaria, Madurial, Kalugayan, Dihingia, Chatai-alia, Barukial and Miri-Sandikai. The several Barpatra-gohain families were Nagapatra, Kenduguria, Kalugayan and Moran-patra, but they did not all spring from a common ancestor. The Barbarua and the Barphukan were selected from the following families, Dihingia, Lahan, Sandikai, Duara, Ghora-kowanr, Patar, Buragohain, Bakatial and Lukhurakhan. A few Barbaruas were selected from Moran Barpatra, Chengdhara, Charingia-Letao, Kachari, Chiring and Khamti families; and a few Barphukans from Langi, Lanmakharu, Chetia, Pikchai-chetia and Tarun Duara families. The Ahom priestly families were those of the Deodhais, Mohans, Bailungs and Chirings.

An officer was generally mentioned with reference to his family, as Bakatial Barbarua, Sandikai Barphukan, Kuoigayan Buragohain and Madurial Bargohain. Personal names were used very scarcely and they had to be ascertained by identification with existing lists maintained in state archives and from the genealogical tables of the several families. The author Srinath who was a member of the Duara family and held the office of Barbarua has consistently referred to himself as Duara Barbarua; and Purnananda, the Prime Minister, appears in the chronicle as the Mahamantri Buragohain Dangaria of the Kuoigayan family. In paragraph 336 is inserted a full list of the principal officers of the reign of Kamaleswar Singha but not a single personal name has been mentioned anywhere. The total eclipse of the personal names in the more brilliant effulgence of the toponomous official titles has its parallel in Frederick Edwin Smith and James Lyle Mackay being overshadowed by the more popular appellations Lord Birkenhead and Lord Inchcape.

The adult population of Assam was divided into *khels* having to render specific services to the state, such as, arrow-making, boat-building, boat-plying, house-building, provision-supplying, fighting, writing, revenue collecting, superintendence of elephants, horses, hawks and forests, etc. Each *khel* was placed in charge of a Phukan, a Rajkhowa or a Barua, who was assisted by a gradation of officers, Hajarikas, Saikias and Boras. An adult male was called a *paik*, and four *paiks* constituted a *got*. One man in a *got* had to serve the state for three months in a year, and the remaining three *paiks* looked after the cultivation and other domestic concerns of their absent comrade. In cases of emergency two and even three men were recruited from each *got* for state purposes, or the *got* maximum was reduced from four to three *paiks*. The levy of one man from each *got* was called the *mul*, of two the *dewal* and of three the *tewal*. The standing army at the capital was a very poor one. In 1809 it consisted of 300 up-country sepoys and 800 native troops. In cases of war or other public occasions the officers-in-charge of the various *khels* mobilised their respective quotas of men. The vast body of subjects was thus a standing militia and their loyal co-operation did not infrequently depend upon the personal sympathies of the intermediate *kheldars* or barons. The *Chamuas* or the higher rank of subjects were exempted from personal service. Up to the year 1772 all Phukanships were confined to the members of the various Ahom families, and the first departure was made in favour of a Kalita Bhuyan as a reward for his leadership in the royalist reaction which ultimately restored the throne to Lakshmi Singha after the temporary overlordship of the Moran rebels. The second batch of non-Ahom Phukans were a few members of the Brahman Kakatia family on whom that unique distinction was conferred as a reward for their loyalty and devotion to the Ahom crown. A large number of Muhammadans were appointed in the several departments of the state, and their principal occupations were the deciphering and interpreting of Persian documents, curving inscriptions on copper-plates and other metals, minting of coins, embroidery work, painting with fast colours, carpentry, sword and gun-making and the manufacture of gunpowder. Several Muhammadan religious leaders known as Dewans were granted revenue-free lands, generally known as *Pirpal* lands.

The sons, wives and other near relations of a reigning monarch were maintained out of public funds. The estates granted to them were known as *mels*, each managed by a Phukan or a Barua as the importance of the *mel* demanded. The Charingia *mel*, the Tipamia *mel*, the Namrupia *mel*, the Saru *mel* and the Maju *mel* were generally conferred on the sons, brothers and nephews of the kings and the beneficiaries held the title of Raja. The chief queen was granted the Raidangia *mel*, the second queen the Parvatia *mel* and the other consorts the Purani *mel* and the Na *mel*. The daughters, nieces, sisters and daughters-in-law were maintained out of the Gabharu *mel*; the queen-mother was entitled to the emoluments of the Khangia *mel*, the king's nurse to that of the Kolichengar *mel* and the grand-mother to that of Enaigharia *mel*.

Succession to the throne was rather systematic in the beginning, being based on the law of primogeniture, with occasional departures in favour of a brother or a nephew. Later on a powerful Gohain or a Barbarua could manoeuvre the support of his colleagues in placing on the throne any prince from the collateral branches and the rivals were disqualified by the mutilation of their limbs. The princes who had no deformity in their body generally enlisted the support of some minister and made a dash for the throne. The problem of the princes was a very acute one, and in the absence of a proper solution the efficiency and internal harmony of the administration were jeopardised to a considerable extent.

Shifting of Capitals

The shifting of capitals was a favourite hobby of many oriental monarchs. Even Akbar was not satisfied with Delhi and Agra and in 1569 he removed his capital 23 miles to Fath-pur Sikri. The first Ahom conqueror King Sukapha had stayed for some time at Sologuri, Habung and Simaluguri, after which he fixed his headquarters at Charaideo in 1238. King Sudangpha who had been brought up in a Brahman family shifted his capital in 1403 to Cheregua on the Dihing river in the midst of Hindu surroundings; and Charaideo was relegated since then to the position of the metropolis of Ahom religion. Suklengmung ascended the throne in 1539 after having contrived the death of his father. Cheregua became reminiscent of his unholy patricide and it began to sting Suklengmung's monarchical conscience. He transferred the capital to Gargaon, and encircled it with a ring of walls and ramparts which gave the name to the new city, Gargaon or the city of ramparts. A very auspicious moment was selected for the king's exodus to the new capital. The magnificence and splendour of Gargaon were an amazement to the Mogul invaders. Sulikpha Lora Raja preferred to live at Lechang. Gadadhar Singha first stopped at Barkola and then at Meteka. His son Rudra Singha founded the city of Rangpur near the site where his mother Jaymati had been tortured to death. The importance of Gargaon was not bedimmed by the ascendency of Rangpur; it continued to be the capital, and the king and his court frequently visited that hoary city associated with the best days of the Ahoms. Lakshmi Singha proposed to abandon Gargaon and erect a new city at Kupoukhat, and Changrung Phukan, the royal architect, was asked to collect the necessary building materials; but the Deodhais and Bailungs vehemently opposed this proposal saying,—"Our ancestors had established their capital at Gargaon as they had found it suitable after having very carefully examined the numerous alternative sites. We cannot now advise His Majesty to abandon this old city." During the flight of Gaurinath Singha and the occupation of Rangpur by the Morans, Purnananda Buragohain had shifted the headquarters to Jorhat, which continued to be the capital of the Ahoms till the termination of their rule. Notwithstanding these two rivals of later growth Gargaon figured in the imagination of the people and in their unsophisticated parlance as the premier city in the good old days of Ahom supremacy. The viceregal capital was at Gauhati, and during the occasional occupation of Gauhati by the Moguls it was shifted to Kaliabar in the upper rapids of the Brahmaputra.

The Author, Srinath Duara Barbarua

The major portion of the present book represents the work of a very influential potentate of Assam. Srinath Barbarua had served the Ahom government in several capacities, first as a commander of the king's household troops and then as chief justice. He held the office of Barbarua for full seventeen years from 1800 to 1817. The compilation of the chronicle was commenced in March, 1804. The events are brought down to November 1806. The present manuscript being incomplete we are not in a position to ascertain the actual downward limit of his entire Buranji. Srinath's brother Harnath Senapati Phukan was a highly distinguished personage of the time. He served in several campaigns and rose ultimately to the rank of the Barphukan. Srinath was a participator and an eye-witness of many of the events he describes in his chronicle and about the rest he had heard from people having direct knowledge of the same. Srinath Barbarua was a strong supporter of the policy of Purnananda Buragohain the Prime Minister, who had to adopt vigilant measures to counteract the grave situation of his country, brought about by the interminable hostilities of the Moamarias. The Premier's motives were misjudged by a large section of his contemporaries, and nepotism and usurpation of sovereign powers were not infrequently attributed to him. Srinath Barbarua enjoyed the confidence and trust of Purnananda Buragohain during the entire period of that minister's dictatorship.

Srinath has written his chronicle with dignity, restraint and seriousness which was expected from a man of his eminence and political vision. The author had at his disposal all the papers and correspondences at the state archives; and the habit of shifting evidence which he had acquired in his capacity as the highest judicial officer of the state have been brought to bear upon his marshalling of facts in due order of importance. The result is an Assamese historical classic of the highest importance. The chronicle presents a complete picture of the Ahom court, of the machinery of the Ahom government in relation to both its internal and external affairs, the working of the different branches of administration, the methods of warfare and the engagements of peaceful times. The observant and critical student of history will be able to glean from the pages of the chronicle a full picture of Assam in the days of its prosperity and peace, and also of the first throes of its deadly struggle for existence.

September 1, 1933. S. K. BHUYAN.

TUNGKHUNGIA BURANJI:
OR
A CHRONICLE OF THE TUNGKHUNGIA KINGS OF ASSAM.

CHAPTER I.

INTRODUCTION.

Invocation.

Salutation to Sri-Krishna! Salutation to Ganesa! Salutation to the Goddess Parvati! This is the Buranji written in *saka* 1725 under the orders of the Duara Barbarua. Keep it secretly. Do not give it even to your son if you have no confidence in him. Show it to one who is unhostile and well-disposed towards you. Pandits have prohibited the betrayal of princes: and if trust is violated it amounts to an insult shown to one's mother. So keep it in confidence; more specially it is an unfathomable Sastra, who ever finds its bottom? Even great sages become victims of confusion in such matters which I have handled with whatever judgment I can command. So Pandits should not at random find fault with this book. If one is bent upon detecting blemishes he will find many. This is the Vamsavali or history of the Swargadeos or Kings of the Tungkhungia Dynasty. This history was caused to be written on Thursday, the twenty-second of Phalgun, on the Panchami *tithi*. 1.

Synopsis.

In the month of Sravan of the *saka* era 1603, Sri-sri Gadadhar Singha became king at Garagram after banishing Lora Raja to Namrup. He had two sons. In the year 1617 King Gadadhar Singha went to heaven. Then his elder son Rudra Singha became king at Garagram in the same month of the same year. His brother was given the Namrupia *mel*. In the year 1636 King Rudra Singha died at Gauhati. after a reign of nineteen years. Then in the same month of the same year his eldest son Siva Singha became king at Gauhati. Swargadeo Siva Singha breathed his last on the sixth day of the month of Aghon in the year 1666. He reigned for thirty years. In the same year and month and on the same day Pramatta Singha ascended the throne at Rangpur. Pramatta Singha went to heaven in the year 1673 after a reign of seven years. Rajeswar Singha's elder brother, the Batgharia Gohain, had an attack of smallpox, and Rajeswar Singha after being king drove away his brother to Namrup. Then in the same year, in the month of Ahin his brother Rajeswar Singha ascended the throne. His younger brother was born at Kalsila, hence he was called Kalsilia Gohaindeo. Rajeswar Singha on ascending the throne conferred on him the Namrupia *mel*. Swargadeo Rajeswar Singha died at Dewargaon after a reign of nineteen years. In the year 1691 his brother Lakshmi Singha ascended the throne, and died in the year 1702 after a reign of fourteen years. In the year 1702 his son Gaurinath Singha became king. He died at his camp at Jorhat near the Dichoi river in the month of Sravan of the year 1717. The length of his reign was fifteen years.[1] After the death of Gaurinath Singha, no other prince being considered worthy of the throne, the Premier Purnananda Buragohain and his colleagues brought the prince Kinaram Gohain as he was considered suitable for the succession. He was the son of Kadam-dighala Gohain, son of Ayusut Gohain, son of the Namrupia Raja Lechai who was the brother of Maharaj Rudra Singha. The Dangarias or the three ministers placed Kinaram on the throne and offered him the usual homage on the twenty-third day of Sravan in the year 1717. Kinaram Gohain after becoming king assumed the name of Swargadeo Kamaleswar Singha. After his death his brother Chandrakanta Singha, the Charing Raja, ascended the throne on the 6th Magh, 1732 *saka*. During the invasion of Assam by the Burmese, Ruchinath Buragohain and other officers deposed Chandrakanta, and placed on the throne Purandar Singha, son of Brajanath Gohain, a grandson of Rajeswar Singha Swargadeo, on the 11th Phagun, 1739 *saka*. Having failed to gain victory over the Burmese Purandar Singha left his country, and Alungmingi the Burmese Bargohain made Chandrakanta king for the second time, on the 25th Phagun, 1740 *saka*. Chandrakanta fought with the Burmese, but being defeated he made his escape to Bengal. The Burmese then set up Jogeswar Singha, son of the Tungkhungia

---

[1] In this synopsis of the reigns of the Tungkhungia rulers the abstracts of the reigns of the kings, Kamaleswar, Chandrakanta and Purandar Singha, could not evidently be given by Srinath Barua. They have been compiled from other sources and inserted here by the editor.

prince Baga Kowanr, just for the sake of pacifying the people, and they began to rule of their own accord, from the 3rd Chaitra of 1742 *saka* to the 21st Magh of 1746 *saka*. This period is called 'Manar Din'. Chandrakanta Singha collected a considerable force and fought with the Burmese at Mah-garh to the north of Jorhat in Jaistha, 1744. But being defeated in the battle he retreated again to Bengal. David Scott took possession of Assam from the Burmese on the 22nd Magh, 1746, from whence commenced the rule of the British. From the 1st Bahag, 1755, Purandar Singha governed Upper Assam or *Junior Khanda* as a feudatory chief under the British. On the 30th Bhadra, 1760, Purandar Singha was deposed, and the *Junior Khanda* was amalgamated with the *Senior or Namani Khanda*, and thus was constituted the Province of Assam. 2.

CHAPTER II.

THE PERIOD OF MINISTERIAL SUPREMACY.[1]

A narrative of the circumstances leading to the ascendancy of the Tungkhungia Dynasty of Ahom Kings, from the death of Chakradhwaj Singha in 1592 SAKA, *to the accession of Gadadhar Singha in* 1603 SAKA.

King Udayaditya put to death.

Swargadeo Chakradhwaj Singha Maharaj died of dropsy on the 15th of Bahag, 1592 *saka*. He tried his utmost to oust the invaders from the land thinking 'It is better for one to die than to remain under the domination of the Bangals'. After his death his brother, the Charingia Raja, ascended the throne with the name Udayaditya. During his reign Raja Ramsingha of Amber, a general of the Emperor Aurangzeb, and a son of Mirza-Raja Jai Singha, was defeated at the battle of Saraighat by Lachit Barphukan, the youngest son of Momai-tamuli Barbarua. On the demise of Lachit Phukan a few months after, his elder brother Laluk Nimati Phukan

---

[1] The present chapter and the four following, dealing with the history of the period 1592–1603, and the reigns of Swargadeos Gadadhar Singha, Rudra Singha, Siva Singha, and Pramatta Singha, have been compiled by the editor from several old manuscript Assam Buranjis to supplement the chronicle of Srinath Barbarua which unfortunately commences from the reign of Raj-

was appointed Barphukan. During the reign of King Udayaditya, a Bairagi or itinerant Sannyasi of Gakulpur in Brindaban, Paramananda by name, exercised great influence upon the hearts of the King and his subjects by the display of wonder-working feats. The King commanded that the twelve Assamese Thakurs or religious heads should be produced before the Bairagi to be initiated by the latter as he believed that no one among the twelve Mahantas could be as potent as the Bairagi. One Lechai Debera of the Lukhurasan clan, who was a disciple of the Makajan Mahanta, knelt down before the Mahantas and said,—'Only bestow upon me the protection of Your Holinesses' feet, and I will do whatever remedy is necessary'. Debera then conspired with Saru-Gohain the brother of the Swargadeo. The King was taken to Charaideo Hill where he was put to death on 1st Aghon, 1594 *saka*. They also killed Pelan Barbarua of the Charingia family. 3.

King Ramadhwaj put to death.

After becoming king Saru-Gohain assumed the name of Ramadhwaj Singha. The Bairagi was also put to death after a good deal of torture. Debera who was hitherto a Hajarika was now appointed Barbarua by Ramadhwaj Raja. This King also suffered from dropsy and his illness took a serious turn. Having seen this the King summoned to his presence Tangachu and other Phukans and said,—'My end is near. I hand over my nephew Kalia Gohain into your hands. You should make him king'. Debera was not invited to take part in the deliberations. 'The Swargadeo has not taken my advice in such a serious matter', thus thinking Debera remained prepared for action and began to kill men. He further said,—'Why should the King spare me after he recovers his health?' With this fear he used to move about armed with two *nakoi-daos* or hook-like swords. The Swargadeo asked Tangachu to put an end to Debera after going out of the King's presence as if he had received an order to that effect from His Majesty. Debera used to carry on amours with a mistress of the King. One day after having passed some time with Debera she said,—'To-day is the last occasion when I see your face. You will be killed to-morrow by Tangachu Phukan. Thus it has been desired by His Majesty'; thus saying she related the entire plot to her paramour. From that moment Debera became extremely careful. When Tangachu was coming out of the King's audience-chamber with *daos* concealed in a roll of soft mats Debera fell upon him and cut him into two pieces. He killed other people as well including Phukans, Rajkhowas and Hajarikas. He then requisitioned the services of a physician named Kharmaju who was asked to kill the King by mixing poison with medicine. The *Bez* or physician accordingly poisoned the King to death on the third day of the month of Aghon, 1596 *saka*. 4.

The first Tungkhungia King.

After this Debera came to know that the Tipam Raja, named Naran Gohain, brother of the deceased king, was marching down from the Charaideo Hill with the object of becoming king. Having heard this Debera rode on a white pony, pursued the prince and fought with him on the road from the hill. Being defeated the prince fell into the wayside ditch. Debera then said,—'Oh, prince, come near and don't be afraid. Whom shall I appoint king but Your Highness?' Debera had two followers named Ratanpuria and Dakhinpatia. After having brought the prince near and having dressed him in the attire and ornaments of a king, Debera said,—'Well, Ratanpuria and Dakhinpatia, what are you looking at? Make the Gohaindeo king'. Saying this Debera put to death the Tipam Raja and fourteen other princes, as well as the Namrupia Raja. Thus the family of Ramadhwaj Singha became extinct in the hands of Debera. Debera then brought a prince from Tungkhung[1] and made him king, but he reigned only for some twelve days or so. The daughter of Momai-tamuli Barbarua was made by Debera the Barkuanri or chief consort of the King. The Barbarua then killed whomever he liked and could lay his hands upon by strategem and treachery. 5.

Samaguria Suhung Raja.

Debera then put the Tungkhungia King to death and placed a prince of the Samaguria family on the throne. The daughter of Momai-tamuli Barbarua then said to the King,—'You are a king only in name if Debera is allowed to wield power like this'. The King at the instance of the Kuanri planned to arrest Debera. Having heard this Debera said,—'You were only a Tamuli-kuanri or a consort of an inferior rank of Jayadhwaj, the *Bhagania Raja* or

[1] This first Tungkhungia King is mentioned only in one chronicle, viz., the Buranji borrowed by the late Hemchandra Goswami from the family of Sukumar Mahanta of North Gauhati. The daughter of Momai-tamuli was a consort of Jayadhwaj Singha, Chakradhwaj Singha, the first Tungkhungia prince and of Suhung Raja.

fugitive king, and it was I who raised you to the rank of the Barkuanri, and you dare to speak like this?' He then killed the Samaguria King who reigned only for some twenty days. Momai-tamuli Barbarua's daughter, the royal consort, was also killed and her body was placed at the feet of the deceased monarch. 6.

The second Tung-khungia King.

Debera then placed on the throne one Gobar Gohain of the Tungkhungia family who was a descendant of the Gargayan Raja, on the 18th Puh, 1596 *saka*. Thus Debera committed many misdeeds and practically assumed sovereign power. 7.

Leadership of the Bahgaria Bura-gohain.

When Debera was thus acting, the Phukans, the Rajkhowas and the Hazarikas consulted together and said to the Bahgaria Buragohain at Gauhati,—'Your Lordship is living in flesh and blood. One single man Debera is making and unmaking kings and deposing and killing us as well. Your Lordship should come to our rescue at this critical juncture. We the people have accepted you as our head, and Your Lordship should not disclaim us.' Saying this the people bowed down to the Buragohain seven times. The Buragohain said in reply,—'Now that the people have acknowledged me as their leader I am never going to leave them'. Having left a few officers at Gauhati the Buragohain Dangaria accompanied by Laluk Sola Barphukan, the son of Momai-tamuli Barbarua, and other Phukans, Baruas, Hajarikas, and Saikias, marched to Upper Assam. 8.

Debera put to death.

Debera then encountered the Saraighatias or officers of Gauhati in a battle at Bahgara. Being defeated Debera took to his heels, but was subsequently captured. He was placed in a pig's cage and brought out with his senior wife raised on his head. At the trial before the Barphukan his junior wife was placed on his shoulders. The Bura-phukan asked Debera,—'Well, Debera, why did you behave like this?' To this Debera replied,—'Have you not heard that we are all made of the same stuff? I have finished composing my share of the *Dasama* verses; you shall also do the same'. Debera was then killed at Rajahat, being hoed from head to foot by the Haris. 9.

Sujinpha Dihingia Raja.

The Buragohain and his followers consulted together and killed the Tungkhungia Raja Gobar who had been placed on the throne by Debera. He was first of all removed from Haithaguri to Bhogbari where he was killed. He ruled for only twenty days. The Phukans offered the crown to the Buragohain, but he said,—'I am a minister and so I cannot be a king'. He then searched for princes in the company of his four sons and found one at Dihing which pleased the hearts of the counsellors and ministers. The Buragohain brought from Dihing the Dihinghia prince Arjun, a descendant of Swargadeo Pratap Singha, and made him king with the name Sujinpha, on the 8th of Magh, 1596 *saka*. He was then forty years of age. 10.

The Dihingia Raja put to death.

At that time the Katakis, the Kakatis, the Dolois, the Baras and the Buruks were all subservient to the Buragohain. When the Buraphukan was returning to Gauhati after having placed the affairs of the capital on a systematic basis, the Dihingia Raja killed all the descendants of the Gargayan Raja. The wife of the Dihingia Raja who was a daughter of one Kekora Sandikai and his four sons said to the King,—'We are kings only in name: the Buragohain is all in all. So we should seize his person'. The King did not first accede to the proposal. But a woman of ill repute carried tales and instituted a friction between the Buragohain and His Majesty who with his four sons now resolved to kill the Buragohain. A fight ensued between the two parties. The Swargadeo escaped by Barghat, and his four sons also fled. The Buragohain having remained at Sakbari brought the King and had his eyes plucked out on the night of one Tuesday, and he died on the day following. Some say that the King fearing that the Buragohain was going to kill him committed suicide by wilfully knocking his head against a stone. While others maintain that during his flight from Gargaon after being defeated by the Buragohain, the *Namanials* or the officers assigned to Lower Assam chased the King and having captured him they placed the King under the vigilance of Bhatdhara, the brother of Laluk Buraphukan, after which they retired to their respective homes. Bhatdhara is alleged to have beaten the King to death with the end of a gun on the twelfth day of Sravan, 1598. The Buragohain had the three princes brought to Bhogbari where they were put to death; while the eyes of another prince named Kalia Gohain were plucked out. All those who were to be killed were killed; similarly those who were to be preserved were preserved. 11.

Sudaipha Parvatia Raja.

After this there ensued a period of anarchy. The counsellors and the ministers were all looking upon the Buragohain as the centre of authority and power. The Buragohain in his turn remained in charge of the state for three fortnights after which he said,—'This is an untoward act on the part of a minister'. He then brought from the vicinity of the Burha-raja's grave at Charaideo Hill a prince to whom the counsellors and ministers bowed down as he was a descendant of the Deka-raja, and with due honour and affection they made him king. He assumed the name Sudaipha. The Saraighatias returned to Saraighat. Thus from the reign of King Udayaditya the monarch became a creature in the hands of his counsellors. 12.

Attempt to kill the King.

Then Mecha Barbarua who was a son of the Phukan of the Rangachila family took as his wife a princess, the daughter of one Laho. Having heard this the King asked the Buragohain to enquire saying,—'Is he a descendant of any king that he dares to marry one of our princesses?' An enquiry was made as a result of which the Barbarua was removed from office, and one Chakrapani was appointed in his place. The other people interceded on behalf of the Barbarua and the King did not intend to proceed further against him. Yet the ex-Barbarua being seized with fright fled down to Saraighat. In the month of Bahag, 1600 *saka*, an assassin struck the King with a sword. The King did not die, but he lost his left thumb. Blows were inflicted in five places, one on the head, a third on the hand, a fourth on the back and a fifth on the palm. The King escaped as if by fate which had decreed an allotted span of life. The ruffian made his escape having left an axe-like *dao* in the *Marang-ghar* or latrine. Being unable to find out the culprit the Buragohain and other nobles and ministers said,—'The ex-Barbarua who was turned out by His Majesty has inflicted these sword-cuts upon the King, or has instigated others to do so. The Saraighatias are in league in this affair'. Charged with complicity in this crime one Jai Tamuli was put to death as well as other men from Dihing and the brothers and nephews of the Tamuli. The King acted as he was made to do by the counsellors. The elder son of the Duara Phukan became Barbarua in place of the younger one. 13.

The Barphukan, Bhatdhara, the younger son of Duara, these three went down to Kaliabar. At the council-chamber or Dopdar at Saraighat the Deka-phukan said,—'The King alone can make or unmake a Phukan. It is highly improper that a Phukan should be dismissed or appointed by a Phukan or a brother officer. I have been dismissed to-day and you will be dismissed to-morrow. But who is he to make and unmake us in this fashion?' This was reported to the Buraphukan at Kaliabar, who with all the members of his family hastened down to Saraighat. He discussed the situation with the Saraighatias and decided as follows,—'It now transpires that we shall all be undone having placed our reliance upon the Buragohain. It is God alone who has saved us somehow. If we depend upon others' help something disastrous may come upon us, while no harm can proceed from any quarter if we are strong ourselves.' The Buraphukan then despatched three men to Nawab Mansur Khan through Baduli who had formerly eaten the bread of the Bangals. The Buraphukan's messengers said to the Nawab,—'The Barphukan has sent us with this message: "Please arrange the appearance of some two hundred horses on the north and south banks at Sarai, and some twenty boats on the waters, and we shall abandon the garrison of Gauhati and proceed upstream. But I shall have to be made King of Assam in return".' The Nawab directed the Phukan's men to go to Dacca in the company of one of his own men and deliver the message to Azamtara, son of the Padshah. The prince having heard the message replied, —'I have taken this solemn vow that I shall without fail make my maternal uncle the Barphukan[1] King of Assam'. He also promised to pay four lakhs of rupees in return for the evacuation of the stronghold of Gauhati. 14.

The Buraphukan solicits foreign aid.

About that time the Buraphukan arranged the dismissal of the elder son of the Duara Phukan from his office of Barbarua and procured his flight to Kaliabar. In the meantime some Saraighatias reported to the

Chintamani rampart.

[1] Laluk Barphukan was the maternal uncle of Ramani or Nangchen Gabharu. Laluk was the brother of Ramani's mother who was a daughter of Momai-tamuli and a consort of Jayadhwaj Singha, who presented her to Aurangzeb's harem in January, 1663 A.D., at the termination of Mir Jumla's invasion. She was married to Sultan Azamtara on May 2nd, 1668, with the name Rahmat Banu Begum.

Buragohain the despatch of emissaries to Bengal by the Buraphukan. The Buragohain having heard this kept the whole thing in his mind. He expressed his opinion diplomatically as follows.—'The Barphukan is a wise man; why should he act like this? The men who informed my agents at Saraighat must have spoken falsely.' The Buragohain then said to the King,—'The elder son of the Duara Phukan has fled to Saraighat out of fear in connection with the murderous assault on the King. I have also heard many other rumours about the state of affairs there. If we slip from our strongholds at Gauhati and Samdhara there is no other place to rest upon.' Having said so he, in the name of the Swargadeo, raised *dowals* or a levy consisting of the second man from every *got*, and employed them in erecting a rampart from the extremity of the hill at Tulasijan to the Dihing. The rampart was named Laimati, but it became famous as Chintamani-garh. 15.

Surrender of Gauhati proposed.

Laluk Buraphukan as well as other Phukans heard this and said,—'We are stationed at Gauhati always prepared to repel the attacks of our enemies. For whom then has the rampart been constructed in the heart of the kingdom? It must be meant for us'. Having said so they deliberated jointly and decided to negotiate with the Bangals with the object of surrendering Gauhati to them. In the meantime the Buraphukan's messengers who had been despatched to Mansur Khan returned and said,—'Our mission has been successful. Baduli accompanied by a force is arriving shortly'. The Saraighatias reported this development to the Buragohain who said,—'It is well and good that I have been informed. If such a juncture actually takes place I shall myself go down to Gauhati as well as other men. Let anybody come, whether he be the Padshah or his son, why should we give up Gauhati?' He then despatched the Khanikar Barua to ascertain the facts. 16.

Bloodless occupation of Gauhati.

The Bangals conspiring with the Buraphukan came as far as Agiathuti with a view to capture the Buragohain. The Pani-phukan and the Miri-Sandikai Phukan reported all the details of the situation to the Buragohain through the Khanikar Barua, saying,—'Nobody seemed to believe in us though we reported the matter so many times. Now, Baduli has actually come. Let the Buragohain do what he can.' The Bangals abstained from entering into Gauhati for three days suspecting that the Assamese might be hiding somewhere in the hills and come upon them unawares. The Buraphukan then assured the Bangals by sending one Kalia of the Buruks who enjoyed the confidence of the Phukan; the Bangals then entered Gauhati. Thus on the 15th of Phagun, 1600 *saka*, the Buraphukan in a friendly manner surrendered the garrison of Gauhati to the Bangals. He sailed upstream and arrived at Kaliabar where he assumed independence, and began to dismiss and appoint officers. The Pani-phukan was dismissed and one Kari-deka was appointed Phukan in his place; similarly Miri-Sandikai was removed from office and Chetia Rajkhowa was made Phukan, while Dighala Gohain was appointed Buragohain. 17.

The Bahgaria Buragohain made a captive.

Having heard all this the King ordered the three Dangarias to leave the Chintamani-garh half-constructed and proceed to Gauhati. The three Dangarias of Gargaon sailed down the river and encamped at Biswanath, while the Phukans and Rajkhowas went further down and halted at Duimuni-sila. The Saraighatias also proceeded up and stopped at the same place on that very day. Laluk Barphukan arrested the Phukans and Hajarikas of Gargaon. Gidamukali Atan Buragohain Dangaria, the Prime Minister, in view of the dangerous character of the situation, crossed the Brahmaputra at Biswanath; he then proceeded further north and stopped at Lejubaj at the residence of one Ramrai Rajkhowa, from where he marched towards the Naga country through Satsayia. But he was captured and brought down from that place. He was afterwards kept in charge of guards under strict vigilance at Duimuni-sila. 18.

The Swargadeo assured.

After this the Phukans went up to Gargaon. The King being afraid fled to the Charaideo Hill saying,—'I was earning my bread by ploughing land. They brought me here and gave me the title of a king. I do not know anything. If they want to do anything towards me let them come here and do it. They alone will share the sin or virtue as the case may be.' Having heard this the Phukans said,—'We are not to be told in this fashion. Many men have been harassed having had to construct a rampart in the heart of the country. So we have come up to search out the people disloyal to His Majesty after having imprisoned the Buragohain. The state of Gauhati is a casket of gold; and the reason which has compelled us to leave such a place must be a grave and serious one.

What is the good of fighting with the Bangals in the frontier if we accommodate Bangals or enemies in the interior of the kingdom? If no enquiry be made into the matter then why do we remain at Gauhati away from our wives and women living somehow on coarse rice and diet? We have come up to appraise the rebels and pay our homage to His Majesty. The King should return henceforth to Garagram without the least shadow of suspicion'. The Swargadeo being again informed as above came to Garagram where he was saluted by the Phukans. The King in his turn distributed robes and ornaments to them according to their respective ranks. After this the Saraighatias who had gone up to Garagram came back to Kaliabar; while the Gargayans remained at Gargaon with His Majesty. 19.

King Sudaipha imprisoned.

After some time the King said,—'It is curious that one single man, the Buraphukan, has surrendered the fort at Gauhati, imprisoned the Buragohain, Phukans and others, and he alone dismisses and appoints men at his own sweet will. I am determined to appoint the Duara as Barphukan. Let him put an end to the life of the Buraphukan by some stratagem; and I shall capture his brother here'. The King then raised the son of the Gargayan-Sandikai to the position of a Phukan and sent him down to Kaliabar. Bhatdhara, the brother of the Buraphukan, sent a message to the King in which he proposed to seize his elder brother on condition that he was made Barphukan. The King declared,—'I hereby appoint Bhatdhara to the office of the Barphukan. The Burha is forthwith dismissed'. The King then imprisoned Marangi Barbarua, the brother of the Buraphukan, at Garagram. The Barbarua managed to escape and narrated the whole affair to his elder brother at Kaliabar. Having heard this the Barphukan went up to Gargaon and imprisoned the Parvatia Raja in 1601 *saka*. 20.

Sulikpha Lora Raja.

The Buraphukan then fetched one Saru-Gohain of the Samaguria family, aged only fourteen years, and made him king at Barnaosal on Thursday, the fifth of Aghon, 1601 *saka*. The new King assumed the name of Sulikpha, and Ratnadhwaj Singha according to the Hindus. The Buraphukan arranged the murder of the Parvatia Raja in the hands of the new Swargadeo. Marangi, brother of Laluk Barphukan, was made Barbarua, and Bandar of the Lanmakharu family who was Saru-Abhaypuria Rajkhowa, was raised to the rank of a Phukan. The Lora Raja first lived at Lechang. The Buraphukan's daughter aged five years became Barkuanri, and the daughter of Bhatdhara his brother, aged twelve years, became Parvatia Kuanri. The King then removed his residence from Lechang to Meteka. 21.

The Bahgaria Buragohain put to death.

As regards the Buragohain who had been imprisoned at Kaliabar, the Buraphukan communicated the King's orders to Khona Gohain who was Chaodang Barua and a member of the Bargohain family, and one Banchengia Khamcheng Gohain of the Barpatra clan. The two went down at the instance of the Buraphukan, and murdered the Buragohain with his family in the compound of the Solal Bargohain on the second day of the white moon in Aghon. The Buragohain's elder brother who was Naobaicha Phukan, his nephew and his son Lankham Deka were also put to death. 22.

The Buraphukan in royal attire.

After this Azamtara, the son of the Padshah, despatched to the Buraphukan a letter with an impression of the Sultan's palm and fingers. The purport of the letter was as follows,—'You should send down your King and the three Dangarias as captives to us, as well as other men who are your enemies by which act you will attain prosperity and happiness. More so, because I will appoint you King of Assam. For whom should you fear?' The above letter was brought by the Bangal Kataki Govindaram who was accompanied by our own Katakis, one Madhacharan of Sola and one Jadu. The Buraphukan removed from the royal store-house the canopy used by kings on the occasion of the ceremony of receiving foreign ambassadors. The Buraphukan dressed himself in the attire and ornaments worn by the kings, sat under the royal canopy and thus received the Bangal envoy Govindaram at his own residence in Meteka. 23.

The Buraphukan killed by Bhotai.

After this the Bar-deodhai once said to the King,—'We should offer some human sacrifices to the temple at Sadiya, as the miseries of the country have not known any abatement.' The King asked the Buraphukan to search for suitable men. A bear had at that time entered into the house of the Buraphukan. One Bhotai of Nagaon who was living with the Buraphukan killed that bear by thrusting his sword. Having seen such courage and pluck on the part of

Bhotai, the Buraphukan thought of sacrificing him at the Deoghar of Sadiya. At this the three men who lived with the Buraphukan, Madhav Tamuli, Aghona Kachari and Bhotai consulted together saying,—'If strong and healthy men are annually sacrificed to the goddess then how will it be possible for good Hindus to survive?' Thus saying the three conspired and pierced the Buraphukan to death in his bed, on the night of Tuesday, the tenth day of Aghon, 1602 *saka*. The three sons of the Buraphukan, Angora, Tholoka and Jagara were also put to death. The King then appointed one Alan Burha of the Dihingia family as Barbarua, and Bandar of the Lanmakharus as Barphukan. 24.

Prince Gadapani, a fugitive.

Sri-sri-mat Gadadhar Singha Maharaja, a descendant of Sri-sri-swarga-narayan-deva Maharaja, was born in the village of Tingkhang where he and his brother passed half the measure of their lives. At that time the Samaguria Lora Raja, Laluki Barphukan, the son of Momai-tamuli Barbarua, and Marangi Barbarua, the youngest son of Momai-tamuli, were managing the affairs of state at Meteka. A search was then instituted for scions of the royal family; and Gadapani being seized with fear deserted his home, his wife and sons. He roamed over hills and forests, towns and villages in his own country as well as in foreign lands situated in the north and the south banks. At this time Laluk Sola Buraphukan was pierced to death by Bhotai Saikia of Nagaon; and in his place the King appointed Bandar of the Lanmakharu family as Barphukan. After this the Lanmakharu Barphukan, the Neog-phukan who was a son of the Gargayan Sandikai, Khamrak Charingia Phukan son of Pelan Barbarua, and Laithepena Bargohain, proceeded to Kaliabar to fight with the Bangals. 25.

Gadapani at Dakhinpat Satra.

Previously to this the prince out of fear for the Buraphukan had kept his two sons in a Naga village. His wife breathed her last with a child in her womb in the midst of punishment and torture.[1] Thus travelling under extreme hardship and difficulty he ultimately

---

[1] In another chronicle, we get this reference to the martyred princess Jaymati,—'At that time the Buraphukan, after informing the King, caused the murder of the two brothers of the Bahgaria Gohain at Kaliabar. He then instituted a search for royal princes, and killed those whom he could find. Not having found the Burha-raja (Gadapani), he caught hold of his wife and caused her death in the midst of punishment'.

obtained the assistance of Silmania Niran, a Bartekela of Rajmai, and of Ramdhan, a member of the Dhanuchocha or bow-makers' clan. Through their instrumentality he gained the support of the Gargayan Sandikai-Phukan and of the Charingia Phukan, the son of Pelan Barbarua. He stayed for some time at the Satra or monastery of Chota Banamali Bapu of Dakhinpat situated at Kalabari in the North Bank. The prince asked the Gosain to acquaint Bandar Barphukan, the grandson of the Lanmakharu Chetia, with the details of his project in order to enlist the support of the Phukan; but the Gosain did not give any encouragement or hope to the prince in his candidature for the throne as it would mean the overthrow of the reigning King, the Samaguria Raja, who was his own disciple. The provisions and necessaries supplied to the prince and the reception meted out to him at the Satra were of the character generally accorded to ordinary individuals. Besides, he was allowed to put up outside the barracks occupied by celibate disciples. During his stay at the Satra the prince witnessed the wealth and splendour of religious practitioners; even Phukans, Rajkhowas, Hajarikas, Saikias and Baras were selected from among the Bhakats or disciples; the Gosains enjoyed the services of the full quota of functionaries attached to a king's household, such as goldsmiths, blacksmiths and scavengers; and they also enjoyed all the prerogatives of a sovereign excepting Kekora-dolas or royal sedans and elephants. The prince also noticed the same state of affairs at Auniati and other Satras. Having failed to receive any support from Chota Banamali Bapu, the prince went of his own accord to Kaliabar, where, he with the help of the Gargayan Sandikai-Phukan and the Charingia Phukan succeeded in winning over Bandar Barphukan to his side by tact and persuasion. 26.

Gadapani made king at Kaliabar.

In the meantime Bhatdhara, the brother of Laluk Barphukan, proceeded to Gauhati and asked Mansur Khan to give him some men and soldiers with the help of which he promised to extirpate the Ahoms. The Nawab sent Bhatdhara to the court of Sultan Azamtara at Dacca. Bhatdhara made repeated entreaties to the prince who said,—'All right, remain here for some time, and I will tell you my decision later'. Bhatdhara remained there accordingly. The Phukans stationed at Kaliabar consulted together and with the object of attacking the Bangals at

Gauhati arranged to bring down the Buragohain, the Barbarua, the Phukans and the Hajarikas from Gargaon to Kaliabar. The Barpatra Gohain and Moupia Phukan alone remained with His Majesty at the capital. After the Dangarias, Phukans, Rajkhowas and Hajarikas of Kaliabar and Gargaon had assembled at one place, they deliberated on the problems of the state, saying,—'How will it be possible for a weak king to protect the country? Only a strong monarch will be able to do so'. Having thus decided, Sri-sri Gadadhar Singha Maharaja, generally known as the Burha-raja of the Tingkhangia family, was declared king at Kaliabar on Thursday, the 20th of Sravan, 1603 *saka,* after 18 *dandas* had elapsed. The party then sailed up the river. Chota Banamali Bapu came up and began to persuade the Barphukan in order to induce the party to return to Kaliabar. The new King and his adherents proceeded up and reached Gargaon on Thursday, the 27th of the month when four *dandas* had remained for the expiry of the night. The party encamped on the bank of the Padum-pukhuri or lotus-tank inside the walls of the capital. They subsequently put to death the Samaguria boy-king at Namrup after having removed him there on the pretext of making him the Namrupia Raja.[1] 27.

---

[1] It is difficult to get in one place a detailed account of the anarchy and disorder that prevailed in the country during the period from the death of Chakradhwaja Singha in 1670 A.D. to the accession of Gadadhar Singha in 1681 A.D. It was during this time that princes of the Tungkhungia clan first sat on the Ahom throne; besides, the history of the period is intimately connected with the events of the subsequent reigns. No account of this disruption of the country is to be found in the chronicle of Srinath Duara Barbarua. Similarly the history of the reigns of Gadadhar Singha, Rudra Singha, Siva Singha and Pramatta Singha has unfortunately been omitted in the Duara Barbarua's chronicle which begins only with the reign of Rajeswar Singha. He has, however, given in the preamble the dates of the accession and death of all the Tungkhungia sovereigns up to Swargadeo Gaurinath Singha, 1780–1795 A.D., though his chronicle comes down to 1806 A.D. In order to place before the public a complete chronicle of the Tungkhungia rulers we have inserted in the present volume an account of the period from the death of Chakradhwaja Singha to the end of Pramatta Singha's reign carefully compiled from several ancient chronicles. Passages have been taken bodily from old buranjis and inserted at the appropriate places; not a single sentence has been reproduced here which has not been found in some old chronicle; and we have also refrained from inserting any fact which has been obtained from sources other than ancient Assamese manuscript chronicles.—S.K.B.

CHAPTER III.

SWARGADEO GADADHAR SINGHA.

Accession.

In the month of Sravan, 1603 *saka*, Sri-sri Gadadhar Singha Maharaja became king. On Saturday, the twenty-first day of Phagun, the residence of the King situated at Charaideo was struck with lightning. On Sunday the twenty-second, the King ascended the Singari-ghar, and on Monday, at the fourth *danda* he sat on the lion-seat. On Tuesday, the twenty-fourth, at the tenth *danda* he ascended the throne. After being placed on the throne he assumed the Ahom name Chao-supatpha, and on the same day he took the Hindu name Gadadhar Singha. The Majumdar wrote that name with a pen of gold, and announced it to all the counsellors and ministers. 28.

Omens.

On Wednesday, the twenty-fifth, a cow fastened down a man at Chunpura with her tail. The man was released afterwards by other people. On the sixteenth day of Chaitra some mysterious agent took away Lo Bhandari from his house. On Monday, the twenty-third, two suns appeared in the sky at the fourth *danda*. In the month of Bahag in the year 1604 the King planted the banyan tree of longevity. 29.

Punishment.

Bhatdhara and his son were mutually fed with the flesh extracted from their bodies. The heart of the son was ripped open with an axe and after being extracted it was cooked, and the father was made to eat it. Then he (Bhatdhara) was also executed. Aka Phukan, a relation of theirs, was killed as well. All their relatives were assigned to the Barpatra's *khel*. On Monday, the twenty-seventh day of Ashar, 1604, the King was offended with Jabang Bargohain and executed him. The son of the merchant Ahina was also killed. 30.

The Battle of Itakhuli.

Then the King consulted the three Dangarias, the Phukans and other officers and commanded them to attack the Bangals at Gauhati. The following officers were members of that war-expedition, —the Gargayan Dangaria, Dilihial Langi Buragohain, Chengkham Solal Gohain, Alun the Dihingia Barbarua, Pikchai Hulou

Phukan, Lanmakharu Phukan, Lanmakharu Bandar Barphukan of Lower Assam, Khamang Pani-phukan, Khamrak Charingia Phukan, Chengrai Phukan son of the Dilihial Buragohain, Khamchin Phukan of Lankhentau, together with the Rajkhowas and the Hajarikias. Our army first captured Bahbari. 31.

Mansur Khan's defeat.

Kajali was then attacked by our men. The Buragohain, the Solal Gohain and the Barphukan encamped at Kurua. The other Phukans accompanied by the Pani-phukan pitched their camps on the south at the fort of Saund. The Barbarua and the Phukan remained outside Kurua. Hulou Phukan, the grandson of Pikchai Chetia Barphukan, joined them from Bahbari. At the mouth of the Barnadi the Bangals or the invaders came to fight with their war-vessels. Our men also chased them in boats and fell upon the invaders. The invaders not being able to stand in battle left their larger boats and fled away in their canoes. The Barbarua then occupied Itakhuli. The general Mansur Khan Nawab also fled being discomfited in the battle. Two cousins of Raja Ram Singha were found there. Our men chased Mansur Khan up to the Manaha, from whence they returned. Several cannon of brass and other steel guns of large and small dimensions as well as other weapons of war were obtained by our men. They also secured plenty of money, men, horses, camels, bullocks and buffaloes. The spoils obtained in this engagement exceeded the amount captured in any other previous warfare. At that time Nawab Mansur Khan had sent the ambassador Syamsingha who was detained by the Swargadeo, and the messenger died here. This war came to a victorious conclusion in the month of Sravan of the year 1604, *saka*. 32.

Conspiracy of the nobles.

On Wednesday, the fifth day of Puh, a flock of bees hived at the principal door of the palace. On Wednesday, the twenty-sixth, the King excavated a tank at Tingkhang. On Monday, the twenty-fourth, the Sandikai Neog and the Bihparua Phukan informed Ram-krishnai Kataki of the Bahbaria clan that the attitude of Bandar Barphukan, and of the Pani-phukan, the son of the Phul-barua, was unsatisfactory. The Gargayan Sandikai-Phukan, Khamrak the Charingia Phukan, Chengrai Phukan of the clan of the Dilihial Buragohain, and Khamchin Phukan son of Lechai of the Khentau clan, these four consulted together, and finding that the two Phukans were attempting to rebel against the King, kept them under watch and guard, and communicated the fact to His Majesty. The message was delivered to the King at his hill residence at the time of offering worship to Charaideo. The King on hearing this commanded that the two Phukans, the Barphukan and the Pani-phukan of Gauhati, should be sent up to Upper Assam. The Barphukan and Pani-phukan were accordingly sent to Gargaon, and the King ordered the three Dangarias to sit at a tribunal to try the offenders. As commanded by the King the Dangarias took the two Phukans to the court in front of the Holong and enquired into the allegations in order to find out the truth. The two Phukans confessed their guilt, and said,—'Seeing the gravity of our offence we deserve to be killed. We are also the servants of the King for the last seven generations. We place ourselves at the mercy of His Majesty.' The King hearing of the details accused them of high misdemeanour. The Barpatra-gohain, the Bargohain, the Buragohain, the Barbarua, Moupia Phukan, Hulou Phukan and Tancheng Phukan son of Kirkiria, interceded at the feet of the King on behalf of the accused. On Sunday, the third of Bahag in the year 1605, at the fourth *danda*, the King accordingly condoned the crimes of the Barphukan and the Pani-phukan; and he only sent them to their respective homes. The Sandikai Neog was appointed Barphukan, and Bheba of the family of Laluki was appointed Phukan, while the post of Pani-phukan was conferred upon Bhakati, son of Dihingia Lakheng Phukan. 33.

Tank at Tingkhang.

In the month of Aghon, 1606, the King ploughed at the sacrificial site of the tank at Tingkhang. The King invited to the sacrifice the three Mahajans or religious leaders of Auniati, Bengena-ati and Katanipar. They organised a religious assembly accompanied by music and recital at the bank of the tank, and the King buried or placed the *Nag* or the sacred pillar. After the ceremony of consecration the tank was named Rahdoi. In the month of Chait the principal entrance to the palace was constructed by our men as well as the Bangals with stones and bricks. On Sunday, the thirteenth day of Jeth in the year 1606, the *Bardhak* or the big drum was placed on its stand at the Barholong. 34.

Further conspiracies.

After this, Chengrai Phukan, Khamrak Phukan, Khamchin Phukan of Khentau, the Pani-phukan, these four Phukans met together and conspired to rebel against the King. The Barphukan, hearing of this, robbed the four Phukans of their retinue and followers, and imprisoned them under safe custody. A few Gargayans or officers attached to the capital such as the Dilihial Buragohain, the Hulou Phukan and a few other Hajarikias were also parties to this conspiracy. On hearing this the King consulted with the three Dangarias and the Phukans and proceeded to Lower Assam. He stopped at Gajpur for two nights, and then after collecting his men he despatched them to the north and the south to halt at the fort of Samdhara. The King despatched the following by the northern route,—the Charing Raja, the Barpatra-gohain, the Barchetia Barbarua, the Duara Phukan; while the Bargohain, the Hulou Phukan and the Naobaicha Phukan proceeded by the southern route, the latter marching by the sands. Then all of them stopped at the Samdhara fort. The King pitched his camp to the east of Samdhara, in the sands to the south of the river Brahmaputra. After remaining there for some time the King proceeded upstream as far as Kaliabar and contrived to bring the Pani-phukan, the brother of the Barbarua, by despatching the following,—Burapachani or his senior attendant, Kalia Kataki, one Phicha who was a Tekela-Bara or head of the *Tekelas* or emissaries of the Bargohain, an Ahom *Jakharia* or supplier of saltpetre in the service of the Bargohain, and a Dihingia boatman of the Barbarua. The Barphukan then arrested the Khamrak Phukan and Chengrai Phukan, and sent them up the river in a boat. The Barphukan proceeded by land and met the King. While the King encamped at Kaliabar on the bank of the Kalang river, he dismissed the Buragohain and sent him home, and appointed Mou Gohain of the Kuoigayan family to the post of Buragohain. In the meantime the two phukans were brought up under proper escort; they were made to wear iron chains and imprisoned in the Hatisal or royal elephant-stall. The King out of consideration for the Barbarua sent his brother the Pani-phukan home and did not kill him. Tancheng, the son of the Barbarua's uncle, was appointed Pani-phukan. In the month of Aghon, 1607, the two Phukans, Khamrak and Chengrai, were killed, and their bodies were placed in a frame on a barge of plantain trees with betel-nut kerchiefs on their necks, and the barge was floated down the Brahmaputra. The King then proceeded up to Gargaon. 35.

The King's return to Gargaon.

At that time the King while at Kaliabar allotted the men belonging to the Namdangia Phukan to the five Phukans including the Barphukan, and from that time only five Phukans served in the establishment at Gauhati. The King on hearing that Hulou Phukan had not joined the service of the Barphukan dismissed him from his post and sent him home; and Lahan Rajneog was appointed Dekaphukan in his place. Then the King halted at Kaliabar for a few days more passing his time in amusement and pleasure, and gave the new name Manpur to the encampment at Kaliabar. He then bade adieu to the five Phukans including the Barphukan after having bestowed on them the usual presents. Then the King went up and arrived at Gargaon. 36.

Suppression of rebels.

In the month of Phagun, 1606, the Barphukan traced out the Namdangia Phukan, and having imprisoned him after being made to put on iron fetters communicated the fact to the King, who despatched the Dola-kakharia Bara, the Chaodang Bara and the Dadhara Bara to fetch the Namdangia Phukan. The Phukan was first cudgelled and then pressed to death between wooden cylinders at Rajahat on Saturday, on the ninth day of Chait. On the first day of Jeth, 1607, the King gave a feast to his subjects. 37.

Dismissal of the Barbarua.

The King was seriously offended with the misdemeanour of the Pani-phukan, the brother of the Barbarua; and desiring to effect the murder of the Pani-phukan, he wanted to dismiss the Barbarua from his post. He also dispensed with the Parvatia Aikuanri, she being the daughter of the Barbarua. In the morning of the twenty-ninth of Jeth when the hour of the fourth period of the day or noon was announced, the King sat at the court at Luklukan and posted the Charing Raja at the Chunpora gate with bowmen, shieldsmen and musketeers, and the Dihingia Phukan of the Duara family at the Barduar or the principal gate, while the Kathalbaria Dola-kakharia Barua was placed in charge of the Meghai gate. Then the King deputed the Chaodang Barua who was a member of the clan of Khamun to the residence of the Barbarua, saying,—"Tell the Barbarua that I have dismissed him home to-day. Take with you a company of men; and see that they remove even the most trifling articles from the official residence of the Barbarua to his home in the country, except the arrows, shields, guns, *daos* and swords which will be found in the former place. Send to my place the three hundred *Kanris* of Dihing allotted to the Barbarua." After this instruction the King despatched with him the Chaodang Bara, the Dolakakharia Bara and the Dadhara Bara. The deputation sent, in accordance with the royal command, the three hundred *Kanris* of the Barbarua and the three Saikias to the King under the escort of the Chaodang Bara. The Chaodang Barua communicated this message to the Barbarua,—"Please come out. The orders of His Majesty should be obeyed." Being thus informed the Barbarua was seized with fright and sent this reply to the Chaodang Barua,—"If the King has issued any command regarding what is to be done towards me then please say so and come in. I shall also be careful. Please utter no falsehood; if any false statement is made then you will suffer on the spiritual scale." Then the Chaodang Barua sent back this message,—"There should be no fear. Nothing is meant for the body. If anything untoward happens then I will suffer on the spiritual grounds." Then the Barbarua came out and enquired about the nature of the royal command relating to himself. Saying so he knelt down on the ground to receive the orders of the King. The Chaodang Barua also did the same, and announced the royal mandate as follows,—"I have dismissed the Barbarua home to-day. I have sent herewith a company of men who will remove all his belongings from the Barbarua's metropolitan residence to his home at Dihing. The military accoutrements in possession of the Barbarua should however be left at the capital." Hearing this the Barbarua asked,—"I want to go in for a moment and come back. May I do so?" The Chaodang Barua permitted him to go in but enjoined upon his quick return. The Barbarua went in and after a while came back with a seer of silver and a suit of clothes together with a pair of ear-ornaments which he offered to the Chaodang Barua. The latter accepted the ornaments and the clothes, but he returned the seer of silver. The Barbaua gave to each of the Chaodang Baras a sum of rupees four and a suit of clothes. He then saluted the King from his residence. After this he started for his home at Dihing. No sooner did he reach Chokihat, a Chaodang Bara ran after him and halted in front of him. The ex-Barbarua was a bit afraid and enquired,—"Well, Chaodang Bara, what is the matter?" He replied,—"The King has desired that you should go home riding on your black pony. You can keep it for your use. You have been asked to mount the pony in my presence." The ex-Barbarua then presented five rupees to the messenger who brought his horse and rode home upon it. On Friday, the thirtieth of Jeth, Lahan Phukan was appointed Barbarua. The Pani-Dihingia Rajkhowa was dismissed from his post, he being the brother of the ex-Barbarua, and the Chaodang Barua who was a Khamun was appointed Rajkhowa in his place. The office of the Pani-phukan was taken away from Laokali-khowa and bestowed on the Dolakakharia Barua of Tingkhang. 38.

The ex-Barbarua's loyalty proved.

On the fourth of Bhada, 1607, the King despatched two confidential spies in the name of the Charing Raja. They were supplied with gold earrings and a suit of clothes each, one being sent to the deposed Barbarua and the other to his brother the ex-Pani-phukan. The spy sent to the ex-Barbarua told him as follows,—"The Charing Raja has sent me to you with these presents of ear-rings and clothes, saying that the Barbarua should act in concert with him to place him on the throne." The deposed Barbarua bound the messenger and sent him to the King with the message,—"I am a disinterested devotee of the King. I am living as it has pleased His Majesty to keep me. The man says that the Charing Raja has sent him meditating the ruin of the King; His Majesty will properly judge it. And the Heavenly King should not try so persistently to kill and destroy me. May I enquire why the King dismissed me home without uttering a word?" 39.

The ex-Pani-phukan's disloyalty proved.

When the other messenger communicated the message to the ex-Pani-phukan after handing over to him the present of the earrings and clothes, the latter said,—"All right, I will wear these presents and render all possible help to the prince. He should only exert himself." The two emissaries informed the King of the results of their interviews, whereupon the Swargadeo was convinced of the loyalty of the Barua; whereas he brought the Pani-phukan from home and imprisoned him at the elephant-stall, saying,—"He formerly conspired my ruin; then and there he should have been executed, but I let him scot-free. Even now there is no alteration in his character." After this the offender was pressed to death at Rajahat on Monday the third day of Ahin. 40.

Miscellaneous events.

On Friday, the eighth of Phagun in the same year, the King entered his house at Charaideo Hill. On Sunday, the twenty-ninth of Kati, the deposed Marangi Barbarua was brought from his home and executed in recollection of his previous attempt at rebellion. In the month of Puh, 1608, the King proceeded through Teok and encamped in the vicinity of the Dichoi river and caught elephants at Holongapar. In that year he established an encampment at Tokolai. In the month of Puh, 1609, the King despatched the Mou Buragohain of the Kuoigayan family with a number of the *dualias* and constructed the fort of Samdhara. On Saturday, the second of Kati, 1610, at the sixth *danda*, the foundation of the house at Barkola was laid. In that very month a number of nondescript *Bebejias* or vagrants of the North Bank were collected and settled at Tokolai. In the Phagun of the same year he retained in their respective positions the celibate disciples living in the Satras or monasteries and removed the married ones. In the Chait of the year 1611, the King fell ill, but he recovered soon after. At the second *danda* of the night of Friday, the twelfth of Puh, 1612, the King started for Sola, and performed a sacrifice by one hundred and eight Brahmans at Biswanath. Katyayan Bhattacharyya and the Mukalimura made offerings of *til* and *kusa* and blessed the King with the longevity of a hundred Brahmans. On Wednesday, the ninth of Magh, the King proceeded upstream to Gargaon. 41.

Miri incursions.

Then the Miris set fire to the house of the Rup-Sandikai at Sadiya and burnt the children and inmates to death; the Gohain however escaped with his life. The Miris further killed two hundred of our men. On hearing this the King despatched Moupia Phukan to suppress the Miris. The Phukan accordingly proceeded to the spot, attacked the Miris, and destroyed some of their men. The Phukan brought their heads, as well as a number of women and children belonging to the tribe. He also obtained a large quantity of *daos*, skeletons and mithans. At the command of the King the Phukan constructed an earthen rampart enclosing the villages inhabited by our men, and entrances were also constructed. The wall had its terminuses at the Brahmaputra. The Phukan presented all the spoils consisting of men and articles which were obtained in the expedition to the King and saluted at his feet. The Heavenly King said to Bih Gohain,—"Why did you not join and render help to the Rup-Sandikai?" Bih Gohain was executed being charged with this offence. In the month of Sravan, 1609, the King accused Kanu Gohain and dismissed him from his post of Rup-Sandikai, and appointed the Kanri-Deka or the headman of the guild of archers, who belonged to the family of the Miri-Sandikais, to the post of the Rup-Sandikai. 42.

Harbouring of princes.

Some time after this, Chungamua, a hereditary bondsman of the Dilihial Buragohain, complained to the King through his Burha-pachani or steward that the Buragohain was harbouring the prince of Diroi by giving him food and shelter, a fact which was known to the relatives of the Gohain. On hearing this the King arrested the cousins and nephews of the Buragohain and imprisoned them at the elephant-stable and enquired into the matter. He further commanded that the Buragohain should be asked at his residence whether the allegations were true. The Gohain averred that the charges against him were unfounded and pleaded his ignorance of the matter. The King said,—"His relatives have affirmed the allegations which have been supported by the bondsman, and still the Gohain dares to deny the charges. Such a man should never be allowed to live." Saying so the King killed Langi Buragohain at his own residence in the month of Bahag, 1612, as well as his relatives. The following were also executed at Bahgara,—Tanchek Kalia, son of Latung Gohain of the family of the Bargohain, and a few cousins and nephews, two men of Metekatal. Three months after this, two brothers of a prince living at Diroi made their appearance of their own accord and declared as follows,—"We have not been given shelter or food by any one, and no one knows who we are. We get our food by begging from house to house; during the day we live in the woods, and at night we live in the burial-grounds of the Ahoms. Why should others be killed for our sake? Seeing that many men have been killed on our account we have come out and offered surrender of our own accord." The King executed the two princes at Jathipota. 43.

In the month of Aghon, 1612, the King personally went to Cheuni and established a settlement there which he named

Laibacha. In Aghon, 1613, a dome was built on the summit of the hillock in the vicinity of the one sacred to the god *Lankuri*. In the same month elephants were captured at Jarapung and brought. On the twentieth day of Ahin, 1613, the King turned out Katyayan Bhattacharyya and other Pandits beyond Bahgara with pitchers suspended from their necks, their offence being their refusal to eat rice on the *Ekadasi*, or the eleventh phase of the moon, following the Durga-Puja. On Thursday, the twentieth, a few kinsmen of the Sola Phukan were traced out, and they were all killed. On Monday, the seventeenth of Kati, a site was dug out to construct a dome or temple at Charaideo. On Tuesday, the twenty-fifth, the foundation stone was laid. After this the Nagas killed our men at Mahang. Having received this intelligence the King despatched the Duara Phukan and the Abhaypuria Bandar Phukan by the Namchang and Barhat passes respectively. The two Phukans marched to the place, and on the pretence of a *pourparler* succeeded in capturing the Nagas with their Khunbao or headman. The captives were imprisoned at the Hatisal, and were removed later on to Langkak where they were all executed. Latha, the brother of the Khunbao, was appointed Khunbao. The King got a number of elephants captured at Maibela in the month of Bhada, 1613 *saka*. In Phagun of the same year a temple was consecrated to the gods. A tank was excavated in the vicinity of the temple; it was also consecrated and named Bhogdoi. Another tank was dedicated at Langkak and named Sonadoi. 44.

Minor events.

Just at that time a panic was caused by the scare that some mysterious being was going to devour and destroy men. There were two floods that year in the month of Sravan within three days of each other. The five lower rungs of the main ladder of the Holong-ghar were submerged under water. The two floods were named *Saka* and *Sakini*. On the thirteenth day of Ashar, 1614, the King uttered religious incantations on the Brahmaputra and performed sacrifices attended by prayers and accompanied by the offerings of goats and ducks, where he implored the gods to bless him with a life consisting of a hundred years. 45.

Disasters and omens.

On the twenty-third of Ashar, 1614, the Nagas of Namchang murdered twenty-three of our men. On hearing this the King commissioned the Dihingia

Naga expedition.

Phukan of the Duara family by giving him appropriate presents and the usual quota of men to suppress the Nagas, and the latter proceeded on Monday, the twenty-second Bhada, by the Namchang route. The ex-Barphukan of the Abhaypuria Chetia family was despatched with soldiers by the Barduar or the main gate. Then the generals attacked the Nagas, killed them and compelled them to submission. The Nagas came and paid their homage at the feet of the King. Latha Khunbao was put to death on the bank of the Jamuna. Those whose attitude to the King was found to be pure and loyal were given presents and sent back to their respective villages. 46.

Naga princesses offered to the King.

Soon after there was an insurrection of the Nagas near about the Dayang, and the King despatched Tancheng Phukan, son of the Duara, to this Naga war. The Phukan searched the houses of the Nagas for two days but could not find them out. The Nagas then approached the Phukan and said to him,—"For ages past we have been eating the crumbs thrown off from the dishes of the King. We have not committed this misdeed. The Abors have done it. But still as we have been cornered we shall offer to the King two of our princesses with slaves and female attendants. The Phukan should intercede on our behalf at the feet of the King and bring about our salvation." The Phukan agreed to the proposal and asked the Nagas to bring their princesses which they did accordingly. The Phukan delivered the princesses to the King and also presented the Nagas before His Majesty, who forgave their crimes and made presents to them. 47.

Repression of monks.

In the year 1614 *saka*, the religious leaders and disciples of the Thakuria denomination, as well as their brothers and nephews were taken to Namruk and killed; their names are as follows :—Jadumani of Bahbari, Jagabandan of Dagi, his son Satrushan, Kanthabhushan, Brahmananda of Sechamukh, Sahadev, Jaydev, Ramgovinda, Sundarishan of Katanipar, Bijoy of Budbari, Ratikanta of Lengdi, his son Jaygopal, Binandasyam of Namati, Sadaykhora Moamaria, Madhai, Baikuntha, his son Raghunandan, Keho of Gajala and his two brothers. A few children and relations fled and thus escaped from punishment. 48.

In 1615 the King seized the persons of the disciples, and this is the reason of their incarceration.—When the King during his princehood was wandering as a fugitive over the country he stayed for a few days at the Kalabari monastery belonging to Dakhinpat. There the prince had an alteration with the Deka-gosain or the heir-presumptive to the leadership of the Satra, who uttered abusive terms to the prince. This was remembered by the King. When he was made King by the Phukans at Kaliabar, the aforesaid Deka-gosain left Kalabari and proceeded down-stream to talk to the Phukans with the object of removing him from the kingship. When the King had been stopping at Biswanath on his voyage up, he saw a boat in the river and enquired who was travelling in the boat. The steward of the King intimated that he surmised from the appearance of the vessel that the Deka-gosain of Dakhinpat must be travelling therein. The King ordered his attendant to request the Gosain to confer his blessings upon him. Our men plied their boats towards the Gosain and told him accordingly, but he did not condescend to come. This is one reason. The King had also remembered the image of gold made by Banamali Gosain. 49.

Causes.

The Bhandari Barua, or officer in charge of the royal store, named Rangacharan Bejdoloi, complained to the King in the following words,—"Why should there be wealth and property in the establishment of a religious devotee? A few grains of rice constitute his only article of necessity, and even this is given to him by his devotees and disciples. If the King permits I can acquire this wealth for His Majesty." The King replied,—"Yes, I have also an umbrage against them. All right, Barua, please arrange for the acquisition of this wealth of theirs by sending Chaodangs. I will tell the monks what I should say and do the needful." On receiving this royal command the Bejdoloi instructed Kola Chaodang as to the desire of the King in this matter, and despatched him with Kana-chekerai and Achubulia. They in their turn harassed the Mahajans or religious leaders and extorted their wealth from them by force and torture. The golden image of Dakhinpat was removed and melted, and placed on the turret of the temple at Charaideo as its pitcher. As a punishment for his past offence the eye-balls of Ram Gosain of Dakhinpat were extracted. In the month of Bhadra, 1616, the wealth of the Auniati Gosain was confiscated and the Gosain banished to Sadiya. The King also ordered that the sacred image of Govinda-Thakur should be

Confiscation and torture.

thrown into water. However, the original image of Govinda-Thakur was secretly kept concealed, and in its place a replica of the image was thrown into the Brahmaputra at Changinighat. The other Mahajans were removed from their localities, and settled at Namrup, Tokolai and Cheuni. The King despatched Achubulia and punished the Gosains incarcerated at Namrup on the full-moon of the month of Bhadra. He also extorted money from all the other *Medhis*, and established them at Cheuni. The Satras were also set fire to. This was done through the instrumentality of Rangācharan Bejdoloi Bhandari-Barua. 50.

Death.

In the month of Magh, 1617, the King went to hunt deer near Bardubi, ahead of the Dikhou. The King was witnessing the hunting operations by standing on a rock. He was suddenly seized with a thrill followed by an attack of fever. The King then returned home, but the fever did not leave him. He had besides an abscess on the neck which gave him excruciating pain. The King died of this pain on Tuesday, the fourteenth day of the month of Phagun, 1617, after a reign of fourteen years, eight months and one day. 51.

CHAPTER IV.

SWARGADEO RUDRA SINGHA.

Accession.

In the month of Phagun, 1617, Rudra Singha, the son of Gadadhar Singha, ascended the throne. In the same year and the same month and on the same day King Rudra Singha reinstated the Mahajans or pontiffs in their original places. In the month of Ahin, 1618, the King ascended the Singari-ghar and took the name of Chao-Sukhrungpha. He distributed presents according to the rank of the recipients. The coronation festivities and amusements continued for seven days. 52.

Earthquake.

In the month of Puh, 1618, Bandar Phukan of the Chetia family constructed a fort at Pungdang under the orders of the King which took two months. In the same year there was an earthquake which continued for six months in an abortive fashion, from Phagun to Saon of the following year. The earth was rent asunder at Sadiya, and *magur* and *kawai* fish appeared in the breaches. As sands and waters appeared at that place the sides of the hills crumbled down. 53.

Conspiracy.

In the month of Bhada, 1619, the Charing Raja, the brother of the King's father, conspired with some men of Tingkhang and attempted to rebel against His Majesty. The Barua of the Chungis living in the neighbourhood of Changtak was also his accomplice. The King was then staying at Charaideo Hill engaged in offering worship. The conspirators designed to murder the King on his return journey to the capital after witnessing hawk-flights. Just at the time when the King was starting for the metropolis, a Dom or a man of the fisherman's caste who looked after the ducks of the Charing Raja apprised the King of the plot to assassinate him. On hearing this the King returned and despatched men to arrest the Charing Raja and the Chungi Barua, who were accordingly seized and imprisoned. After his return to the capital the knee-caps of the Charing Raja were extracted and the offender deported to Namrup, while his accomplice the Chungi Barua was executed. In the month of Bahag of the same year the following persons in joint consultation concealed a prince by giving him food and shelter in the house of Lahoi of the village of Papang,—Cheogam the Hazarikia of the guild of musketeers, Ramjay of the family of Chaorai, his two nephews, Langu the Deodhai of Nangkum and his son, Angka of Kakajan who was a supervisor of horses, a Brahman of Namtial, two men of the clan of Bakara Khanikar the artisan or image-maker. The King was intimated of this fact by men who heard it. The King caused the arrest of the prince and of Lahoi and his son. They were commanded to disclose the names of the conspirators. The prince as well as Lahoi said,—"All the men whose names have been mentioned know of this fact. They have been giving food and shelter." The King executed the prince together with the accomplices. The eye-balls of the two Deodhais were extracted. The relatives and children of the accused were transported to Namrup and settled there. All the members of the family of the Parvatia Phukan who was the grandson of Lechai, an archer, were also removed to Namrup. His offence was the alleged friendship contracted between the bondsmen of the Phukan and Ramjay of which he was aware. 54.

In the month of Agrahayan, 1619, the excavation of the tank

consecrated in the following Phagun by holding an assembly of the Mahajans, and named Jaysagar. In the month of Phagun, 1620, the construction of the three dome-shaped temples on the bank of the tank commenced, and an establishment was erected to the north of the tank and named Rangpur; and in Magh, 1622, the three shrines were dedicated. The images of Bishnu, Kesavrai, Siva, Durga, Ganesa and Suryya and others were placed in those temples. The town was also formally occupied sometime after, and it was named Rangpur. 55.

Jaysagar and Jaydoul.

In the month of Chaitra, 1622, Sarujana Gohaindeo, the younger brother of the King, made an attempt to rebel against him. In this conspiracy the prince acted in concert with the following whom he had met very frequently,—the Bhitarual Phukan of the Sandikai family, Bandar Naibaicha Phukan of the Lanmakharu clan, Bailung Dekaphukan, Chekham Hajarika or chiliarch of the Hilaidaris or musketeers of Bhadaru, Lochan Bara of the Ghorachowas or guild of oslers. The King was intimated of this conspiracy by Damodar Phukan of Mechaghar belonging to the camp of the refractory Gohain, when His Majesty was putting on his shoes in his palace. The King was satisfied with the evidence against the accused and issued orders for their execution. Desiring to save the lives of the three Phukans, the King had the three Dangarias taken out on the pretext of witnessing the game of cock-fighting. Apprehending the drift of the King's intention the Dangarias interceded on behalf of the Phukans, who were accordingly let off without punishment while a few others of the accomplices were executed including the Ghorachowa Bara and the Hilaidari Hajarika. The Phukans were dismissed from their office and sent to their homes in the country. Sarujana Gohain was deported to Namruk, and a few of his followers were decapitated while others were expelled after having their noses and ears chopped off. Soon after, the King despatched his steward Ghansyam of Cheregua, and had the eye-balls of his rebellious brother extracted. 56.

Revolt of Lechai.

After this the King constructed his royal premises at Rangpur by employing up-country or Bangal architects. A palace called Talatal-ghar with a few stories underground was constructed at Tengabari, as well as a temple for placing the sacred image of Rangnath. A

Importation of foreign costumes.

dome was also built for performing the sacrifices connected with the *Holi* festival. During the celebrations of the ceremony in 1626 the King put on a cloak, turban and shoes, and presented similar robes to his nobles. The three Dangarias, Laithepena Bargohain of the Madurial family, Darab-dhara Buragohain of Kuoigaon, and Kancheng Barpatra-gohain of Kenduguri protested and said,—"Why should we wear these presents imitating the fashions of the Bangals or foreigners in supersession of our own indigenous costumes?" Saying so they returned the presents. A fresh set of presents were sent by the King which included the *Kunmin* or the chief item of the national dress. They were worn by the Dangarias. The Buragohain, however, implored the King to give him the cloak, turban and shoes, and His Majesty granted his prayer. It was from that time that the custom of making presents consisting of turbans and cloaks was introduced. 57.

Naga raids.

In the month of Aghon, 1623, the King proceeded to Kaliabar. In Puh at Barhat a Jugi merchant of Bandarkhel killed some sixty Nagas who had entered our fort. During the confusion which followed the Nagas also killed a large number of our men at the *Lonsal* or salt-emporium. The King was apprised of this incident of the slaughter of our men by the Nagas when he was staying at Biswanath on his return journey from Kaliabar. The Heavenly King resumed his journey upstream towards the end of Phagun, and reached Gargaon on the second day of Chaitra. In consultation with the Dangarias and Phukans, the King despatched Basang Phukan of the family of Khimrat Patar, son of Sonapuria Gabharu, to fight with the Nagas. The Phukan proceeded and halted in the plains to the north of the Dilihi opposite to Barhat; from there he sent men to the Naga villages who negotiated and subdued the hillmen. He then came and bowed down to the King who forgave the offence of the Nagas and dismissed them by offering presents to them. A stone bridge was constructed at Namdang. 58.

Synod of Gargaon, *saka* 1624.

In the month of Jeth, 1624, the King promulgated an order to the Medhis or religious leaders of the Sudra caste to the following effect,—"I have not come across any text in the scriptures authorising a Sudra to offer initiation to a Brahman. Hence no such initiation should be offered. Besides, if any text can be cited which authorises such an initiation, the manuscripts where the relevant passages are to be found, should be brought to me. The preachers should also attend in person. I will investigate into the matter." All the other Medhis pleaded their ignorance of the matter, and declared their intention to carry out the command of the King. But the following five preachers,—Ram of Naroa, Madhavananda Bhatnokhowa the grandson of Barbhakat, Bareghariа Siram, Ramananda grandson of Gopal of Bhavanipur, and Chaturbhuj of Sechamukh,—stated that they could produce texts proving that a Sudra could initiate a Brahman, and that they should be summoned and questioned on this point. Each of them sent a letter to this purport. The five aforesaid priests were brought within the walls of Gargaon, as well as numerous Brahmans and Pandits. The King consulted them all, and investigated into the subject by opening piles of books; but in no manuscript could any passage be found empowering a Sudra to initiate a Brahman.

Then the King said,—"There is no passage in these scriptures to support such an initiation. The five Medhis should now proceed to show in which *puthis* or manuscripts they had found such an authority." The five priests failed to refer to any *puthi*, nor could they cite any authority. They could not also utter a single word. The Brahmans also became furious. The King ordered the five Medhis to be imprisoned in the elephant-stall. The Baruas and the Phukans implored for mercy, and the King said,—"I wanted to execute them but as my officers have begged for mercy I forgive them this time." Then five earthen jars were painted with lime and suspended from the neck of the five Medhis, and the King commanded that they should be sent back and settled as follows,—Sriram Thakur at Katanipar, Chaturbhuj Thakur at Mawamara, Ramchandra of Naroa at Koamara, the Bhatnokhowa Thakur at Elengi, and Ramananda the grandson of Bhavanipuria Gopal at his own place. The King then issued an order to all the Sudra Medhis to the following effect,—"The Brahmans who are now living in the Satras should no longer be given shelter there. The Brahmans of the neighbouring villages should not also be permitted to visit the Satras. Any violation of this order will be attended by due punishment which will be extended to the Brahmans as well." In the month of Ahin, 1625, the spies informed the King that two Brahmans were seen at Moamara. The King caused the arrest of the Moamaria Medhi and punished him

3

in the open courtyard. The two Brahmans were also given a thrashing, and had their ears and noses clipped. The Brahmans who were formerly disciples of Sudra priests were initiated again by religious preachers of their own castes. On information being received that the Kamalabaria and Madhupuria priests were not offering worship to images, they were also whipped and turned out with pitchers suspended from their necks. 59.

Expedition against Cachar and Jaintia.

Jai Singha, the Kachari Raja sent an ambassador with diplomatic letters and presents; he came and said,—'Our state extended formerly up to Mahang; I request the Heavenly King to restore to us our old territories.' Our King gave an audience to the ambassador, but considering the demand to be an unwarranted one he said,—'How does the servile Kachari venture to make such a proposal?' Then the Bargohain said to our Katakis or ambassadors as follows,—'What are you looking at? Sieze him by the neck and turn him out!' Then he was turned out of the Holong-ghar, during which tussle the beads of his necklaces were torn and dropped down. The letter was also torn to pieces. Then the King in consultation with the three Dangarias as well as other Baruas and Phukans came down to Biswanath where he encamped. From there he despatched by the route through Naga-choki at Marangi the following officers:—Darabdhara Buragohain of the Kuoigayan family, the Barchetia of the Bahbaria clan who was the warden of the Marangi frontier. The Gohain was placed in charge of the commissariat to arrange for the supply of rice. The two, viz., the Barchetia and Deka-Barbarua, son of Alan Barbarua of the Dihingia family, led the expedition being accompanied by Phukans and Rajkhowas. The Pani-phukan of the family of Phul-barua of Saraighat or Gauhati was sent by the Kapili route with the usual quota of Phukans and Rajkhowas. The two contingents proceeded by two separate routes and reached Demera and Maibang. The Kachari Raja fled and escaped into Jayantia. Our men sent a request to the Jayantia Raja to deliver up the Kachari chief, but the Jayantia Raja refused to comply with the demand on the principle that a refugee should not be betrayed. In the meantime the Swargadeo heard that the Barbarua was lying ill at Maibang, and he ordered the return of the army from the expedition. The Barbarua died at the fort at Gelemu during the return of the expedition. Our officers came back to Biswanath and presented the spoils obtained in Kachar to the Swargadeo and saluted him.

A year after, the King came down again and despatched the Gargayans headed by the Barbarua by the Kapili route. The Barphukan and the contingent stationed at Saraighat were sent by the route through Gobha. The two parties arrived at Jayantapur. Ramsingha, chief of Jayantia, offered his submission to the Barbarua, and sent the Kachari Raja to the Swargadeo. The Kachari Raja had previously informed the Barbarua as follows,—'You should contrive to send the Jayantia Raja to the Swargadeo. If this is not done then the Saru-kowanr or junior prince of Jayantia will come and rescue the chief. It will be difficult for you to escape; besides, they have designed to get you into the capital by a stratagem. I would advise you not to act up to his words.' Hearing this the Barbarua and Barphukan, after mutual deliberation, brought the Jayantia Raja on the pretext of giving him a reception, and subsequently imprisoned him. The Raja said,—'I am going to die like a woman being incapable of offering any defence.' Bijayram Kataki said,—'I told you before that the Assamese are unrivalled for their secret diplomacy, and that it is difficult to read their mind. You did not pay any heed to my advice at that time. What can Bijayram do now? An urchin has now fallen into the grip of a veteran; how is it possible for him to escape?' Then the Baruas and the Phukans after joint consultation decided to start on the third day to escort the Jayantia Raja to the capital for an audience with the Swargadeo. On that very day the Jayantia Raja was sent by the Gobha route. The Saru-kowanr was also waiting in full preparation, and hearing that the Raja was removed, he came out of his mountain fastnesses, chased the escorters having demolished the fort Sāt-koth, but returned to his own village not finding any trace of the Raja. One Barkrishna Thakur, attached to the Devi temple, was despatched with men to fetch the image of Jayanti-Devi. While bringing the image our men were waylaid by the Saru-kowanr of Jayantia, who killed the men and rescued the image. Krishna Thakur climbed up a tree, but he was brought down by an arrow-shot and killed. The two Phukans had in the meantime returned with the Jayantia Raja and reached Gobha. On hearing of the destruction of Sāt-koth they handed over the custody of the Jayantia Raja to the Dihingia Phukan, and without the permission of the King they pursued the Buragohain Phukan, cleared their paths and ultimately joined their own forces. The passage was obstructed when the fort was destroyed. The Buragohain was deputed formerly to regulate the duties of the men assigned for the supply of provisions. But he came out. The King, aggrieved at hearing the destruction of Sāt-koth despatched the Buragohain again to seize the person of the Saru-kowanr of Jayantia. They tried jointly to the best of their ability but no trace could be found of the Saru-kowanr, and it was accordingly reported to the King. The King ordered all of them to return which they did accordingly. The King returned to Rangpur and amused the Rajas of Jayantia and Kachar by arranging the celebrations connected with Phaku-yatra or the Holi festival. The Rajas of Jayantia and Kachar saluted the Swargadeo by kneeling before him. 60.

Ram Singha dies at Rangpur.

The Raja of Jayantia died at the place Jankhana which was allotted to him for his residence, and the Swargadeo arranged for the cremation of his body and the usual funeral obsequies. Two years after the King went down to Sariahtali and placed the Barkowanr or the crown prince on the masnad of Jayantia. The new Raja agreed to the annual offering of tribute to the Swargadeo. Krishnai Kataki of the Bahbaria family was deputed to escort the new Raja to Jayantia. The Baruas and the Phukans were sent to arrest the Saru-kowanr or the younger prince, but they returned being unsuccessful. 61.

Omens.

The stone domes situated at the two doors of Bahgara gate were broken by some mysterious agent at night. The domes of the temple at Tingkhang were also broken as well as those at the subsidiary temple on the Charaideo Hill. The King then went down to the mouth of the Barnadi where he performed the Holi festival, and offered alms and bounties. After offering worship to the god Madhava he went back to Rangpur. 62.

The King at Gauhati.

With the object of invading Bengal, the Swargadeo went down to Saraighat in the month of Bahag, and pitched his camp near the rampart of Raja Parikshit. A few days after a Changtalia Hari, or sweeper who used to work under *chang* or platform, entered the house of the dancing girls adjoining the main hall of the King

The sentinels saw him when coming out and said, 'Who is there ?' There was a great commotion. The King was startled in his sleep, and stood up with his sword and called in Ghanasyam of Cheregua, headman of the attendants, from the gate-house to whom he said,—'Well, Ghanasyam, enquire into what is afoot.' He accordingly enquired into the matter after pacifying the hubbub. He was told that the commotion was due to the sudden appearance of a man there. The men then examined the place with torches. There was rain before and footprints were left on the soil. The footmarks indicated a toe detached from the remaining fingers. Enquiries were made as to who was the trespasser, and every one denied. The King, on hearing this, ordered that the man with parted toes should be found out by an identification of his footmarks. The Pachani-Bara or chief steward investigated into the matter and came upon such a man in the wood, and his footprints bore evidence to his being the culprit. The matter was reported to the King who ordered him to be imprisoned. In the morning, after a prolonged enquiry into the matter, some three of the suspects were killed in the vicinity of the rampart of Raja Parikshit by having their chests ripped open with axes. A few others, who served in the inner chambers of the King's residence were turned out after having their noses and ears clipped, and the Haris or sweepers who had served outside were admitted for inner service.

63.

Hunting at Dirgheswari.

While at North Gauhati, the King once started for a deer-hunting excursion to the Dirgheswari Hill. On the way a buffalo issued out of the woods and dispersed the procession of elephants and horses as well as that of the archers and shieldsmen. The brute further rushed through the line of palanquin-bearers and stood between the palanquin of the King and of his two sons. The buffalo had, after killing a man, come alongside the Dhirgheswari Hill from north to south. A deer-slayer pierced him with a spear, and the buffalo ran up to the Dhirgheswari Hill. The King after entering Khajikhowa went out again and ascended the raised platform erected for the purpose of shooting deer, and busied himself in killing deer. Then a large number of monkeys assailed the hunting loft and perched on the royal canopy as well. They could not be driven by any means. The King alighted from the machang and ordered his men to open fire at the monkeys. On the return journey, at the Kanai-barasi-bowa rampart, the elephant Prabalsing attacked a palanquin-bearer who was on the point of being gored with the tusks, but his body was not penetrated through. The man stood between the tusks. The man being released was running for his life, when the elephant again caught hold of him by a sudden move, snatched away his head-apron and chewed it. The elephant became infuriated and rolled down from the rampart, head downwards, into the ditch. The Buragohain of the Pukhuriparia family was serving as the Mahut or elephant-driver; he also rolled down but he firmly clung himself to the head of the animal, and managed not to have a fall. The King placed two elephants and a few men in charge of the mad elephant and forbade them to lift him till he came to his senses. Thus saying the King came away. 64.

Invasion of Bengal.

Previously to this in the month of Bhada, the King conferred with the following on the subject of the invasion of Dacca or Bengal,—the Bargohain son of Laithepena Gohain, Kuoigayan Phukan Buragohain, Kenduguria Deka Barpatra-gohain and the Baruas and the Phukans, whom he addressed as follows,—'Well, I intend to invade the territories lying between the boundaries of Dacca and Rangagara. What is your opinion?' The Barpatra-gohain of the Kenduguria family supported the King's proposal and said,—'The King's proposal is reasonable. The territories bordering on the Karatiya are ours. The enemies have got possession of them only on account of our indifference and inaction. The duty of a king is to destroy the enemy, and to recover lost possessions with a view to preserve the ancient boundaries of his kingdom. We have a large fleet and naval soldiers, and abundance of war-materials. If the King orders, the enemy will be crushed and destroyed.' The Phukan-Buragohain of the Kuoigayan family then added,—'The King's proposal is reasonable, and what the Barpatra-gohain says is equally reasonable. The ancestors of our King had, by virtue of their prowess and courage, crossed the boundaries of Rangamati, and washed their swords at the Karatoya-Ganga. They found it inconvenient to fix the boundaries of Assam at the Karatoya, so they made the river Manaha the western limit of Assam and established a garrison at Gauhati. In the reign of Jayadhwaja Singha there was an abundance of provisions and men, and still he acquired the title of 'Bhagania Raja' or the 'Deserting King'; arms and ammunitions, materials and supplies are torpid and impotent:

the followers and subordinates of the King are symbols of life and animation; they alone can infuse into the immobile war-provisions a dynamic force. Still we should measure the strength of our own equipments as well as of those of the enemies. We must be prepared for both success and reverse, and our measures should be advanced in full recognition of these factors. At the same time the King's command will be obeyed."

At this the King became angry and said,—'At all times and ages the counsels of the Gohains have been of this character,' and then dismissed them from his presence. Then the Baruas and the Phukans said,—'Oh King, you can dispense with the Gohains; command us and we shall attack the territories up to the boundary of Dacca.' Then the King cleared all the places on the two sides of the road from the principal gate to the Lohit or Brahmaputra and fed his people. The King in order to witness the amusements of the people on the two sides of the road had erected a house there. There he sat and all the people blessed him with longevity. While in that house the King felt unwell and came back to his camp. From that day his illness grew on apace. The King had previously levelled down a neighbouring hillock in order to extend his camping grounds. The King had a dream at night where he was told that his illness was due to his bringing down the hill made by God. Then the hill was reconstructed and the old trees and creepers were replanted there. The King distributed alms and presents, but still his health was not restored. 65.

Death.

On the eighth day from the first attack of illness, the twice-glorious King Rudra Singha died just a *prahar* before sunset on Sunday, the second day of the black moon on the thirteenth of Bhada, 1636, after a reign of eighteen years and six months. 66.

CHAPTER V.

SWARGADEO SIVA SINGHA.

Accession.

On the same day when King Rudra Singha died, the Barjana Gohain, the eldest son of the deceased sovereign, was placed on a raised platform in the principal court-chamber, where the three Dangarias and all the Baruas and

Phukans knelt down before him and declared him to be the king. All of them, in fear of the Patar Barphukan guarded the new monarch throughout the night, and remained watchful in the Barchora or principal court-chamber being properly armed. The Bhitarul Phukan of the Duara family was posted at the principal gate, while the Dihingia Phukan of the Miri-Sandikai family remained at the river-side gate. 67.

Return to Rangpur.

A few days after, the officers and nobles conferred about the desirability of going back to Upper Assam; but one of the three dancing girls who were to accompany the King became impure, and the royal party had to postpone their departure for four days more. On Friday the body of the deceased king was placed in a boat; and Ghanasyam, the head of the royal attendants, was ordered to press to death the three dancing girls, and their dead bodies were placed at the feet of the deceased king in the boat. The vessel was sent up in charge of the Phukan-Buragohain of the Kuoigayan family, and of Barchetia, son of Japarjal, as well as the two Gohains. The King then imprisoned the Barphukan, and with him he arrived at Rangpur. The body of the deceased king was kept at Chunpora, where the Phukan-Buragohain died in Ahin a fortnight after. In Kati, a mound was raised where the remains of the dead king were buried, and in Aghon the *Sraddha* ceremony was performed by burning the effigy of the dead king. The heads of the monasteries were invited to attend the *Sabah* or assembly where alms and religious gifts were distributed. In Phagun the new King entered the Singari-ghar, and sat on the throne when he assumed the name Siva Singha. The festivities connected with the coronation continued for seven days, and the King bestowed presents on the three Dangaries and other nobles according to their rank and dignity. Then in the month of Bahag the King planted the *Ao-bar* or banyan tree of longevity. 68.

Phuleswari Barkuanri.

The King had a nurse who was the daughter of one Lakhtakia Koch. She was admitted into the royal chambers. The King had a dancing girl, named Phulmati, daughter of a *nat* of Chinatali. She was made the Barkuanri or chief queen and named Bar-raja. The King gave her the royal umbrella and permitted her to ride on elephants. Her brother was appointed Barpatra-gohain, and her paternal uncle was raised to the rank of the Tipamia Phukan, while another was made Dhekial Barua. The queen in contravention of the ancient customs of the Ahoms introduced the custom of burning the dead. She organised an assembly of the religious preachers of the Thakuria denomination, and made them bow down before the heads of the Auniati and Garamur monasteries. They were asked to offer worship to the gods with the help of images, the Bhagavat and Salagram stone under the priesthood of Bhagavatis and Dewris. Besides, she perpetrated many more insults and misdeeds. This is the most significant dark spot in her career. She caused the images of all the temples including Phulbari to be thrown into the river Luit or Brahmaputra, and she personally conducted the desecration staying in her camp at Sonarijan. Then she substituted stone and brass images in all these temples. This is another stain on her character. She excavated a tank near Namdang, and erected a temple which was named Gaurisagar. In consequence of her impious deeds she suffered protracted agonies after which she died. 69.

Draupadi Parvatia Kuanri.

The younger sister of the deceased queen had previously been married to the Solal Bargohain of the Miri-Sandikai family, by whom she became the mother of two sons. The King snatched her away from her husband and made her his Parvatia Kuanri. She had a son through the King, who was made Tipam Raja. Of her two sons by her former husband, one was appointed Bargohain and the other Sadiya-khowa Gohain. She excavated a tank near the village inhabited by the Kalanchu-paria Gohains. A temple and other domes were also constructed. They were afterwards dedicated to the gods, and the tank was named Siva-sagar. After this she went with the King to the newly constructed residence in the north of Chinatali, where they amused themselves by killing fish and deer. The Parvatia Ai-Kuanrideo died there of griping pain in the stomach. Her body was taken to Charaideo Hill and a mound was raised over the same. A temple was also erected at the spot at Chinatali where the queen had breathed her last. 70.

A new Buragohain.

At this time the young Buragohain of the Railungia family died in the month of Kati. On Sunday, the ninth of Aghon, King Siva Singha went to his residence at Charaideo to perform the ceremony of Khun-mung. He admitted to his chamber the Maut Gohain who was a Bara of the Pukhuriparia clan. The King placed his feet on the head of the new Gohain and blessed him, saying,—'I appoint you Gohain. With my blessings you will live up to a ripe old age. You will become very old and your head will touch your knees.' Saying so the King gave him a bunch of betel-nuts and a pair of suits, one of which he was to wear when he listened to his appointment as Buragohain and the other on his return home. The King commanded him to wait at the extremity of the court-chamber. The Majindar was then asked to appoint him Gohain after proper instructions. The Majindar accordingly announced to him the royal command and appointed him Gohain at the extremity of the court-chamber, saying,—"Gohain, the King has desired me to tell you as follows on his behalf,—'You have been appointed Gohain in consideration of the pleasure which I have received from your satisfactory conduct in the past. If you accord me similar pleasure in future, the bread which you will earn as Gohain will continue down to your descendants'."

The Gohain then replied,—'The King has said that I have been made a Gohain in recognition of my past services. But I do not believe that I have been able to give any satisfaction to His Majesty. God desires nothing but the sincere devotion of His worshippers; and when He becomes pleased He merely displays His own graciousness. Nothing in fact has been done by me; and what the King expects from me in future in the shape of satisfaction is also not to be had from me. God is pleased to ordain the birth of a boy, and gives him proper understanding and knowledge while still in the womb of his mother. If my Lord the King be pleased to train me properly and obtain satisfaction from me then only my bread will be permanent and will filter down to my descendants. Nothing will come out of me alone.' His son was also appointed Lari-Gohain or heir-presumptive to the office of the Buragohain. They were given two horses on which the father and the son were allowed to ride back to their residence. 71.

A new Barkuanri.

After this the King married Akari Gabharu and made her the Barkuanri or chief queen in 1661 *saka*. She was the daughter of the deposed Solal Bargohain, son of Laithepena Bargohain of the Madurial family. She was first married to the Barpatra of Kalugaon. 72.

Death.

In the month of Push, 1665, there appeared in the sky a comet and it was visible in the sky for three successive months, Push, Magh and Phagun.

On Friday, the tenth of Aghon, 1666, when four *dandas* had remained to complete the night, Maharaj Siva Singha passed away.

The Charing Raja, the Batgharia Gohain, Bhobola Gohain, the Kalsila Gohain,—these four younger brothers were on the bedside of the King. His son the Tipam Raja poured waters of holy unction at the appointed place near the heels and pressed the main toe of the dying King. The following officers and nobles also attended the King at his bedside,—the Buragohain of the Pukhuriparia clan, the Kalugayan Barpatra-gohain, Solal Gohain of the Madurial family, his brother Birai Na-phukan, and his uncle the Katha-sodha Phukan, Rupchandra Barbarua of the Bakatial family, the Bhitarual Phukan of the Lanmakharu clan, the Abhaypuria Phukan son of the Duara Barphukan, and a few other Baruas and Chamuas. The Dihingia Phukan of the Miri-Sandikai family was at the central door. The Hati-Barua and the Dekaphukan were posted at the western projection of the court-room, while the Rajneog of the Bakatial family was in the centre of the court-chamber. 73.

CHAPTER VI.

SWARGADEO PRAMATTA SINGHA.

Tipam Raja's bid for the throne.

The Kalugayan Barpatra-gohain, the Dihingia Bargohain and the Dihingia Naobaicha Phukan took up the cause of the Tipam Raja, and assembled the attendants and servitors employed in the interior of the royal household in one place, and made up their minds to install the Tipam Raja as king. After King Siva Singha had passed away, the Tipam Raja left his feet and took his bath. He then armed his adherents with swords, shields, spears, arrows and bows, and asking them to remain ready for action he himself waited in full preparedness. 74.

Suppression of 'king-making' attendants.

At that time the Pukhuriparia Buragohain and the Bakatial Barbarua said to the Tipam Raja,—'We have the brothers and sons of the deceased king entitled to sit on the throne. If you do not become king then who will fill up that exalted office? You have come out prepared with your attendants; is there any fighting going on anywhere? A king is properly installed on the throne if he is appointed by the three Dangarias and the Baruas and the Phukans. Can these urchins of slaves ever appoint a king?' The Buragohain asked the Charing Raja to seize the hands of the Tipam Raja, which he did accordingly. The Charing Raja had a sword in his hand. The Tipam Raja asked him to throw off the sword, and he snatched away his hand from the Charing Raja's grip. The Buragohain advised the Charing Raja not to part with the sword. The Tipam Raja requested his followers to give him a *dao*, but the Buragohain intercepted and threatened by saying that the man who would give him a *dao* would have even his son in the womb hacked and quartered. Saying so the Buragohain took out the four brothers of the deceased king as well as the Tipam Raja, but they were confronted at the michang or ante-chamber by the bevy of household attendants. The Buragohain then said to the Barbarua,—'What are you looking at? Don't you see that we are going to be massacred?' Just at that time Laidhan, who was a Changmai-ligira or an attendant of the royal cookshed, gave the Buragohain a sword which he pointed at the miscreants and they dispersed. The Buragohain's party then came out to the gate-house, and there also they were confronted by the rebels, who were also dispersed after some altercation, and the party then reached the courtyard of the palanquin-bearers. Even there, one Naga Ligira, an attendant belonging to the Dihingia family, having placed himself at the head of forty shieldsmen of the Lukhurasan clan, confronted the royalists on the way. He was also disbanded. 75.

Accession of Pramatta Singha.

The Buragohain and the Barbarua then received the Charing Raja at the principal court-chamber and said,—'Charing Raja, we hereby appoint you king.' The Buragohain then led the new King to the elevated platform and announced as follows,—'The brother of the deceased sovereign has become king. All the subjects including the Baruas and the Phukans should now offer their homage and kneel down before him.' Then the people assembled knelt down before the newly appointed monarch. 76.

Advice to the new monarch.

The Buragohain then counselled the new monarch as follows,—'The great God has conferred on you the position of a sovereign. Your duty will be the protection of the virtuous, and punishment of the wicked, and investigation into the weal and woe of your subjects. Just as a person does not feel heat when sitting below a huge tree, so under the shelter of your elder brother's government you were not tainted by the merits or demerits of the subjects. From to-day you have become the fountain of all their actions, virtuous or wicked. Your Majesty should regulate the acts according to the principle of their inspiring wicked or virtuous deeds. You have three younger brothers. They should also be protected and maintained by you as your own sons. They in their turn should pay homage to you regarding you as their father. They will succeed to the kingly office according to their seniority. You should not reject from your protection the Tipam Raja as well. Your Majesty should love him as your own son.' After saying so the Buragohain bathed the body of the deceased king and ascended the royal chamber for laying on the winding-sheet. On Sunday, the twentieth of Magha, the Buragohain removed the body of Siva Singha to Charaideo and buried it there. 77.

Punishment of rebels.

On the ground of revolt against established authority, the Kalugayan Barpatra-gohain was dismissed, and the son of the Barpatra-gohain of the Kenduguria family was appointed in his place; and similarly Khamchang Gohain, son of Laithepena Bargohain, was appointed Bargohain in place of the Dihingia Bargohain who had been dismissed. In addition to the above punishments the following were also chained and imprisoned in the elephant-stall,—the Dhekial Barua, and his son the Lari-Gohain, the Tipamia Phukan and the attendants Birah and Naga, and a few other shieldsmen. In the month of Phagun, the *Sraddha* ceremony of the deceased king was performed to which all the religious preachers were invited. They sang hymns to the glory of Hari, and alms and presents were distributed to them. In the month of Chaitra the trial of the rebels was taken up; those against whom the charges were light were let off with slight punishments and sent home. The Tipamia Phukan, the Dhekial Barua, his son Naga, and a few other miscreants had their ears and noses clipped and deported to Teji. 78.

Coronation of Pramatta Singha.

In the morning of Friday, the third of Ashar, 1667, the King ascended the Singari-ghar. When four *dandas* or midday had been announced the three Dangarias knelt down before the King and laid earth at the appointed place. Then the King commanded Parmai Maut the elephant-driver to bring the elephant named Mithabagari and to erect a howdah on it. The King rode from Tangkak to bring the image of Chengdeo. At the shrine where the image was placed, the King proceeded from the elephant to the platform and wore the image suspending it from his neck. He came back by Tangkak and sat in the appointed chamber screened from public view. There also the King had the image suspended from his neck. Outside the screen the lion's seat or throne was placed in a north-southernly position. Three wooden seats were also placed with graven images of dragons or unicorns as supports, each leading to the throne, and they were lower on the north than on the south. The three seats were placed on the north of the throne like a series of stairs. They were covered with a sheet of cloth each. The Buragohain caught hold of the eastern supports to the right when the King was ascending the throne. The Bargohain seized the western supports, the Barpatra and the Barbarua the two southern supports. On the throne again there was placed a raised seat with dragons as supports. The image of a snake was engraved on the western side of that elevated seat.

The King with the image of Chengdeo hung down from his neck ascended the throne from the south having placed his hand on the head of the Buragohain. He faced the east with his back to the west and leaned against the graven image of the serpent. The Bailung or the Ahom priest uttered benedictory verses or *bakhams* whereupon nine volleys were fired accompanied by the music of *Bardhak* or drums and other instruments. There were at that time only the three Dangarias, the Barbarua, the Ahom Barua in charge of the royal store and the three Bailungs. The King descended from the throne with his hand placed on the head of the Buragohain. The Deodhais or Ahom priests again uttered benedictory incantations, and the King kept the image of Chengdeo inside the space screened, and came out and sat on a *Nara-pira* or a large wooden seat in the balcony. Then the Baruas or officers employed in the royal store accepted the gifts of betel-nuts, betel leaves, rice, duck-eggs, and clothes presented to the King and made an inventory thereof. The screens were then lifted and the three Dangarias as well as all the Baruas and Phukans knelt down nine times before the image. After this they all came out and the three Dangarias sat in the Chatai court-chamber. They were also treated to a feast in the Holong-ghar. Then, when two *dandas* had remained for the termination of the day, the King came and sat on the throne which had nine steps. There again the Dangarias and the Baruas and the Phukans saluted the King seven times in due order of precedence. The King alighted from the throne and sat down on a *Nara-pira* to the west of the Holong-ghar. He then rose from his seat and pierced to death a white buffalo with his spear, while the three Dangarias killed a black buffalo. The festivities and amusements continued for seven days more attended by the similar slaughter of buffaloes.

On the eigth day the image of Chengdeo was returned to its shrine in the manner in which it was first brought; the King returned therefrom in a palanquin. The Dangarias were sitting at the Chatai-chora according to the approved procedure. The King commanded that the ambassadors of Jayantia and Kachar should be invited to witness the festivities held in connection with his coronation. He consulted his three Dangarias, and the Bargohain and the Barpatra-gohain said,—"Yes, they should be brought to such a function." The Buragohain added,—'The two principalities of Jayantia and Kachar have been recognised and protected by the Heavenly King since the days of his ancestors. The father of Your Majesty in order to punish their untoward attitude invaded their territories, and brought down their chiefs together with their ministers and potentates. Kachar has abided by the terms settled with its ruler at that time, but Jayantia has failed to ratify the terms of the agreement. Sȯ its ruler has been imprisoned for fourteen years. Kachar should be invited to send its representative to witness the festivities of the coronation but it is not proper that this privilege should be conferred upon Jayantia. If the consul for Jayantia be shown round the amusements now going on in full swing, then there was no necessity of imprisoning its ruler for fourteen years.' But even in spite of the opposition of the Buragohain the ambassador of Jayantia was taken to the assembly and allowed to witness the functions. The following presents were offered to the King,—a large sheet of embroidered cloth as well as a complete suit of royal apparel with *Kunmin* placed on a *sarai*, a lime-pot made of five tolas of gold, a pair of earrings with filaments made of three tolas of gold, a pair of *kalak* made of two tolas of gold, a silver *bata* weighing twenty-eight tolas, a pair of silver *kalak* weighing two tolas, two pigs, two pairs of fowls, two pairs of geese, a pair of male and female slaves, two he-buffaloes, a pair of milch cows. On Tuesday which was the fifth day of the ceremony, at the fourth *danda* at noon the three Dangarias saluted the King from the balcony of the royal palace, and made presents of similar articles. In the month of Magh the King planted the *Ao-bar* or the banyan tree of longevity. 79.

Embassy from Rani.

In the month of Phagun, 1667, the Buragohain received the Rup or ambassador deputed by the Raja of Rani. Vidyanivas Kataki introduced the representative of Rani. The Buragohain then said,—"Vidyanivas, ask the Rani ambassador whether at the time of his departure from his country, the subjects of the Swargadeo living in plains and hills were in enjoyment of peace and plenty. When did he arrive here? Has he encountered any fear or trouble in his journey?' On being thus interrogated by Vidyanivas the Rani ambassador said,—'When we left our territory, the subjects of the Heavenly King living in plains and hills were all well. We have been absent from our country for full five fortnights. We have not experienced any fear or trouble in our journey either in the roads or in the ferries." The Buragohain again added,—'It is our wish that the subjects of the Swargadeo living in plains and hills should pass their days in peace and happiness.' The ambassador of Rani then replied,—'We Mikirs and Garos live in the interiors of hills. The Heavenly King used to give us the bones of cows looking upon us as insignificant as shrubs on the way or dogs on the road. But for many years we have not been blessed with the good grace of the Swargadeo. We have also been comparatively weakened by the cessation of royal favour. I have been deputed by my countrymen to win back the kindness of the Heavenly King. How shall we meet the great King unless the three Dangarias come to our rescue?' The Buragohain then replied,—'Vidyanivas, tell the ambassador that the prayer of the wild monkeys even was granted by Lord Ramchandra as it was made with proper reverence and love.' 80.

Temples and edifices.

King Pramatta Singha erected the Ranghar at Rangpur. It was made of brick, and had two roofs like the ordinary houses of bamboo and wood. He also caused the gate-houses of Gargaon to be built of brick. He also erected the temple at Sukreswar in Gauhati. Besides, in 1673 *saka,* he raised a temple at North Gauhati at the place where Rudra Singha had breathed his last; an image of Siva named Rudreswar was placed in the temple, and lands and paiks were endowed for the maintenance of the temple on the system of Devatra tenure. Hence the village was named Rudreswar. Settlement operations were initiated in Kamrup and arrangements were made for the maintenance of records of rights. Nothing particular was achieved during the reign of this King. 81.

Death.

King Pramatta Singha breathed his last on the twenty-ninth day of Aswin in 1673, *saka,* the *tithi* being the Navami or the ninth day of the black fortnight. He ruled for six years, ten months and five days. 82.

CHAPTER VII.

SWARGADEO RAJESWAR SINGHA.

Accession.

On the death of Pramatta Singha his younger brother ascended the throne with the name Rajeswar Singha. Three sons were born to him when he was a prince. The eldest of them was named Kandura Gohain. His younger brother the second prince was given the *Charingia mel,* while the *Saru mel* was bestowed on the youngest prince the Sarujana Gohaindeo. Rajeswar Singha on ascending the throne thus gave the three princes the charge of the three *mels.* On Rajeswar Singha's assumption of the royal office a fourth prince was born to him who was termed *Pat-kowanr* or the throne-prince. Kandura Gohain died at Gargaon, and a mound was raised on his remains at Bhogbari. On the occasion of his ascension to the Singari-ghar in 1674 *saka,* the King invited all the religious preachers and the Rajas of Darrang and celebrated the usual festivities for seven days, and made presents to the three Dangarias and other officers employed in the capital of Gargaon and the viceregal headquarters of Gauhati according to their rank and dignity. In 1675 *saka,* the King ascended the *Pat-ghar.* 83.

Royal tour.

In the year 1678 the King desired to proceed to Gauhati, and accordingly commanded Kirtichandra Barbarua of the Bakatial family to erect encampments at different places. In obedience to the royal mandate the Barbarua erected temporary residences for the King at the following places,—one on the bank of the Sonari river, another at Gajpur, one at Dergaon, one at Jatiarang opposite Biswanath, one at Kaliabar, one at Sariahtali, one at Bardowa, one at Beki, one at Kalsila, one at Barnadi and one at Hajo. The King halting at these encampments and amusing himself by hunting deer and buffaloes, and catching fish, arrived at Gauhati. The Barphukan escorted him from Latasil, and many people were killed in the crowd being trampled on by elephants. In the month of Chaitra, 1679 *saka*, the King travelled back to Upper Assam halting at his camps, and arrived at Rangpur. 84.

Embassy from Nara.

Four Phukans then visited the Ahom court as ambassadors of the Bar-Naras. The old Chiring Phukan received them duly in the residence at Ramanibazār. Bhagi Buragohain of the Kuoigayan family entertained them at his house at Bokanagar according to the customary procedure, and also the Doulbandha Chatai-alia Bargohain at his camp at Chatai-ali. At all these three places the Nara envoys were feasted with buffaloes' heads roasted along with the horns, which were served on *mehengas* or raised dishes. The King himself received the messengers at the *Holong* at Gargaon; the three Dangarias as well as the Barbarua, Phukans, Rajkhowas, Chamua-phukans, Baruas and Hazarikias were ordered to attend the function in their turbans, cloaks, cloths and ornaments according to their rank. The Saikias, Baras, and Paiks of the Kanris were also ordered to appear in ceremonial costumes. The foreign ambassadors were placed at the elephant-stalls near the Barduar. As commanded by the King the officers and men were given three sets of robes of different sorts which had to be worn alternately; and they were expected to make their exits and their entrances in these different costumes with a view to give the impression of numerical superiority. The Nara ambassadors said,—'Yes, the number of men belonging to our Bhai-raja or brother-king is certainly great, yet the grass in the roads has not yet withered.' 85.

Bangal jugglers.

The King brought from Bangal a company of jugglers under an Ostaz named Bahpati who was accompanied by a handful of other female artificers. The Swargadeo arranged for the entertainment at the Ranghar. This is what they showed,—mangoes were made to appear on tender mango plants having only two blades; dances were performed on the point of a trident, and several other feats were exhibited before the monarch, who became pleased and gave the performers one thousand rupees. 86.

Murderous attack on Kirtichandra.

At Rangpur, in the month of Kartik, 1685, after passing the day at his town residence, the Barbarua proceeded to his watch in the evening when the night had advanced one *danda*. As he entered the gate-house, an assassin struck him at his neck with a *dao* from behind; somehow the windpipe was not severed. The Tekela-Bara caught hold of the miscreant, and Ram-krishnai, son of Jada Tamuli, clasped round the body of the Barbarua and with other men he removed the Barbarua to the guard-house by bandaging his neck with a piece of cloth. His son Choladhara Phukan or the master of the ward-robe, who was then at the store of royal costumes, was informed accordingly. On receiving this news the Phukan being afflicted with grief hurried to the King's quarters, fell prostrate at the feet of the monarch with eyes full of tears, and said,—'An assassin has hacked the King's servant the Barbarua inside the principal gate: it is inexplicable as to who the miscreant is'. The King was mortified and said,—'All right, the matter will be properly investigated. I shall institute an enquiry as to who dares to hurt my Barua knowing that I am living in flesh and blood'. The Barbarua was guarded that night by a regular bevy of watchmen, and the muzzles of the royal cannon were turned towards the residence of the Barbarua. The Naobaicha Phukan of the Miri-Sandikai family was seen at his residence at a prohibited hour, and he came to the capital that same night hearing of a murderous fray inside the city-walls without any torch. 87.

Trial of the conspirators.

At day-break, the murderous criminal was recognised by all; he transpired to be one Ratikanta, a Ganak of Nazira-hat. At the instance of the monarch Ratikanta was asked,—'Who are the accomplices at whose instigation you have committed this act?' Ratikanta admitted his guilt and gave out the names of those who had accompanied him,—one Barchamua of the Chaodangs, Mani Dhekial Barua of Lukhurakhan, his sister's son the Dayangia Deka of Sandikai family. The last two persons being found guilty in the trial were fettered with iron chains and imprisoned at the Hatisal at the entrance of the Barduar. The Naobaicha Phukan was also accused of having entered the city at a prohibited hour and was imprisoned with fetters. The Gharphalia Barua of the Barukial Bargohain family was going out after discharging his duties at the guard, when he was accosted by the Dhekial Barbarua from the place of imprisonment, who said,—'I have no *hăchati* or handkerchief on my head. Please send me your *hăchati*.' The Gharphalia Barua in his sincerest motives sent his *hăchati* to the prisoner. The Tekelas on guard saw this and communicated the fact to the Barbarua, who reported the same to the King. The Swargadeo having heard this charged the Gharphalia Barua who was the brother-in-law of the Barbarua, of the offence of giving a handkerchief to a prisoner, and removed him from office and drove him away. Barbarua's own elder sister was given in marriage to the Gharphalia Barua. In the trial the Dhekial Barua as well as his nephew were both convicted and pressed to death under wooden cylinders; their dead bodies were placed on a raft, with a *hăchati* on the nephew's shoulders, and were then made to float adrift. In a similar trial Jhabuli and Naobaicha Phukan had their noses and ears cut off, and they were placed at Nibok. The Barchamua, Mandhaj, was fried to death in oil, and his three accomplices were hewn with axes. Ratikanta Ganak was also torn asunder with axe. The blacksmith who made the *mit-dao* or dagger with which the Barbarua was struck had his ears, nose and eyes destroyed. At this time, the Barbarua obtained the King's permission to arm one man out of every twenty retainers with a club. From that time clubmen were attached to the Barbarua, who also became entitled to daily guards. 88.

Jai Singha seeks Swargadeo's protection.

After this the Miri-Sandikai was appointed Naobaicha Phukan, and his son Khangia Phukan was promoted to the office of Dhekial Phukan. The Barbarua also recovered from the wounds. Then, the king of Burma having occupied Manipur or the kingdom of the Magalus, the chief of the latter took shelter in the Kachari country from whence he sent word to our Chokial Barua that should the Barbarua be pleased to lead him, he would take refuge at the feet of the Heavenly King. The Kachari Raja also sent a communication to the same effect. The officer in charge of the Chauki or military outpost reported the matter secretly to the Barbarua. The Barbarua placed the matter before the King, saying,—'The Kachari Raja as well as the Manipuri Raja intend to come here to take shelter at the feet of Your Majesty. They have sent words to us accordingly, so I have informed Your Majesty. If Your Majesty orders me, I, your servant, expect to fetch the two chiefs and cause them to pay obeisance with the help of the divine prowess of Your Majesty. Besides, the Kachari and Manipuri Rajas have said that I, your servant, should go and bring them in person, and so I have informed Your Majesty.'

On hearing this the King commanded the Barbarua to escort the two Rajas. The Barbarua with due submission replied as follows,—'Since Your Majesty has commanded me, your slave, I will go. I pray that Your Majesty might be pleased to confer the title of Deka-Barbarua on the Choladhara Phukan'. The King said,—'All right, the Choladhara Phukan will be made Deka-Barbarua'. The King then permitted the Choladhara Phukan to take his seat at the place reserved for the Barphukan, and conferred on him the title of Deka-Barbarua. 89.

The Barbarua at Raha.

Then in the month of Aswin, on the Bijaya-Dasami day, the Barbarua started with a large number of men, elephants, horses and provisions. He marched forward, and pitched his camp at the military outpost of Raha. The Barbarua despatched Katakis to both the Rajas on a day which marked the passage of five years from the time when the murderous attempt was made on his life. The message ran as follows,—'As requested by both the Rajas I have come to escort them with the knowledge and permission of the Swarga-deo. So they should both come without any delay.' Thus being informed by the messengers, Jai Singha, the Raja of Manipur, and his son Juvaraj Anupananda, with the Kachari Deka-raja came to the Chauki at Raha in the month of Jeth and held an interview with the Barbarua, who being delighted at the sight of the Rajas signalised the event by firing seven volleys of cannon. He also arranged various festivities and amusements. During the month of Jeth, the Barbarua excavated a canal from the Kalang to the Lohit to permit the passage of boats and rowers. The Barbarua came out by that canal with the two Rajas, and began to advance upstream. He also came upon an image of Hara-Gauri on a hill which he took with him. At last he reached Rangpur, and halted at Rangnath at the entrance of the Barduar. The Rajas were accommodated at Mataimora. The two Rajas had a retinue of nearly 500 men with them. The Barbarua then sent the following message to the King,—'I, your slave, have brought both the Rajas by virtue of Your Majesty's divine grace.' The King having heard this called in the Barbarua to the principal audience-chamber. All the Dangarias, Phukans and others assembled in the gathering. The King summoned the Barbarua and the three Dangarias to the *chang*. The Barbarua bowed down his head before the King. 90.

Achievement of Kirtichandra.

The Swargadeo asked the Barbarua,—'Has the mission for the execution of which you were despatched been fulfilled? What fear and privations did you feel in your travels and sojourn? How many men have you lost? When did you resume your return march and when did you reach this place?' Being thus asked by the King orally, the Barbarua replied,—'Oh King and Lord, by virtue of Your Majesty's sacred power, Jai Singha, the chief of Manipur, as well as Sandhikari Raja, the paramour of the Kachari Raja's mother, have been brought to your presence by me, your slave. An idol of Hara-Gauri has also been brought alongwith.' The King praised the Barbarua for thus bringing the two Rajas. He allowed the Dangarias to retire from his presence after giving them the *bata* containing betel-nuts. The King feasted the Barbarua at his dinner. The King ordered the three Dangarias as well as the Phukans and the Baruas to sit at the court from that day wearing their turbans and cloaks. 91.

Reception of Jai Singha.

Then the Swargadeo granted an audience to the Kachari and Manipuri Rajas in the Barchora of his palace at Rangpur. The two chiefs bowed down their heads before the Ahom King, and the council too assumed a gala appearance. On that occasion the band headed by Jayananda supplied a musical *soiree* to the accompaniment of *Pasouj*, at which the Rajas were exceedingly delighted. The King conferred upon the Barbarua the following marks of distinction,—a single velvet piece for use as carpet, a *Japi* or wicker umbrella with a peak made of gold; it was also ordered that musicians would sing and blow their horns in front of the

Barbarua as he would pass to and from the principal gate and his town residence. 92.

Kuranganayani.

The Barbarua then made the following recommendation to the Swargadeo,—'The chief of Manipur has a daughter named Kuranganayani. The Manipuri Raja was descended of old from Babrubahan. He is a Kshatriya, and there is no doubt about it. I hope, Your Majesty will marry the princess.' Having heard this the King replied,—'Very well. As recommended by the Barbarua, I will marry the princess.' The Barbarua then despatched Khangia Phukan, and Ghumuria Dualia Phukan of the Dihingia family to bring the Manipuri Raja's daughter, mother, brother and son from the Kachari kingdom. They were brought and stationed at Gaurisagar. The Swargadeo then married the princess at the Sonari river by performing the Chaklang ceremony. The Barbarua served as the bride's father and supplied all the necessary articles of marriage. Golden ornaments, dowry and other provisions for food were all supplied from the Barbarua's house. The princess excavated a tank, and made an establishment at the village Manaimaji in the Sarucharai forest lower down the Dichoi, where the Magalus or Manipuris forming part of the marriage settlement were allowed to live. 93.

Rawan-badh Bhawana.

A *bhawana* or dramatic performance enacting *Rawan-badh* or the killing of Ravan, was held for the entertainment of the Manipuri and Kachari Rajas. From that time the Barbarua used to sit against the *fukam* or main pillar in the transept while the Barphukan down to other Phukans sat in the Bhawana hall. The Deka-Barbarua was the *Ostaz* or master of the revels in connection with the performance. Seven hundred men took part in that *bhawana*, and it was an extraordinary success. The Manipuri and Kachari Rajas were extremely delighted. 94.

Aid to Jai Singha.

The Barbarua submitted the following recommendation to the Swargadeo,—'This chief of Manipur has taken refuge with Your Majesty being driven from his kingdom by the Burman king. The Sastras have said that a fugitive should not be denied protection; so, if Your Majesty can contrive to reinstate the Manipuri Raja in his own kingdom, the act will bring in to Your Majesty both fame and piety.' After the Barbarua had thus informed the Swargadeo the latter said,—'Very well, let him bring the Dangarias, and let us discuss with them about the proposal of the Barbarua.' The Dangarias set forth their advice on being consulted regarding the matter. The Swargadeo then made the Manipuri princess his chief queen. The King then took the three Dangarias as well as the Barbarua to his *chang*. He asked the Dangarias,—'This Manipuri Raja took shelter in the Kachari kingdom being pursued by the Burmese. Through the instrumentality of our Barua he has come here and sought our protection. What do you say regarding the reinstatement of the Manipuri Raja in his own kingdom? What is your individual opinion in this matter?' Having heard this from the King the Dangarias gave the following reply,—'If Your Majesty can restore the Manipuri Raja to his kingdom, your fame, piety and glory will be resounded in your own land as well as in other regions.'

The King then ordered the Barbarua for the collection of men, provisions, powder and ammunitions as well as the recruitment of *dowal* soldiers belonging to Gauhati and Gargaon establishments. Receiving the above command of the King the Barbarua humbly submitted as follows,—'The King's orders can be carried out only by virtue of Your Majesty's divine prowess. What can be achieved from us alone, Your Majesty's slaves and servants?' The King then ordered for the presentation of the *bata* containing betel-nut and leaf to the Dangarias, and he also gave the same to the Barbarua who accepted it in his *hāchati* covering his head. The Barbarua saluted the King and all the counsellors retired from the presence of the sovereign. 95.

Harnath Phukan appointed general.

As commanded by the King the Barbarua arranged for men, provisions, powder, munitions, arms, and weapons and all other requisites for an expedition; he also ordered all the officers of Gargaon and Gauhati to mobilise the army of *dowal* soldiers in the month of Kartik. In Aghon, the King commanded the Sandikai Dekaphukan of the Edabaria branch, and the Bhitarual Phukan of the Lahan family to accompany the expedition. As the aforesaid Dekaphukan fell ill, he was removed from office, and a man from the Gajpuria Hati-Barua family was appointed Dekaphukan. The Bhitarual Phukan also had an attack of diarrhœa; on account of his inability to go he was dismissed, and the Dualia Phukan of the Duara Barphukan's family was presented with a golden sword and appointed commander of the expedition being placed at the head of all. The army consisted of nearly 40,000 men, and included Gargaon and Gauhati recruits consisting of the *muls* and the *dowals*, as well as the *meldagias* or men attached to the various *mels*. To each assortment of soldiers the King attached the respective Dualia Phukans and Rajkhowas. 96.

Farewell to Jai Singha.

When all the men were ready, the King bade farewell to the Manipuri Raja at the audience-hall in his residence on the bank of the river Sonai. When the preparations were completed for the march, the Swargadeo asked his three Dangarias and the Phukans to impart necessary instructions to the Raja of Manipur. 97.

The Barpatra-gohain's parting advice.

The Lechengial Barpatra-gohain Dangaria then addressed the Manipuri Raja,—'Oh, Raja of Manipur, your kingdom was occupied by the Burmese. Being unable to stand in your dominion you took refuge in the Kachari territory, from where you sent your prayer to the Swargadeo through the Barbarua. Our King then sent the Barbarua and brought you from Khasampur, and you placed yourself at the mercy of the Heavenly King. Our monarch, in his turn, has greatly favoured you by despatching a large number of soldiers and attendants charged with the commission to reinstate you in your own kingdom. On reaching your land you should collect your old ministers. If you have received any wrong from any man you should pardon him and accept him again into your good graces, as required by the exigency of the situation. Our King has particularly desired that you should not forget him, after you have regained your kingdom through the favour of God and the Goddess. You should keep yourself acquainted with our safety and welfare by sending to the King envoys and letters through the Barbarua.' Thus was the Manipuri Raja instructed. 98.

Jai Singha's reply.

The Bargohain, the Buragohain as well as the Phukans instructed the Raja more or less in the same manner. Being thus advised, the Manipuri Raja made the following reply,—'What you have said to me is wholesome and proper. The saying "My kingdom is gone and I am an exile" has become applicable to me. A householder plants a mango tree, and waters it so that it may grow. If through some mischance, the tree does not bear fruit, the owner may utilise the tree for some other purpose. What service can be rendered by me? Yet, the Barbarua has stepped into the position of a father to me, and the Swargadeo into that of God. If I be restored to my kingdom, the fame and piety of the King will shine eternally in this earth as the moon and the sun.' The words of the Manipuri Raja were listened to by the King as well as by his ministers and advisers. 99.

Advice to the general.

The Lechengial Barpatra Dangaria then addressed the Senapati Phukan,—'O, Phukan, you are a member of the Duara family, whose pedigree is ancient and not modern. So His Majesty has specially commanded you to place the Manipuri Raja in his dominion, and has provided you with a large number of soldiers and attendants as well as materials. So you should proceed with the King's army with care so that you and the contingent may not suffer hardship and loss in the journey. After reaching Manipur, you should make the most strenuous effort to consolidate the Manipuri Raja in his kingdom by the adoption of strategic measures, by war or by any other means.' The Barbarua also instructed the Phukan in the above manner at the instance of the King. 100.

Harnath Phukan's reply.

Being thus instructed, the Senapati Phukan then said,—'What the King and the Dangarias have ordered, and the instructions which have been imparted by the Dangarias and by my elder brother the Barbarua, are logical and true. Yet what can be achieved by me alone? What may occur by the favour of God and Goddess as well as by the righteousness and might of the Heavenly King will only take place. And so, what should I beg of you? I pray that the King and the Dangarias will bless me. Then only all our objects will be achieved.' On that occasion the King deposed the Barchetia Marangi-khowa of the Japarjal family for not being able to speak. 101.

The Lata-kata Ran.

The general, Bhitarual Phukan, then entered through the mouths of the two rivers in the company of his army, and proceeded through some hills, but having lost his right way ascended up the country, and arrived at a place facing the Charaideo Hill. Not being able to find out the way to Manipur, the men roamed about in the forest, where for want of food their knee-caps became enlarged. The juice of wild plantains served the purpose of water. The price of rice rose up to one rupee for a quantity contained in the average *temi* or lime-pot. The provision-suppliers could not reach the army being killed in their march by the Nagas. The army made their march by cutting and clearing the jungle. The Nagas also refused passage to the soldiers and killed a large number of our men, while many more died of fever and dysentery, and others by the bite of snakes and spiders. The Manipuri Raja had previously taken upon his own shoulders the task of conducting the army by showing the correct way, but having entered the forest he also became nonplussed.

Then the officers including the Senapati Phukan conferred together about the situation, and not being able to find the way by any means sent a report to the Swargadeo fully informing him of the facts,—"The Nagas have killed many of our men, and our food-stuff has also fallen short. Many have died of fever and dysentery. We, your slaves, have been compelled to apprise Your Majesty of the situation not being able to find any other solution." This was told to the Barbarua. The Barbarua communicated the news to the King, who ordered the withdrawal of the expedition in the month of Jeth. The army returned in the month of Ashar. Two-thirds of the men and provisions were lost, only a third could come back. At the time of coming out of the forest, the soldiers reached the Manipuri Raja to the other bank having placed him on a raft for crossing the river Baraka. The army returned in the month of Ashar. 102.

Harnath Phukan accused.

When the remnant of the force arrived at Rangpur, the King ordered them to stop at the Hatisal in front of the Barduar. Then under orders of the Swargadeo, the Senapati Phukan was charged with the following offence,—'Why has he caused the destruction of so many of my men and such a large quantity of my materials? Why could he not advance by opening his way by killing the handful of Nagas who had offered resistance? Oh, I see, he has neglected in his duties entrusted by me.' 103.

Harnath's explanation.

Being thus accused the Phukan submitted the following prayer to the King,—'Whatever may be the charge His Majesty has brought against me, I am within it. My forefathers, His Majesty's servants of old, could not escape from similar charges, and how can I avoid them now? The Manipuri Raja promised to conduct us by showing the way, and so we undertook the march. On entering the forest we could not trace the way by any means. Besides, many of our soldiers died of blood dysentery, and our food-provisions also failed. There were no provision-suppliers, and the Nagas did not allow us passage; they used to roll down stones from hill-stops and kill our men by that method. We proceeded one month's journey by clearing the jungle, but could not find out any clue whatsoever. So, I, His Majesty's slave, have been made liable to blame. If I had neglected Your Majesty's commission, having had somebody to show the way, then only, I, his slave, would be guilty of remissness in duty. Besides, if there had been suppliers of food-stuff, such loss of men would not have occurred. Yet, how can I escape from offence against His Majesty? So I, his slave, is within the bounds of punishment."

This supplication of the Phukan being submitted to the King, His Majesty pardoned his offence and permitted him to go to his residence. After a few days he was allowed to resume his duties at the watch. This expedition was termed *Lata-kata Ran* or the creeper-cutting expedition. 104.

Death of Rajeswar Singha.

Then after a year, in the month of Jaistha, *saka* 1691, the King Sri Rajeswar Singha passed away at Dewargram. He reigned for nineteen years. 105.

Cremation.

The body of the deceased king was conveyed upstream for burial at the Charaideo Hill. The ministers and counsellors consulted together, and arranged for the return of the cortège when it had reached the vicinity of the temple at Gargaon; the body was conveyed down and burnt below the big *Simalu* tree on the banks of the Lohit adjoining the royal residence at Sonai river. One of the princes, in the company of the Chetiapatra Phukan, conveyed the bones to the hill. The *Sraddha* ceremony was performed according to Brahmanical rites. From that time was inaugurated the custom of burning dead bodies, and of performing the *Sraddha* according to Brahmanical rites. 106.

CHAPTER VIII.

SWARGADEO LAKSHMI SINGHA.

Accession.

On the twenty-first day of that month of Jaistha, of the year 1691 *saka*, the following nobles and ministers jointly deliberated and installed the Namrupia Gohaindeo, the younger brother of the deceased monarch as their king at the royal camp at Dewargaon,—the Lechengial Barpatra-gohain, the Buragohain of the Kuoigayan family, the Madurial Bargohain, Gendhela Barbarua of the Bakatial family who was also called Kirtichandra after he had brought the Magalus, Dholpeta Naobaicha Phukan of the house of Dihing, Rungrungia Bhitarual Phukan of the Duara family, Puthao Dekaphukan, the Dihingia Phukan of the Rup-Sandikai family, the Balia Na-phukan of the Madurial family, the Rajneog of the Bakatial family. The new monarch known previously as Kalsilia Gohain now took the name of Lakshmi Singha.

At that time, under orders of the King the Maju-Gohain and the Saru-Gohain were exiled to Namrup where they were maimed. The Pat-kowanr was placed at Barkola. Then the King kept with him a son of Pramatta Singha by conferring on him the Tipam *mel*. The King was then brought from Dewargoan to Rangpur. 107.

Spectre of the Moran revolt.

In the same year, in obedience to royal orders, the Barbarua sent some men to cut Bardhaks or drums. These men came back and reported to the Barbarua that they could not cut the drums, as the Hati-chungi Morans acting in a heretical and disloyal manner had made their own Raja and Barbarua and launched a war or rebellion. And Manchoka, the *Tekela* of the Barbarua, came back and submitted detailed information to the following effect,—'The Hati-chungis under the Barbarua as well as those under the Phukans have assembled together and recruited devotees or followers; they have made two women Radha and Rukmini, and after holding diabolical conferences they have launched a war of insurrection.' Having received this information, the Barbarua reported the matter to the King, who ordered the former to make enquiries. In obedience to the King's command, the Barbarua investigated into the matter, and concluded that it was a mutinous revolt. Bez, the Bara of the *Tekelas*, was despatched at the head of a force consisting of one thousand Bhitarual Chutia *Kanris*, and one thousand musket-men attached to the Barbarua, commanded by their respective Hajarikas. This contingent marched forward and reached the place where the Morans had made their belligerent preparations. There ensued a provoking altercation between the two parties. 108.

Triumph of the mutineers.

Our Bez Bara said to the rebels: 'You are common men. Why do you lift your sword against the King? Why are you launching hostilities? Will the King keep you now in safety?' Thus he said many other things to the Morans, who without listening to the prohibition killed a number of men by some stratagem. The Hajarikias died there; and very few men could escape. The Morans robbed our men of their provisions. Bez Bara escaped somehow, and gave all particulars to the Barbarua of what he saw and heard, and concluded by saying,—'The war has assumed a serious character, and it cannot be combated with a small army'. The Barbarua then submitted detailed information to the King. 109.

A fresh contingent under Harnath Phukan.

The King deliberated with his three Dangarias, the Barbarua, and the Phukans and Rajkhowas, and appointed the Bhitarual Phukan of the Duara family as Senapati or commander-in-chief, who was given a detachment of 6,000 men consisting of *muls* and *dowals*. Besides an additional force of 8,000 soldiers was placed at his disposal with the respective Hajarikias,—one thousand of the Bajua Dimarugurias, Bajua Kowanr's thousand, Bajua Kowanr's musketeers thousand, two regiments of Bakal, Dhadum's thousand, Bhitarual Chekeratalia's thousand, in their *muls* and *dowals*. The Dola-kasharia Bara, the Chaodang Bara, the Barbarua's Tekela-Bara, *i.e.*, the informer Bez Bara, Telgaj the Chabukdhara Bara, and Anadar the Kalita Bara were also appointed to accompany the expedition. Besides, eight tuskers and twelve horses were given to the army. The Bhitarual Phukan was made general at the head of all. He was presented with a golden *hengdan* or sword, and then despatched to the war ahead. It was in the month of Kartik of the year 1691 *saka*. 110.

Ahom reverses.

The army proceeded accordingly and encamped on the southern bank of the Dibaru. Then they erected a bridge over the Dibaru river and crossed it. When they had made preparations to construct a fort in the compound of Manchoka the Morans fell upon them by surprise. Fortunately, only a handful of the King's own troopers fell in that encounter. The army halted there in a stockade being ready for engagement. A few days after the Morans destroyed the bridge over the Dibaru, and intercepted the movements of our men. The rice-suppliers could not proceed, and our men suffered misery from want of food. They began to eat *outenga* or dilennia, *dhekia* or fern, *kachu* or arum and tender shoots of *kaka* bamboos. Their knees became enlarged and there was an outbreak of fever and dysentery. 111.

Moran strategy.

The Morans then held a council. They contrived to call in the three exiled princes, Batgharia Barjana Gohain, brother of Rajeswar Singha, who was driven away by that King; Maju-Gohain and Saru-Gohain, sons of Rajeswar Singha, who were expelled during the reign of Lakshmi Singha. The Morans said to these three princes,—'Come over to our side. When necessary we shall appoint one of you as king. When you become king, you should appoint your Baruas and Phukans from among us.' Thus saying the Hati-chungi Morans and the three Gohains interchanged oaths and promises. The Morans reminded the princes,—'For no fault of yours, the Bakatial Barua had previously poisoned the ears of the King against you, and contrived to banish you to Namrup, and caused mutilation of your limbs. So let us proceed to put the Bakatial Barbarua to death'. Having heard this proposal, the three princes became delighted, and accepted the proposal of the Hati-chungi Morans, being unable to foresee the consequences. They placed reliance on the words of the Morans though they knew them to be promises coming from low quarters. The Batgharia Gohain was then placed on the back of an elephant, as well as the Maju-Gohain and Saru-Gohain. Then the princes, in the company of the Morans marched post-haste towards the camp of the Senapati Phukan. 112.

Mohanmala's justification.

Mohanmala Batgharia Gohain then addressed the Senapati Phukan as follows,—'Phukan, you are sprung from the Duara family, your line is not of yesterday's growth. Seven generations of your ancestors have paid homage to us. There have been established also bonds of relationship between the two families. Now I alone am entitled to the throne. The Bakatial Barbarua by a diplomatic manœuvre instigated the King to banish us to Namrup. So we have waged war to exterminate the family of the Bakatial Barbarua. The offices and honours attached to the family of the Dangarias and of other Ahom houses will continue as before; we will not do any harm to the common paiks, nor shall we kill any one'. Thus the prince spoke to the Senapati Phukan and others. 113.

Harnath imprisoned by the rebels.

To this the Senapati Phukan made the following reply,—'You Gohains are banished princes, how can we take you as king? At present the Heavenly King is sitting on the throne. So we cannot accept you as king.' The Gohains then said,—'If you can, open fire at us from your guns.' Saying so they rushed forward and demolished the fort by their elephants. After getting down from the elephant they seized the Phukan by his hand and took him away with his men. The Phukan was kept under guard in a house built at some distance from the scene. The captives were admitted to the contingent of the Gohains. Of them the three Baras,—Bez, Telgaj and Kalita, were pressed to death between wooden rollers. 114.

Moran regime.

The Morans in consultation with the Gohains appointed Raghab as Barbarua; one Khora named Nahar was appointed Deo-Gosain, his two wives being named Radha and Rukmini. Then the Morans secretly administered poison to Saru-Gohain and Maju-Gohain, and thus killed the two Gohains; the Batgharia Gohain was the only survivor. He was also placed under surveillance in a house at some distance. Then Ramananda the son of Khora was made king, though the Morans proclaimed to the people as a make-believe that the son of the Batgharia Gohain was their king. The secret of the Morans was known only to the Morans, and they went on saying falsely that the Batgharia Gohain's son was their king. 115.

Renewed war deliberations.

Then the soldiers of the Phukan's garrison came and informed the Barbarua of the capture of the general by the Morans who had been accompanied by the Batgharia and other Gohains. This news was announced in the council, whereupon the persons assembled became dispirited. The Barbarua then went to the King and communicated to him the news at the balcony of the principal house, saying,—'The Batgharia Gohain, the Maju-Gohain and the Saru-

Gohain, in the company of the Morans, came and destroyed the Phukan's fort and took him and his men as captives.' Having heard this the King expressed his sorrow and asked the Barbarua of the means to be adopted. The Barbarua advised the King to convene a meeting of the three Dangarias, the Phukans and the Rajkhowas, and deliberate with them so that they might give their own opinions in the matter, and then the King after studying the situation might issue commands to them which would be carried out implicitly.

The King then ordered the Barbarua to summon from Gauhati the Duara Barphukan and the Dihingia Pani-phukan. The Barbarua sent a Kataki or messenger and quickly brought the Barphukan, the Pani-phukan, the two Rajkhowas and the two Rajapowalis or vassal chieftains of Rani and Luki. The King then convened a meeting of the three Dangarias, the Phukans, the Baruas and asked them their advice. They all gave the following counsel,—'Oh King, why should we abandon fighting on the ground that the Bhitarual Phukan has been carried off as captive? Your Majesty has a large number of servants and retainers; whatever order Your Majesty may be pleased to issue to them will be obeyed.' 116.

Appearance of a comet.

Then in *saka* 1691, on the fifth day of Aswin, a star with a tail appeared in the sky, which portended evils. 117.

Fresh encounters with the Morans.

The King then ordered the Barbarua to despatch the three Abhaypurias to protect the store of gold and silver in Namrup and fight with the Morans. The Naosalia Phukan's son Jabakial Gohain, the Bar-Abhaypuri Rajkhowa, the Pani-Abhaypuria Rajkhowa of the Kota Barphukan's family, the Saru-Abhaypuria Rajkhowa of the Bargohain's family, marched towards Namrup but they could not reach that place as they had to fight with the Morans at Dighalighat; and being vanquished in the battle they offered their submission to the Morans.

Then the Guahatia Dekaphukan, the Ghora Barbara, the two sons of Chikan Bangal, with the *dowal* recruits from the Phukan's men, halted at the mouth of Timun where they erected a stockade. Then a contingent of 5,000 Changmais under the command of one Mai Barua, a Buruk by caste, proceeded by the Sariah-hat route, but a fight ensued just when they had reached Changmai. The Dualia Phukan, son of the Dihingia Pani-phukan, was despatched by the way through Dhai-ali with the *dowals* attached to the Pani-phukan. The Barkakati who rose to be Parvatia Barua followed the Dulia Phukan with some men. One Likchan Bara, who was originally a Likchan Ahom by caste, and who afterwards became Bacha Rajkhowa, was sent by the route through Charaideo Hill at the head of his own men. 118.

Moran manœuvres.

Then Ragha Moran came out of the forest with his followers and retainers and obtained the submission of the villages up to the Dihing river. He circulated a false report among all people that the Barjana Gohain's son was the king. Hearing this the people offered their homage. The Morans went on raising devotees and recruits by beating the ground with thick sticks and singing the following song:—

'Ashtabhuj, Saptabhuj and Chaturbhuj are our protectors;
His sword cuts him, his gun kills him, and Chaturbhuj protects.'

This is the song which they went about singing: the villagers being seized with panic and affright used to offer their submission. The privates of a garrison broke open the fort and made good their escape, while the chiefs surrendered themselves to the enemy.

Previously to this, Bayan Deka, son of the Moamaria Mahajan Chaturbhuj, cunningly raised from his disciples a straw bundle, a split rattan and a split bamboo per man, and he also made each of his disciples bring a turf of earth, with which a high plinth was raised at Khutiapota, where a house was constructed with the materials thus collected. By this contrivance he could also ascertain the numerical strength of his followers. He also designed to become king, and his disciples and followers promised to make him king.

There was a man named Abhay Bhandari in the service of the Barbarua; he had a son named Ambarish. There were also a few attendants serving in the royal palace. They communicated to the Moamaria Mahanta all that we said or did. The Mahanta reported the same to Ragha. These secrect communications of the Moamarias were known only to themselves, and not to the Bamunias. 119.

The heroism of Baroi Dualia Pani-phukan.

The chief weapons of the Morans were *tokons* or clubs. They had also other weapons, but they had no confidence in them. Then the Moran leader, attended by soldiers armed with *tokons* stood in front of the Dualia Pani-phukan. Ragha Moran then addressed the Pani-phukan,—'Well, Phukan, with whom do you fight? The son of the Barjana Gohain is now the king. The Bhitarual Phukan has offered his submission to us along with his army. Have you not seen this? So all the people up to Dihing river have also paid their homage to us.' The Phukan then replied,—'The Heavenly King is on the throne. Should I offer my submission at the instance of an insectivorous Moran? I am an offspring of the Dihingia family. I have bowed before the Heavenly King with this head of mine, and why should I now accept another as king?' On hearing these words Ragha Moran rushed with his army towards the Pani-phukan. In the meantime all the men accompanying the Phukan took to their heels; and some were killed by the enemy. The Phukan stood at his post with his back touching that of his *Tamol-kata ligira* or attendant to cut betel-nuts.

Ragha then addressed the Phukan,—'Well, Phukan, still there is time for you to submit'. To this the Phukan replied,—'I have already told you, Moran, that I will not submit to you'. The Phukan had in his hand his bow and arrows, and a sharp sword. The *Tamol-kata* was armed with a sword and a spear. With these weapons they killed a number of Morans. They were then surrounded by the Morans on all sides, yet they stood undaunted. Then there ensued an arrow-fight. A few Morans perished at the Phukan's shot. All the arrows that the Phukan had became exhausted by this time. Ragha said again, 'Well, Phukan, won't you surrender even now?' The Phukan replied,—'I have said before that I am not going to offer my submission to you'. Then the Phukan was wounded by a spear from behind. The lance pierced him through his breast. The Phukan fell facing the ground whereupon he was hacked. The *Tamol-kata* was also decapitated. 120.

Chieftains in Upper Assam.

The Parvatia Barua who followed the expedition having received intelligence of this reverse came back secretly to the metropolis. Then some fugitives from the Phukan's camp came and reported the matter to the Barbarua, who communicated it to the King. On hearing this news the Phukans and the Baruas living in the capital removed their properties in advance to some safe place. Besides, the men who were despatched against the Morans used to submit to the enemy. The Barbarua, realising the frustration of all plans reported to the King,—'I have found that the attitude and feelings of our people have assumed a dangerous shape. Those who are sent to the war submit themselves to the Morans, while others desert the field. So I have informed Your Majesty. If we see that we cannot stay any longer in this place, we shall proceed down to Gauhati after deliberation with Your Majesty'. Saying so he secretly arranged boats and boatmen necessary for the journey. The Barbarua further said,—'I have brought the chieftains of Rani, Luki and Topakuchi. I will send them to war, and see what they can do.' Then the Barphukan of the Duara family said,—'This chief of Rani is a great warrior. He has previously vanquished the Bangals'. 121.

Reverses to Rani and Luki chiefs.

The chieftains were then despatched with the Gargayan Dekaphukan along the Dhai-ali route; while the Tangondhara Rajkhowa of the Adabaria section of the Sandikai clan, who had been appointed Dihingia Phukan, proceeded by the Tamuli-bazar route in the company of his retainers. The Lechengial Barpatra-gohain also proceeded with his men by the Lechang route. Then Ragha Moran encountered the chiefs of Luki, Rani and Topakuchi at the terminus of the Dhai-ali, and there ensued a battle between the two armies. Then Rani and Luki chiefs were vanquished and they left the field. The Morans chased them and killed many of their soldiers. The Barpatra-gohain remained at his own residence. The Phukans returned and joined the King: the other common men retired to their own homes. One or two of the fugitives came to the Barbarua and informed him of all that had happened. The Barbarua communicated the same to the King. 122.

Lakshmi Singha deserts the capital.

The Barbarua, in consultation with the King, proceeded down with the intention of going to Gauhati. Then in the year 1691 *saka*, on the eighth day of Aghon, on Saturday, at the fourth *danda*. the King and his party reached the Sonai river camp at night. The King could not get the boats that were arranged for him. The King's followers too dispersed in all directions, who also took with them the ornaments of the King. 123.

Of the King's followers the following accompanied His Majesty,—the Madurial Bargohain, the Kuoigayan Buragohain, Kirtichandra Barbarua of the Bakatial family, the Rajneog, the Duara Barphukan, the Dihingia Pani-phukan, Jati Rajkhowa of the Buragohain family, the Dekaphukan of the Hati-Barua family, the Dihingia Phukan of the Sandikais, the Deka-Barbarua, the Dhekial Phukan, the King's mother, the queen and a few *dulias* or palanquin-bearers. The following did not desert the company of the King,—the Khanikar Barua, the Habial Barua, the Sandikai Ghora-Barua, the King's son-in-law; the Ligiras,—Kam, Pijali, Lakhar, Latha; and Sivanath of Lanmakharu family. 124.

The King's adherents.

Then Ambarish, son of Abhay, his cousins Pradad and Mahada sent men to inform Ragha that the King had left the city and proceeded down, and that the Morans should come at once and take possession of the capital. 125.

Informers of the Morans.

Having received this news Ragha Moran proceeded with his army and entered the city at midnight on the fourth *danda*. Their entry was signalised by a salvo of gun-fire. In that very night Ragha sent 400 *Baratias* or adherents who surrounded and captured the King and his followers at the Sonai camp in the early part of the day. The King was seized with fright. In the night when the King deserted the city, the Deka-Barbarua left the company of the King and proceeded down in a fisherman's boat. But he was seized and detained by the Kaliabaria Gohain of the Chatai-alia family, to whom the Deka-Barbarua was a son-in-law by relationship. Then the Morans seized the persons of the King and his followers and led them up, and kept them under guard at the Jaysagar temple. At the instance of the King the Barbarua had gone from the Sonai camp to the Moamaria Mahanta to pray for their lives. The Mahanta said,—'All right, if I can I shall protect you'. The Barbarua was captured there and put in chains with all the members of his family. He was kept under watch in the Hatisal or elephant-stall at the entrance of the Na-duar. The other Phukans, Rajkhowas, Chamua Phukans and Baruas were kept in their respective dwellings. After some days, Ragha Barbarua sent some men who destroyed the stockade of Chikan Bangal at Abhaypur. His two sons and the Ghora-Barbara were also captured. The three were hooked to death near the road at Pataghar. 126.

Lakshmi Singha imprisoned.

The Morans occupy Rangpur.

Then Ragha Barbarua sent men to Raja Ramananda with the following message,—'We have occupied Rangpur; and we have seized the King whom we have kept under guard.' Hearing this Ramananda became delighted, and being accompanied by his father Khora, Radha and Rukmini, the Morans proceeded in hot haste with their army and occupied the capital. Their Baruas and Phukans drove away our Baruas and Phukans from their respective dwellings, and occupied them themselves. They also brought with them the Barjana Gohain bereft of his followers, as well as the Senapati Phukan. All the Phukans and Rajkhowas who had offered their submission to the Morans were now brought with them. After occupying the capital in this manner the Morans fired a volley from their gun. This happened in the month of Aghon, *saka* 1691. After entering the city Khora assumed the name Deo-Gosain, and he stayed at the Rangnath Doul with Rukuni; Radha remained at the Hara-Gauri Doul. The Raja resided in the capital. His brother took the name Beli-raja. Ragha Barbarua occupied the quarters of the Bakatial Barbarua. Ragha Barbarua then said that he would take one hundred wives. Thus saying he brought in the queen, who was the daughter of the Manipuri Raja, as well as the daughters of the Phukans and the Baruas. One Khundamara of the Likchan family was Likchan Bara. He used to collect men for the royal council. Ragha Barbarua used to receive all informations from him. One Madan of the Kakati Chaliha family used to hold diplomatic conversation with foreign envoys when Ragha Barbarua sat at the court. He decided cases by sitting at his court both in the forenoon and in the afternoon. The sons of the Bakatial Barbarua were murdered at the Mah-bhandar, literally the emporium of pulses. The Raja, Ramananda, brought in the daughter of Tarimua Bhandari Barua and made her his consort. 127.

Appointment of Moran officials.

One of the Morans was appointed Bargohain, another Buragohain and a third Barpatra-gohain, thus all the Phukans and Rajkhowas were appointed from among the Morans. One Ligiri Kanri who had his home at Kalugoan was appointed Barphukan and sent down to Gauhati. The six Phukans and fourteen Rajkhowas of Gauhati were appointed from the Morans. Only the old Solal Gohain was retained in his office. One of the Garudharias became Sadiya-khowa, one of the Kachari-jowa Chetias who was a Moamaria was appointed Marangi-khowa Gohain.

After this the Rangpuria Raja, Ramananda, in deliberation with Ragha, and other Phukans and Rajkhowas, went to the house of the Moamaria Mahajan at Khotiapota, leaving Ragha Barbarua in charge of the capital. The Senapati Phukan effected his escape and fled down to Chilmari after crossing the Manaha. 128.

The Morans harass the Bamunia Mahantas.

After this Raja Ramananda proceeded to Khutiapota, where he summoned the Auniatia, the Dakhinpatia, the Garamuria, the Kuruabahia Gosains, and other Bamunia and Thakuria Mahantas. He confined them and exacted money from them as follows,—from the Auniatia Gosain Rs. 8,000; from Dakhinpat Rs. 8,000; from Garamur Rs. 4,000; from Kuruabahi Rs. 4,000. Thus he extorted money from all the Mahantas proportionate to their rank and condition. Besides, the Auniati Bagis Bapu was punished by being deprived of his nose, ears and eyes. The Moamaria Mahanta passed a rule according to which all the common men of the villages were brought in crowds and initiated, each new disciple having had to pay only a bunch of betel-leaves. The work of initiation continued for two months. Then the Mahajan took the *Kekora-dola* or sedan which is the prerogative of kings alone. 129.

Dissensions among the Morans.

Ragha Barbarua was then taken from Rangpur, and with him were also taken the Swargadeo, the three Dangarias, the Barbarua, the Barphukan, and all others including the Phukans and the Baruas. Then after a few days the Buragohain, the Bargohain, the Barbarua, the Barphukan, the Dekaphukan and the Kathkatia Barua of Luthuri were all murdered at Khutiapota. After this the Moran Raja and Barbarua along with others came up to Rangpur in the month of Chaitra. In the same month, on report being received about the outbreak of hostilities at Gauhati, Rukuni proceeded down to that place. In the selfsame month Ragha Barbarua said to Raja Ramananda,—'It was I who first occupied the city, captured and imprisoned the King. I am the person who took the lead in all these matters. So the *Kekora-dola* or royal sedan and the mace should be given to me.' The Raja said that he could not confer upon him these insignias. Being thus refused Ragha became displeased and went up to

Chepan with Khora. The Raja brought them back by sending emissaries. Previously to this Bayan Deka had thought of becoming Raja, and accordingly he had organised armed hostilities through the eastern Morans by despatching Khora, which resulted in the acquisition of the kingdom. Then he said to them when they had gone to Khutiapota,—'Formerly you promised to make me Raja, but now I see that Ramananda has been appointed instead, and you do not mean to make me Raja.' Then the Morans including Ragha Barbarua told him that they did not desire to appoint him their Raja. Having heard this Bayan Deka said,—'You have deviated from your promise, and I will see what I can do.' 130.

The Ahoms roused to action.

According to this a number of Moamarias under the leadership of Govinda Goanburha went up and stopped at Sagunmuri after erecting a stockade. Each of them had a *chekani* or slender bamboo stick in his hand. Having struck the sticks against each other they went about singing the following song,—'Praja ou, Jarau-rouwa', literally, 'Oh people, there is something rotten here.' Singing this they advanced with their *chekanis*. This happened in the month of Chaitra, 1691 *saka*. After this, our deposed Dangarias and others said to themselves,—'The Morans had declared formerly that the son of the Barjana Gohain was the Raja, but now we see that a Moran has assumed sovereign power. The Heavenly King has also been removed from the throne; the Mahantas also have been made to pay money under compulsion; the Dangarias, the Baruas and the Phukans have been murdered, deposed or expelled. The Morans have set up an independent sway. Since the advent of King Sukapha to this country till now only the members of the royal family have become kings, and not others of inferior blood. Besides, the Baruas, the Phukans and the Rajkhowas have been appointed from among the members of the Ahom families. The Heavenly King, as an act of favour occasionally raised others or non-Ahoms to power, yet they could not be independent.' Having thus deliberated they resolved to attack the Morans. 131.

Vow to extirpate the Morans.

The following persons participated in the deliberations,—Bailung Gohain, son of the Doulbandha Bargohain; Gohain Hajarika of the Kuoigayan Buragohain family; a member of the Moran

Patar family; the two brothers of Bhadrasen of the Bakatial family; their two uncles; one Deka of the Neog-Gohain family of the Lahan clan; Baghmua of the Lai-Sandikai family; one Deobilia Pachani of the Buragohain family; Ram-krishnai, son of Jada Tamuli; Ramnath, another son of the same; Mohan of the Dafala-duaria family; one Kekeru Hajarikia, a retainer of the Bargohain, by caste a Kalita; Kahan; Apainta; the families of the three Dangarias; some of their sons and brothers; some tenants and servitors of the same. All these men united together at Bhogbari, where they, by the name of their spiritual leaders, took an oath not to desert each other, nor to betray their secrets. 132.

Ram-krishnai and Kuranganayani.

Thus the royalists conferred for about ten days. Ram-krishnai who was charged with the task of capturing Ragha conspired with the Magalu princess: and she promised to do away with Ragha. She had been taken by Ragha Moran as his wife. Then Ram-krishnai hatched a plan with some Magalus and other men. Kahan and Apainta undertook to kill Khora with the help of a party of men. The rest promised to enter inside the city walls. After deliberating in this manner the men who were entrusted with the task of capturing Ragha, on the *Sankranti* of the month of Baisakha, proceeded and stopped at the inner entrance. Having received this news Ragha surmised that Govinda Gaonburha Senapati of Sagunmuri had come with his *Chekani-kobowa* soldiers, and accordingly he came out to escort them with a *sarai* with betel-nuts and leaves. The Magalu princess with a sword in her hand followed him with other ladies each armed with a *dao*. There was not a single male. 133.

Kuranganayani kills Ragha.

Ram-krishnai then gave the hint by uttering a few words. The Magalu princess, recognising the voice, struck Ragha with a sword just below the calf. Ragha fell down with his face towards the ground. Then Ram-krishnai who was also there severed his head. Then the party issued out of Ragha's residence, and approaching the Rangnath temple made a sign by words to be recognised by the men who had been deputed to capture Khora. Having recognised the voice Kahan and Apainta gave a thrust with a spear on the thigh of Khora. Khora was wounded, but he did not fall, and he ran off. He then fell at the entrance of the main gate of the temple. 134.

Those very men pierced Radha to death at the Hara-Gauri temple. The men who had killed Ragha now entered the walls of the city by breaking down the main gate with the help of elephants. Then they went in by breaking open the *Darika* door, where they cut some men, and some Morans as well as some Phukans and Baruas. They set fire to the King's court and also to the houses at the *Darika* door. Then Raja Ramananda made his escape with his chief consort through a secret passage. She was the daughter of Tarimua Bhandari Barua, a Koch by caste. 135.

Murder of Radha.

Then they took down a *dola* or litter from the Dolaghar, where they placed a pillow erect, and paraded the *dola* round the Barchara or royal court. The dola-bearers announced by shouting,—'The former King of the Tungkhungia family has become king again. The people should not disperse.' Then the Kanris and Baruatis became delighted, and the citizens remained in perfect composure. Then the Gohain Hajarikia of the Kuoigayan Buragohain family in the company of a large concourse of men proceeded to escort the King from the Bardoul. The King was seized with fright at the sight of the crowd approaching. Then the people explained all that had happened, and that they had vanquished the Morans; they also gave marks of individual identity. The King then believed it to be true. The royalists placed the King on the sedan, and after bringing the queen-mother, the queens and the prince, placed them under proper guard at the Dolaghar. Then they re-occupied the city on Tuesday, on the Baisakha Sankranti, in 1692 *saka*, when it was still one *prahar* of the night. 136.

Re-occupation of Rangpur.

On that very night the King issued an order that the Morans should be killed wherever and by whomsoever they are found, and they should be brought as captives as well. Then this order was proclaimed from all the roads throughout the country by men on horseback. This proclamation being heard the Morans were captured and put to death. Many were yoked in pairs and made over to the Hatisal. Khora was found by the watchmen in a clump of arum plants; he was captured and made over. He was also put to death after various tortures. 137.

Death of Khora Moran.

On that very day the Heavenly King appointed Bhadrasen,

son of the Bakatial Rajneog, to the office of the Barbarua. Bailung, the son of the Doulbandha Bargohain was appointed Bargohain. Gohain Hajarikia of the Kuoigayan Buragohain family was appointed Buragohain. The office of Barpatra was conferred upon a member of the Moran-Patra family. Baghmua of the Lai-Sandikai family was made Naobaicha Phukan, while the office of Dekaphukan was conferred upon a member of the Lahan family. A member of the Sandikai family was already appointed Dihingia Phukan. The Na-phukan was selected from the members of the Deobilia branch of the Buragohain family. A member of the Bakatial family was appointed Rajneog. The Barbarua's brother was appointed Choladhara Phukan. Kekeru Hajarikia, a retainer of the Bargohain, was appointed Bhandari Barua. The old Pani-phukan of the Dihingia family was appointed Barphukan. Mohan of the Dafaladuaria family was created Ghora-Barua. 138.

New Ahom officers.

In the morning of the next day the King commanded the Prime Minister, the Buragohain of the Kuoigayan family, to capture and bring the Moamaria Mahanta from Khutiapota. The Dangaria too marched with a force day and night to Khutiapota where he acquainted our Kanris and Baruatis with the object of his mission in secret. They became delighted and having consulted together surrounded the Morans on all sides. Apprehending a friction the King despatched Ram-krishnai with some Magalus along with two princes in the rear. The Buragohain by adopting a stratagem brought out the Mahanta and seized his person. The father and the son were packed in bags and placed on the two sides of an elephant. The Buragohain left Khutiapota while there was one *prahar* of the day, and marching day and night reached Rangpur on the third *prahar* on the next day. The captives were then made over to the King, and the Mahajan was asked about his conduct. The Mahajan admitted his guilt. The King finding them guilty got the father and the son executed at the open space in front of the Hatisal near the Na-duar. 139.

The Moamaria Mahajan put to death.

The day after the Morans were captured, the King despatched Dhaneswar Barkataki of the Bahbaria Kataki family to Gauhati in order to arrest Ligiri Kanri, the Moran Barphukan. A few days after, the King also despatched his Barphukan with the same mission.

The Morans quelled at Gauhati.

Then Dhaneswar Kataki proceeded to Gauhati in a swift boat by day and night. After reaching Gauhati, he caused the capture of the Moran Phukans and Rajkhowas, by taking them by a stratagem to the Dopdar or the Barphukan's council-chamber. They were then placed in an enclosure with chains under proper watch. 140.

Rukmini killed at Gauhati.

The Barphukan during his stay at Gauhati killed all the Phukans and Rajkhowas of the Morans. Rukuni was also killed. Dhaneswar Kataki after a march of eight days informed the King of the extirpation of the Morans hearing which His Majesty praised Dhaneswar. 141.

The image of Hara-Gauri.

Previously to this the Bakatial Barbarua had recovered in the Kachari country a stone image of Chamunda which he took with him and placed in the Hara-Gauri temple. A month after the suppression of the Moran revolt, the image was sent back to the Kachari country as it was found to be of an implacable nature. 142.

The Chekani-kobowa revolt.

After four days had passed of the month of Baisakha, the King deputed the Bargohain, the Barpatra-gohain and the Bakatial Dhekial Phukan with a large army to suppress the *Chekani-kobowa* revolt at Sagunmari under the leadership of the commander Govinda Gaonburha. The Dangarias marched to the spot and encountered the Morans in an engagement, in which the Barpatra Dangaria lost his life as well as the Dhekial Phukan and numerous soldiers. The Bargohain Dangaria made his escape with great difficulty. The fugitives from the battle communicated the news to the Barbarua who conveyed it to the King. This intelligence caused a sensation in the city. It was only then that the three Dangarias personally attended the watch at the capital. Each of the three gates was guarded by eighty young men recruited from the several Ahom families. The guards were supplied with food. The King then deputed the Buragohain and the Barbarua with a large force against the rebels, and also sent with them a detachment of Magalus on ponies. A battle took place soon after their halt, where the Morans being unable to stand fled from the field. The Magalus spurred their horses and chased the fugitives who were killed by the pursuers. The Buragohain and the

Barbarua then communicated the news of the victory to the King who was delighted. The other people were also pleased. To signalise the victory drums were beaten in all the roads, and guns were mounted on all sides of the city and fired. Then the Buragohain, who was also the Prime Minister, came back with the Barbarua and related all that had happened to the King, to whom they also made their obeisance. Two days after Govinda Senapati was found at Dihing and captured by Saharias or village watchmen. He was also put to death. 143.

New officers.

Then the son of the Moran-Patra Gohain who fell in the battle was appointed to the office of the Barpatra. After this a messenger proceeded to Gauhati under the orders of His Majesty, and he appointed a member of the Labhabaria branch of the Duara family as Pani-phukan. The son-in-law of the King's nurse was created Chetia Phukan, he was Kachari-kumar or a potter by caste. A member of the Dihingia family was appointed Dihingia Phukan. The Dekaphukan was selected from the Miri-Sandikai family. Kahan was appointed Chekera-talia Hazarikia and Apainta was made Hazarikia of Bakal. Mohan was removed from office, and the Bargohain's son was appointed in his place as Dhekial Phukan; the younger princess was also given to him in marriage. The Ghora-Barua of the Sandikai family was made Khargharia Phukan. A member of the Kuoigayan Buragohain family was made Gandhia Barua. He had also married a princess. His elder brother was appointed Bacha Rajkhowa. A member of the Gajpuria Hati-Barua family was appointed Nibukial Rajkhowa. The office of the Nyaya-sodha Phukan of Rangpur was conferred upon a member of the Dihingia family; while the corresponding office for Gargaon was given to one Lakua of the Bakatial family. Thus the King restored the offices attached to the various families according to their fitness and desert. Previously to this the Solal Gohain had captured the Choladhara Phukan and made him over to the Morans. Being charged with this offence the King had him brought from Kaliabar in a bamboo crate in the position of a man on horseback; on his way he was also subjected to humiliation and disgrace; and he was subsequently dismissed from his Gohainship. Then Barpeta, a member of the Madurial family, who happened to be a relation of the former, was deputed to Kaliabar as Solal Gohain. One Garudharia Gohain who had been appointed

Sadiya-khowa Gohain by the Morans was captured and killed. 144.

Renewed hostilities of the Morans.

After the occupation of the capital the Morans had engaged a few thousand of our men to erect an encampment at Kundil. On hearing that our Heavenly King had re-occupied the kingdom by defeating the rebels, the Hati-chungi Morans treacherously murdered those men, though some of them made their escape. After this the Morans renewed their hostilities. The fugitives from Kundil reported the matter to the Barbarua. The Barbarua enquired as to the ringleader under whom the rebels had taken up arms. They replied that the leaders who had killed our men and assumed a hostile attitude were Lephera, Paramananda, Obhota-numia, and Tanganaram. Having heard this the Barbarua reported the matter to the King who ordered the despatch of an expedition against the rebels. The Barbarua provided the Na-phukan with his six thousand retainers as well as the *muls* and *dowals* of the Bajua Kowanr; he also despatched the Bakatial Nyay-sodha Phukan with the contingent. The deposed Dualia Phukan, a member of the Kharikatia branch of the Duara family, was summoned and provided with a regiment of Lahan and Bacha soldiers; he was then despatched to the war. Further the King commanded them as follows,—'You three should fight in a concerted manner. The rebels have destroyed our stores and villages, and carried away from there our ornaments, and copper and brass articles; you should institute a vigorous search for them.' They were deputed with the above instructions. The expedition set out eight days prior to the completion of Baisakha. 145.

Expiation.

The Heavenly King then issued the following command,—'The Morans have violated the sanctity of many people. And so the Brahmania and Thakuria Gosains including Auniati and Dakhinpat should undergo expiation.' They then underwent the expiation ceremony. 146.

New officers.

The King then instituted an enquiry regarding the persons who had accepted office under the Morans. Phisi of the Dihingia family, the nephew of the Raidangia Phukan of Hatimur who was the Chaodang Barua, were dismissed from their posts and turned out. Khundamara Barbara of Likchan was dismissed and driven away to the settlement of Bacha. Madan, a Kakati Bara, was sent home after being dismissed.

At that time the Senapati Phukan of the Duara family was staying at Chilmari as a refugee. He was brought back and reinstated in his former office of Bhitarual Phukan. The houses of those who had accepted office under the Morans were looted, as well as the residence of the Moamaria Mahanta. The spoils were deposited in the royal store-room at Rangpur. The King instituted a census of the articles in the treasury. One Pijali, a Barahi Bez by caste, who had been the King's attendant before ascending the throne was appointed Khanikar Barua. One Kam Ligira was made Tipamia Phukan. His mother was a Ligiri or female attendant; and his father joined the *khel* of the Bargohain of the Miri-Sandikai family. Lakhar, a Ligira of the Barpatra *khel*, and a Lukhurakhun by caste, was made Senchowa Barua. 147.

Intelligence of Moran insurrection.

In the month of Kartik, *saka* 1692, the Phukans engaged in the frontier warfare in the east despatched intelligence of the conduct of the operations to the Barbarua through Raghunath Kataki. The Barbarua asked as to the persons who had launched the warfare. The messenger replied that the selfsame Morans had taken up arms, and that the contest was of a critical nature. The Barbarua reported the matter to the King who, in consultation with the three Dangarias, deputed the Mahamantri Buragohain Dangaria with his retainers and other soldiers, having placed him as commander over the Phukans previously despatched. The Dangaria pitched his camp near the woods where he halted. From there he entered the forest with his army and appointed the prince as his junior in command. One Bihlangi, a Brahman of the Dimaruguria regiment, was also entrusted with a command. Just at that time the Morans issued out all on a sudden and killed some of our men including the Nyaya-sodha Phukan. Yet the Dangaria stood ready to face Lephera and Paramananda in battle. He was then joined by a reinforcement which had been marching in the rear. The Kowanr Senapati and the Duara Dualia Phukan were in their company. 148.

Repression of the Morans.

Then there ensued a contest with the Morans where Lephera and Paramananda were both killed. The Morans unable to take their stand fled from the field. The Dangaria, seizing an opportunity, halted there by constructing a stockade. From there he attacked the villages of the Holongaguria Morans. Being unable to stand the Morans fled from there as well. The Dangaria threw off a fort at that place wherefrom he destroyed the two villages Saruchakari and Barchakari, and captured Obhota-numia. The Morans dispersed and entered the forest. Being starved to death they came out of their own accord and offered their submission. The Dangaria sent the refugees to the King, who numbered nine or ten thousand with their wives and children. The King confined them in an enclosure at Alikekuri and placed them under guard. Those who belonged to *khels* were restored to their respective units. The Holongaguria Morans were established at Rangdaichong. The Dangaria after a search recovered some of the articles which had been taken by the rebels after destroying the royal stores and emporiums; he came back with these and had also Obhota-noma with him. He waited in the courtyard of the temple of Rangnath and sent report of his arrival to the King. The King admitted the Dangaria and the two Phukans to his own quarters. The Dangaria knelt down before the King and communicated the details of the war. His Majesty being delighted conferred rewards upon the Dangaria and the two Phukans according to their merits and also gave them a feast. The gold, silver, copper, brass and cloths which were obtained by vanquishing the Morans were presented to the King by the Majindar. The King directed the articles to be deposited in their respective stores. 149.

The Pani-phukan dies at Gauhati.

After this the news of the death of the Pani-phukan was transmitted from Gauhati. Having heard this the King appointed Tangandhara, the Dihingia Phukan of the Sandikais, as Pani-phukan. The Sandikai Dekaphukan was living without an office; he was now appointed Dihingia Phukan. 150.

Kalita Phukan.

After this followed a period of amusement including hawk-flight and other pastimes. The King went to Kahmara to watch and participate in hawk flights. He was followed by the Barbarua at some space. Ramnath Bharali Barua went before the Barbarua on horseback. The Barbarua said to himself,—'Ramnath who is my tenant should not go before me riding on a horse'. Accordingly he informed the King who caused the eyes of Ramnath and his brother to be extracted near the tank at Pajikata. This Ramnath was a sworn friend of the Kalita Phukan. As fate would have it there was a secret misunderstanding between the Kalita Phukan and the

Barbarua, and one would not spare the other if there was an opportunity. The Kalita Phukan confidentially informed the King,—'The Barbarua is contemplanting a revolt against His Majesty conspiring with the two Nati-Gosains. His Majesty should ascertain the facts after making proper enquiries.' 151.

Harassment of officers.

The King then assembled his three Dangarias, and after deposing the Barbarua instituted a trial. Finding the allegations to be true, Bhadrasen Deka-Barua, his uncle Neog-phukan, his brother the Choladhara Phukan and his uncle Baga Deka were beheaded near Ranghar. One of the Gohains or princes was also killed near Ouguri. The Tipamia Gohain was orderded to be in Baga's village at Bacha. Their houses were searched and their belongings confiscated. On the selfsame day the King asked the three Dangarias as to whom they would like to appoint to the office of Barbarua. This was in the month of Sravan, *saka* 1693.

The Dangarias nominated the Dihingia Phukan, the Khargharia Phukan and the Pani-phukan, and asked the King to appoint one of them according to his choice. The King then appointed the Dihingia Phukan of the Adabaria branch of the Sandikai family as Barbarua. The Kalita Phukan was appointed Choladhara Phukan. After a few months a member of the Labhabaria branch of the Duara family was appointed Rajneog Phukan. Nedhai, the son of the Dihingia Phukan of the Miri-Sandikai family, was appointed Dihingia Phukan. After this Ukils or ambassadors of the chief of Jayantia arrived with letters. 152.

Naga Majindar Barua.

A Ganak of Nazirahat, named Naga, was appointed Majindar Barua. Bailung Bargohain complained to the King,—'The attitude of my brothers is not satisfactory. This is a matter which concerns the Swargadeo, and hence I cannot refrain from informing Your Majesty. Having known this the King should take steps as the occasion demands.' The King made an enquiry and found the allegations to be true, and accordingly killed the two elder brothers of the Bargohain, the ex-Naphukan of the Madurial family who had become the Rajkhowa of Bacha having suppressed the Morans, and Naga Gohain who was living as an exile, all these four were put to death at the mouth of the Safrāi. The Lechengial Barpatra-gohain and his brother were both cudgelled to death in their residence at Lechang. The two princes, Bapi and Barmura, who had come with the Morans, and a few others were punished or exiled to Namrup. Some forty Magalus were living at Mataimara; all on a sudden they went away by the mouths of the two rivers. Nakua Nyaya-sodha Phukan of the Dihingia family was deputed to bring them back. The Phukan failed in his mission and came back. 153.

Harnath Phukan Senapati.

At that time the Kalita Phukan exercised great influence upon the King. The Senapati Phukan also looked upon the Kalita Phukan as his chief stay. The King once ordered the Kalita Phukan and the Naga Majindar to ask the Barbarua to the effect that the Barbarua should submit an account of the men and provisions which had accompanied the Senapati Phukan in his war-expedition. The report was submitted and explained to the King in his chamber, from which he understood from the large amount of men and provisions that the Phukan did not act as he was expected to do. The Phukan was secretly informed of the matter through the Tamuli Ligira, brother of Bhorola. This is one reason. The Kalita Phukan also confidentially communicated the same news through the Patar-Tamuli-kata. One day the Kalita Phukan sent the following message to the Senapati Phukan,—'The King's attitude towards you is not a favourable one: he always speaks of the submission you offered to the Morans. I inform you as a well-wisher. Knowing this, the Phukan should live in retirement for sometime'. It was the Senapati Phukan's turn to give watch that day. He stayed away at his residence on the plea of illness; and being accompanied by the Jakayal Deka named Dom-vidya, one Kanfairagi, and a youthful retainer, he made his escape that night, and took shelter at Kaiman in the house of the Dulia Barua of the Dilihial Buragohain family, taking advantage of an existing relationship. He was found after a search of seven days; he was brought from his shelter and was confined in fetters in the Hatisal near the Na-duar in a cage. The King then accused him and ordered him to be made over to the Chaodangs. This order was communicated by Naga Majindar, the Bura Tamuli Phukan and the Kalita Phukan to the Barbarua, saying that the King had handed over the Senapati Phukan to the Chaodangs: this was also reported to the Chaodang Barua. The Chaodangs then took the Phukan in their custody after removing his chains. The queen-mother, the Pahumaria Na-gosain senior, and the Barbarua detained the culprit and informed the King accordingly, who then pardoned the Phukan and ordered him to be brought back. At the instance of the Barbarua, the Phukan was returned from the Nalamukh and kept in the space in front of the Barduar. The Phukan and the Majindar came from the royal presence and dilated on the offence as follows,—'The King has said that he would have killed the Senapati Phukan but for the intercession of the queen-mother, the Gosain and the Barbarua; and thus his life has been saved.' The Phukan then supplicated in the following words,—'My enemies reported to me that the King had contemplated my death on the allegation that I had offered my submission to Ragha Moran and caused the loss of men and provisions. Having heard this I was seized with fright and so I took shelter elsewhere. The King has presently offered me pardon as the scion of an ancient loyal family. I have been saved by the queen-mother, the Gosain and the venerable Barua, who interceded before the King on my behalf.' This prayer was offered by the Phukan. The King then made over the Phukan to the Barbarua who informed His Majesty that he would be a surety for the Phukan. The three men who had accompanied the Phukan were deprived of their noses and ears. The Phukan was then settled at Rungrung. Later on he came back to Rangpur by imploring the King. Sivanath, a Tamuli Ligira of the family of Bandar of the Lanmakharu clan, was appointed Bhitarual Phukan. 154.

Lakshmi Singha ascends the Singari-ghar.

Before this, Lakshmi Singha ascended the Singari-ghar at Gargaon, *saka* 1693, when he assumed the Hindu name Lakshmi Singha, and made gifts and charities. All the nobles and officials of Gargaon and Gauhati, including the three Dangarias, were given presents; all the Mahantas were collected and the festivities continued for seven days. Gifts were made to the Mahantas. A daughter of the principal branch of the Gargayan Sandikai's family was made Barkuanri or chief queen, while the daughter of the Khangia Phukan of the Chatai-alia Bargohain family was created Parvatia Kuanri. After ascending the Singari-ghar the King planted the banyan tree of life, when he made gifts to women. 155.

The Kalita Phukan's influence.

At this time the King presented the Kalita Phukan with a complete suit of dress, and he became a great favourite of the King. After this a messenger named Dhanrai came from Jayantia. The Barbarua informed the King about receiving the ambassador. The King sent word to the Barbarua that Dhanrai Kataki was a shrewd diplomat, and the Kalita alone would be competent to receive and negotiate with him. As suggested by the King the Barbarua asked the Kalita to receive the Kataki. The Kalita received the envoy at his own residence. The Kalita Phukan being a favourite of the King used to come down from the King's *chang* and conduct the diplomatic affairs of the court. Thus enjoying the good graces of His Majesty, the Kalita took from the King a pair of gold bangles studded all over with valuable gems and a pair of earrings, to wear on the occasion of the marriage of the daughter of the Mridangia Bap of Dihing. Having thus received these presents from the King the Kalita Phukan became the most influential. The Dangarias also, on their way to the appointed state meetings, stopped for some time to talk and exchange greetings with the Kalita Phukan. The sons of many Baruas and Phukans danced attendance at the residence of the Kalita with the hope of getting preferments. 156.

Complaint against Kalita Phukan.

Having thus acquired influence and prosperity, the Kalita Phukan became blind of his power, and went to the extent of poisoning the mind of the King against the Bargohain. Having heard this as it rolled down from one ear to another ear, the Bailung Bargohain Dangaria conferred jointly with the Kuoigayan Mahamantri Buragohain and the Barpatra-gohain of the Moran-Patar family. They sought an audience with the King on the ground that they wanted to confer about state affairs. The King ordered the Barbarua to bring them up to his presence. The Barbarua brought the Majindar and also the three Dangarias by despatching messengers. The Barbarua himself sat with the Phukans and the Rajkhowas. The Majindar then informed the King of the presence of the Dangarias, and the King took the three ministers to his chamber. The Bargohain Dangaria who was related to the monarch by the marriage of their children made the following prayer to His Majesty,— 'O King! we your subjects are not of one day. We have been your subjects since King Sukapha came down to this place. So we have ventured to inform Your Majesty of what we have thought. This Kalita Phukan is disparaging and insulting us in an intolerable fashion, and is devising means also for killing us. Besides, he was a servitor attached to my *mel*, *i.e.*, under my jurisdiction, and so he should not slander us. This Kalita is a voluptuary and a drunkard, and so he should not remain in touch with the King. He is without any caste or creed. Such a man should not remain in the company of Your Majesty.' To this the King replied,—'I did not know the Kalita before. It was you who said that Kalita was a good man, and that he had distinguished himself by subduing the Morans. Further, you recommended him for high distinctions. So I conferred upon him rank and dignity. If the Dangarias now say that he is a wicked person, I will enquire into the matter.' 157.

The King's reply.

The Dangarias requested the King to send down the Kalita from the royal residence and hand him over to them; they added that if the King could not accommodate their wishes they should be dismissed and turned out from office. The Barpatra Dangaria said,—'This Kalita has saved us all by suppressing the Morans. My revered colleague, why should you abuse him now like this?' To this the Bargohain replied,—'Well, Apa, you have become mad.' The Barpatra then retorted,—'We three Dangarias are of equal rank and status. So you should not speak in this manner.' Saying thus the Barpatra paused for some time. The King having heard all this remained silent. Then he said,—'With reference to the request which the Dangarias have made, I would like to say that they should go to-day, and I will make an enquiry to-morrow.' Saying so he directed the Majindar to present the *bata* of betel-nut and leaf, which was done accordingly. The King then gave them leave to depart. The Dangarias halted at the Barchora or council-chamber, from where they called in the Majindar again and asked him to inform the King of their waiting there, and also to request His Majesty to surrender the Kalita to them. The Majindar informed the King accordingly. The King's mother explained the pros and cons of this action to the monarch, adding,—'O, my son, as you have been importuned by the three Dangarias it is advisable on your part to surrender the Kalita.' The King sent the following message through the Majindar,—'The Dangarias should retire to their residence to-day. I will enquire to-morrow, and if I find the Kalita guilty, he will be punished according to his offence.' The Majindar conveyed this message to the Dangarias. The *bata* was given again at the Barchora, and the King gave them leave to retire. Hearing this the Dangaria s retired to their respective residences. 158.

The Kalita seeks forgiveness.

The Kalita was also present at the conference held by the Dangarias where they informed the King of their intentions. On the departure of the Dangarias to their houses, the Kalita came out in disguise by the Darika gate, and halted at the watch-house of the Barbarua with the Majindar. The Barbarua in his turn sent the Kalita to his (Barbarua's) residence, where he remained secretly for a week. At the instance of the King the Majindar Barua brought the Kalita Phukan to the Barchora and communicated to him the order that the Phukan should attend the court and remain in his residence on alternate days. The Dangarias discovered on many occasions the Phukan's remissness in the discharge of his duties, and reported the matter frequently to the King. The Kalita Phukan then went to the Dangarias and fell prostrate at their feet; yet they did not offer him any pardon. The Kalita offered his prostration to the Bargohain who remained adamantine. On the subject of the Kalita Phukan the King sent word to the Dangarias to the following effect,—'I have invited the Dangarias to reconsider their attitude towards the Kalita Phukan. I have dismissed him from service, and driven him to his home at Tambulbari. Let him remain in the north.' To this the Dangarias replied,—'If the King has removed the Kalita from his Phukanship, we have no objection to his residing at home.' Then in the month of Baisakh, 1694 *saka*, the King despatched boats and boatmen, as well as two Dolakasharia Baras and two Chaodang Baras as guards and had the Kalita escorted and placed at Tambulbari. Then the Tamuli Phukan of the Bantom Ahom family was appointed Choladhara Phukan, in which office he acted only for three days. The Bargohain's son who was a Dhekial Barua was made Choladhara Phukan. The aforesaid Tamuli Phukan was appointed Dhekial Phukan. 159.

The Kalita schemes a rebellion.

Then the Kalita collected in an independent capacity a large number of men at the place to which he was exiled. He equipped them with weapons, and instituting all the four watches he remained in preparedness for war. He was joined by the sons of several deposed Baruas and Phukans. The King's messengers could not bring any man from their camp, and the *Tekelas* or emissaries were captured and detained. Then the Dangarias reported to the King on these high-handed activities of the Kalita. 160.

Expedition against the Kalita Phukan.

The King ascertained all the facts, and concluding that the Kalita was perpetrating misdeeds, sent an expedition against the Kalita for subduing him, under Nedhai Dihingia Phukan, the Lahan Dekaphukan, the Deobilia Neog-phukan, the Kowanr Senapati, the Bargohain's son Lari-Gohain with the forces under their jurisdiction. This was in the month of Jaistha. They crossed the Dihing at Bandardewa-ghat. The Marangi-khowa and Solal Gohains proceeded up the Luhit and joined the expedition. They surrounded the Kalita from all sides. The Kalita's supporters took to their heels. 161.

Death of the Kalita Phukan.

The Kalita fled with his son, and entered the Kechamati-parvat. The Kowanr Senapati pursued them, and having found them at the mountain fastnesses brought the father and the son yoked together. Then they were both killed on the way by assassins. The King had issued order only to seize the person of the Kalita, and now he was killed by assassins. The expedition returned in Ashar; the King was apprised of all that had happened, and the men bowed down before the sovereign. The King accused the Kowanr Senapati saying,—'How has it been possible for prisoners under arrest to be killed by assassins? The Senapati should find out and capture the culprits.' On this offence the Kowanr Senapati was put in heavy chains, and they were taken off only after four months. 162.

Sadiya expedition.

Then the Nakhams with some men came down from the Khamjania Naras to Sadiya, being unable to live any longer under the oppression of their chief. They prayed to the King for some land through the Sadiya-khowa Gohain. The King in consultation with the Dangarias ordered them to be settled in the Maluk territory beyond the outskirts of Sadiya. After living there for some time they murdered the Sadiya-khowa Gohain of the Lankekia family. This news was communicated to the King, who despatched the Mahamantri Buragohain Dangaria attended by the Kowanr Senapati. Hearing of the arrival of the Dangaria at Sadiya, the Nakhams took to their heels. The Dangaria recommended to the King for the appointment of the son of the deceased Lankekia Sadiya-khowa in the office of his father. The King accepted the proposal. The Dangaria after appointing Lankekia's son as Sadiya-khowa as ordered by the King, returned from the expedition and paid his obeisance to His Majesty by kneeling down at his feet. 163.

Bereavements in the royal family.

Then at that time the queen-mother caused a tank to be excavated at Alikekuri. But she died before the tank could be consecrated. Her *Sraddha* ceremony was performed on a profuse and lavish scale, and largesses were distributed to Brahmans. A year after the tank was dedicated by His Majesty; an enclosure was made for Brahmans and another for females, and charities were distributed from there. Almost at that time the Parvatia queen had an attack of smallpox, as well as her daughter. Both of them were kept at the Devighar, where they both died. 164.

Internal affairs.

Then at that time one Krishnapuria of the Lukhurakhun family was made the Parvatia queen. After this in the month of Aghon, 1695 *saka,* the King began to select a site for excavating a tank at Bhatiapar. After two years the tank was consecrated and gifts were distributed. The artisan employed as superintendent of the operations connected with the excavation of the tank was one Mathan, who was the Barbarua's *Tamol-kata*, or betel-nut cutter, of the intermediate rank, belonging to the Darikial regiment. The King also constructed a temple afterwards. After this Nakua Nyaya-sodha Phukan of the Dihingia family died, and a member of the Kharikatia branch of the Duara family was appointed Nyaya-sodha Phukan. In the month of Jaistha the Swargadeo ascended the Patghar. In the year 1696, the King presented to each of the three Dangarias a set of presents consisting of long ear-ornaments of gold, gold bangles, a turban and a cloak, and a frock-coat similar to those used by the Naras. The Barbarua was presented with precious earrings, gold bangles, a turban and a cloak of Karchipi cloth with spotted embroideries. The Phukans were given ear-pendants with suspended filaments, gold bangles, as well as turbans and cloaks. Thus all the officers and nobles stationed at Gargaon and Gauhati were presented according to their rank and position. The King also invited all the Mahantas or religious preachers and held festivities for seven days, and presents were distributed among the Mahantas. The King then deposed Kasi Barphukan of the Dihingia family and appointed the Dekaphukan of the Lahans to the office of the Barphukan. A member of the Tirowal branch of Chiring family was appointed Dekaphukan. After this in the month of Jaistha, the dress of a female attendant employed in sweeping floors caught fire at the back, the hem of her attire having touched the burning wick of a lamp. The wick stuck to her robes, which she flung aside. The fire dropped at a corner of the portico of the King's main residence from where it spread to the thatch of the roof. The King retired to the house formerly inhabited by him when he was a prince. The next day a house was constructed near the Barchora to which the King retired. This fire portended disasters. 165.

Death of Lakshmi Singha.

Then in the year 1699 *saka*, the dysentery from which the King had been suffering took a serious turn. Then the King's son was appointed Juvaraj or heir-apparent. The Dangarias as well as the Baruas and the Phukans were presented with robes consisting of the four requisite pieces. After this the King died a year after, in the month of Puh, in the year 1702 *saka*. His body was cremated at the Hatikhok-ghat on the bank of the Dikhou. The bones were taken to Charaideo, under the escort of the Dekaphukan of the Chiring family and the Chetia-patra Barua of the Madurial family. 166.

CHAPTER IX.

SWARGADEO GAURINATH SINGHA.

Accession.

On the day when Lakshmi Singha died, the ministers and nobles placed his son the Juvaraj on the throne. The rites and ceremonies connected with the death of the monarch were performed according to *Dansagar*, and gifts were also made. Musical recital recounting the praise of Hari was also performed by the Mahantas invited specially for the occasion. It was in this gathering that the Bengena-atia Mahanta was allowed to sit next to the place allotted to the Kuruabahi Gosain. This seat was formerly occupied by the Mahanta of Dihing through the instrumentality of the Bakatial Barbarua. Then the Barbarua of the Adabaria family became a great favourite of the King. The King acted as he was advised by that officer. At that time the Rajneog Phukan of the Labhabaria Duaras was removed from office on the receipt of complaints made by the people. The son of the Barbarua was appointed Neog-phukan. There was an animosity between the Barbarua and the Bargohain since the days of Swargadeo Lakshmi Singha. Having discovered some loopholes the Barbarua out of umbrage reported the matter to the King. The King found out that the attitude of the Bargohain was extremely antagonistic; and so on the Bhishma-ashtami day in the month of Magha, Bailung Bargohain, his sons the Lari-Gohain and the Hati-Barua were beheaded by orders of the King near the Pakighar, literally, a masonry building. His other son the Choladhara Phukan, who was the son-in-law of the former king, was similarly executed outside the gate named Uranar-choki. Their belongings were seized and removed to the palace of the King. Then the eldest son of the Barbarua was made Choladhara Phukan. On becoming a Phukan he exercised great influence upon the King. His maternal uncle who was Chetia-patar Barua of the Rangpuria branch of the Madurial family was appointed Bargohain. He had adopted a son of the sister of the Parvatia queen Krishnapuria; he was now maimed and banished to Barkola along with the queen. By this time the Lahan Barphukan died at Gauhati. 167.

Adabaria Barbarua deposed.

Then the deposed Senapati Phukan of the Duara family was appointed Barphukan. The Barbarua excavated a tank at the terminus of the Tangchuali; but no water oozed out there though it was twenty cubits deep. At the bottom there sprang up a thick cluster of paddy plants as if they were transplanted there. This was a bad omen. A row of bamboos in front of the Rangpur residence of the Barbarua blossomed with flowers; this was also an evil omen. After this the Barbarua constructed the Singari-ghar. Thus the Barbarua conducted the administration of the country in an independent manner. The King then realised that the Barbarua did everything by ignoring the absolute rights of the sovereign. Thus saying the King deposed the Barbarua. His sons, the Choladhara Phukan and the Neog-phukan were also dismissed from their offices; and the Barbarua was driven with his five sons to his home at Adabari. On that very day the King appointed the Khargharia Phukan of the Sandikai family, who happened to be the husband of his elder sister, to the office of the Barbarua. The deposed Barbarua said to the new one,—"Well, my friend, you have become Barbarua, and what fears can I have now?" He further gave him counsels for his guidance and security. Then the new Barbarua kept the deposed Barbarua under guard in front of the Hatisal near the Barduar. In that very night, he was placed on a horse and sent to Adabari with his sons. The articles deposited at the Rangpur residence of the deposed Barbarua were seized and removed to the King's household. This happened in the month of Phagun, *saka* 1703. In the same month of Phagun, the King was initiated by the second of the three sons of one Ramananda of the Pahumara family, who (Ramananda) was designated as Acharyya or a religious preceptor. The King thenceforward became a very devoted benefactor of the Brahmans. 168.

The King ascends the Singari-ghar.

After this, in the month of Baisakh, *saka* 1704, the Namtial Barbarua caused the King to ascend the Singari-ghar; where he assumed the Hindu name of Gaurinath Singha. He made gifts, and collected the Mahantas, and the festivities lasted for a week. He made presents to the nobles and officers of Gargaon and Gauhati including the three Dangarias in order of their rank and dignity. After this he planted an *Ao-bar*, on which occasion also he distributed gifts and charities. On that very day, the Bar-aideo or the elder sister of the King, was given in marriage to the Namtial Barua; he was allowed to have a red covering for his distinctive mace or Arowan. On his return he deposited the hangings of network at the Charaideo house, and planted a *Bat-bar*, when also he made gifts and presents. 169.

The Moamarias burn houses.

The queen-mother, named Edakhati, had brought up a girl of the Sandikai branch of the Adabaria family. She was now made chief queen at Gargaon. The granddaughter of the Chatai-alia Doulbandha Bargohain was made Parvatia queen. After this the King proceeded to Garagram in the month of Chaitra. After ten days had elapsed in Baisakh, *saka* 1705, the King came out of Barkola-duar to Nazirahat and amused himself by plying boats. Night approached, and the King entered the city by the Barduar. Some Moamarias with torches in their hands had accompanied the King's torch-bearers, and entering the city by the Darika-duar they set fire to the stalls where *dolas* or sedans were kept. The Moamarias inflicted a stroke with a sword on the forehead of the Dola-kasharia Barua, named Lephera, who made a hairbreadth escape. The Dhekial Phukan was also wounded. The King was frightened at the sight of the fire; and he arranged to fetch a Makhundi or female elephant named Sarukali, belonging to the Majindar Barua, from the stall attached to the Gandhia-bhandar. With the help of that elephant he caused a breach in the back wall of his residence, after which he entered his old dwelling. He was accompanied by Naga Majindar Barua, the Dulia Barua of the Sandikai family, and a handful of attendants. The queens also entered there with some female attendants. This manœuvre could not be detected by the Moamarias. They cut some men inside the Darika-duar. The citizens began to flee being seized with scare. The Moamarias then came out and set fire to the Barchora, from where the Phukans and Rajkhowas fled away. The Barbarua also went out of his Palighar or guard-house. The paiks also fled away. The Morans came out from there and set fire to the Holong-ghar. The Mahamantri Buragohain Dangaria of the Kuoigayan family heard this from his son the Lari-Gohain; and coming out in the company of the Senapati Phukan of the Duara family, encountered the Morans in a close spear-fight at the entrance of the Barduar. Some Moamarias fell in that affray and also a handful of our own men. Then the Buragohain and the Barphukan with the help of their followers alone drove back the Moamarias; and having entered the city began a search for the King. 170.

Moamaria atrocities at Rangpur.

The King became somewhat frightened suspecting the approach of the Moamarias. But recognising the Buragohain Dangaria and the Barpukhan he became composed. The King gave vent to his sorrow before the two nobles, the Buragohain and the Barphukan, who in their turn expressed similar regret. Then a search was made for the Barbarua who was ultimately recovered; and arrangements were made for strict watch during that night. It was proclaimed by shouting aloud that the King was in the city and that the citizens should not flee. All the main thoroughfares were guarded by the citizens. The Moamarias then set fire to the residence of the Madurial Bargohain Dangaria. The Bargohain fled. The Dihingia Phukan of the Miri-Sandikai family was killed by the

Morans when he came out of his house, seeing the fire in the residence of the King. His followers deserted him and took to their heels. In the meantime the Moamarias set fire to the house of the Kenduguria Barpatra Dangaria; and the Dangaria fled down to Gauhati in a swift boat. Then the Moamarias marched towards Rangpur by the route through Panichoki. It was believed that the sons of the deposed Barua of the Adabaria family were in the company of the Moamarias. The King being unable to ascertain the real fact despatched a Dola-kasharia Bara to the deposed Adabaria Barua, with orders to imprison the Barbarua if he was found in his residence, and chain his sons. The emissary found the Barbarua in his house and acted according to the command of the King. On their arrival at Rangpur, the Moamarias met the gate-keeper of the principal entrance. He was asked to open the gate on the pretext that the King and his associates had come there, the residence at Gargaon having caught fire. The porter did not open the gate, but they proceeded to report the matter to the Phukan. In the meantime the Moamarias broke open the gate and entered inside. Having met the Nyaya-sodha Phukan of the Duara family near the Barchora they captured him. The Gharphalia Barua of the Madurial family fled. One Bakhar Hajarikia of the family of the old Dhekial Phukan was at the Darika-duar; he also fled away. All the female attendants and dancing girls who were found inside were removed by the Moamarias to the Dolaghar or sedan-stall. The Moamarias passed the night within the walls of the city. The next morning they issued out and set fire to the houses of the Nagosain, of the Lanmakharu Bhitarual Phukan, and of the Barphukan. The Parvatia Bhattacharyya Gosain was living in a house on the bank of the Jaysagar tank: and the Moamarias severely abused the Gosain. 171.

The curse of the Parvatia Gosain.

At this the Gosain cursed them uttering the following words, —'The Moamarias will soon be destroyed'. The Moamarias used to shout to the people on the roads that the Opar-Charingia-Raja was the Raja, and that the deposed Barbarua of the Adabaria family was the Barbarua. 172.

After this a wounded Moamaria, who happened to be a member of the Bargohain's family, was caught hold of at Gargaon, from whom all the particulars of the movements and schemes of the

Moamarias were obtained. With the object of attacking the Moamarias at Rangpur, the King despatched the Kuoigayan Mahamantri Buragohain Dangaria, the Madurial Bargohain Dangaria, the Senapati Barphukan of the Duara family, the Dihingia Naobaicha Phukan, the Rajneog Phukan of the Buragohain family, the Chatai-alia Barua, and the Chetia-patar Barua, with a large force and provisions. They accordingly marched onward taking with them all the villagers they could meet from Chatai-ali. The Buragohain Dangaria, the Barphukan and the Neogphukan advanced by the route through Uran-choki; while the rest consisting of the Bargohain, the Naobaicha Phukan and the Chetia-patar Barua, proceeded by the road through Meteka. 173.

Preparations to encounter the Moamarias.

When the Barphukan marching in the van had reached Ghorasal or the horse-stalls, he was spotted by the Moamarias two of whom rushed towards him. Seeing this our men retreated, and were pressed back by elephants. However, the Nagayan shieldsmen accompanying the Phukan saw the two men and severed them to pieces. In the meantime, when the Buragohain Dangaria had reached the Nalamukh, three Moamarias dashed out of the Barduar to attack him; one of them was on horseback, while the two others were on foot. The Dangaria's followers speared two of them to death, and the third ran away and entered the city. The Moamarias receiving the report from the fugitive fled away by the Na-duar. Then our men, on hearing that the Moamarias had fled away from the city, proceeded with the army and occupied the capital. Then the Dangarias, the Phukans and the Baruas despatched some soldiers on horse to inform the Barbarua of the re-taking of the city. The Barbarua received the tidings at four *dandas* of the night; and being pleased he communicated the news to the King, who became greatly delighted, as well as other persons. Guards and watchmen were posted during that night. Next day at about one and half *prahar* the Barbarua sitting in the court sent the following message to the King,—'His Majesty's servants, the Dihingia Phukan and the Nyaya-sodha Phukan, have both perished in the performance of the work of the Heavenly King. The King may be pleased to allow their sons to succeed to their fathers' offices.' The King appointed the sons of the deceased officers as Dihingia Phukan and Nyaya-sodha Phukan. 174.

Re-occupation of Rangpur.

Further preparations.

After this the King commanded the Barbarua to extirpate the Moamarias living near the capital; and the Barbarua had them arrested in flocks and put them to death. The next day the King marched up with his forces to Rangpur. On the day following the King summoned the three Dangarias, the Barbarua, the Barphukan, and other Phukans and Rajkhowas, and solicited their advice in the following terms,—'The Moamarias have been exercising great power; and the Morans have committed many misdeeds heretofore. What is your opinion with regard to the extermination of the Moamarias with their sons and adherents?' Hearing this proposal the officers assembled unanimously expressed their wish to annihilate the Moamarias. Having thus consulted an order was promulgated to all at the Barchora on that very day to the effect that the Moamarias should be killed with their sons and friends by whomever and at whatever place they were met. This order was proclaimed in the interiors by despatching the Dola-kasharia Bara, the Da-dhara Bara and the Tekela-Bara. Having heard this dire command of His Majesty our men captured and killed the Moamarias in all the villages with their sons and wives. Some of them fled into the territories of the Dafalas, the Bhots, the Kacharis and the Jayantas and thus saved their lives. 175.

The ex-Barbarua's sons punished.

At that time the three Dangarias, the Barbarua, the Phukans and the Rajkhowas had to keep watch at the capital during day and night. Next day the King convened a *Barmel* or general council of the three Dangarias, the Barbarua, the Phukans and the Rajkhowas, and said to them,—'It has been reported that the sons of the deposed Adabaria Barbarua came in the company of the Moamarias: the Barbarua should institute an enquiry into this matter and communicate to me his findings.' Having received this order, the Barbarua as well as the three Dangarias and the Barphukan informed the King that the report was true, whereupon the King ordered the eyes of the four sons of the Adabaria Barbarua to be plucked. Then the Dola-kasharia Bara accompanied by one Chidai of Kamalabari put out the eyes of the four sons at their Adabari residence. After this in the month of Jaistha the Senapati Phukan of the Duara family made his obeisance to the King, and he was sent to Gauhati as Barphukan after the King had administered to him the necessary instructions. 176.

Purnananda made Buragohain.

In the month of Ashar the Kuoigayan Mahamantri Buragohain Dangaria died, and his son the Lari-Gohain or heir-apparent was appointed Buragohain After this, Gendhela, the grandson of the Sandikai Pani-phukan, was appointed Choladhara Barua. 177.

The King ascends the Patghar.

Then the Barbarua constructed the Patghar by employing the *dowals* who were raised for the purpose. In Baisakh the King ascended the house, and offered gifts to the officers and nobles of Gargaon and Gauhati, including the three Dangarias, according to their rank and dignity. The King also made appropriate presents to the Saikias and Baras of the *Kanris*. The two chiefs of Darang attended the functions; and they were also given presents. All the Mahantas were invited, and with them the King celebrated the festivities lasting for seven days. The Mahantas were offered gifts and presents. This happened in the year 1705, *saka*. 178.

Naga Majindar's eyes are extracted.

After this, Naga Majindar who was a Ganak of Nazirahat, was charged with an offence by the King; his eyes were extracted at Gargaon, and he was driven home. His belongings were removed to the King's household. A member of the Kayath caste was appointed Majindar Barua. At that time one Brahmachari, who was a great-grandson of the Chatamial Mahanta Basudeva, and who had his home at Naogaon, was living on the bank of Jaysagar. He now intended to rise against the authority of the King. The King having come to know this brought him from his house near Jaysagar and had his eyes put out; after this he was sent to his home at Naogaon. His three accomplices were fried in oil to death. After this the Dhekial Phukan of the Phisi regiment died. The Changmai Barua of the Changmai family was appointed Dhekial Phukan. After this the King went to Adabari, where he met the Barbarua and his four sons at the gate of the residence of the deposed Adabaria Barbarua: the King was moved to great compassion at seeing their deplorable condition. The King spoke to them many words of kindness and sympathy and offered some money and cloths. They also made many prayers and supplications to the King and bowed down at his feet. 179.

Death of Harnath.

After this the King returned to Rangpur. The King's stepmother was a daughter of the Naphukial Sandikai family. She was now given the Khangia *mel*, and proclaimed as Raj-mao or queen-mother. Then a tank was excavated at Naphuk where a temple was also constructed. It was formally consecrated afterwards. After this the Senapati Barphukan of Gauhait died, and the fact was reported to the King. The King then ordered the Barbarua to erect a camp at Sonai river for bathing on the Asoka-ashtami day in the month of Chaitra. As ordered by the King the Barbarua constructed a temporary residence there. His Majesty proceeded to the camp and bathed in the Brahmaputra according to the prescribed rules. During the King's stay in this camp, in 1706 *saka*, he appointed the Choladhara Phukan of the Sandikai family, named Gendhela, as Barphukan. The new Barphukan paid his respects to the monarch, and proceeded to Gauhati after he had received necessary instructions from His Majesty. The King's maternal uncle, one Bhadari of the Sandikai family, was appointed Choladhara Phukan. From the camp at Sonai the King went to the Satra or monastery of the Dakhinpat Gosain, and also to the residence of the Na-gosain of Pahumara. Thus after amusing himself the King returned to Rangpur. At this time, the son of the Na-gosain performed within the city-walls a *Bhawana* or dramatic entertainment, the name of the play being *Padmavati-haran*. In the meantime some men from the interior of Upper Assam informed the Barbarua that a nondescript band of Hati-chungi Morans had commenced hostilities under the captaincy of one Badal Gaonburha. Having received this intelligence the Barbarua communicated it to the King. 180.

Royal marriage in Hindu rites.

Then the King despatched the Na-phukan of the Duara family with his personal force. The Phukan subdued the Morans by diplomacy and stratagem, and returned with Badal and Charal, and knelt down before the King. The King ordered that the two rebels should be put in chains. After this the sentry-house of the Gharphalias at Rangpur was struck by lightning. In *saka* 1707, the King proceeded to Gargaon. Then in Ashar, the King married according to the regular Brahmanical code, the daughter of one Kalia Deka of the Dihingia family. The King offered presents to the three Dangarias, the Barbarua, the Phukans, the Rajkhowas, the Kakatis, the Dolois, and the Deodhais according to their rank. Presents were also given to the Barphukan and other officers of Gauhati. 181.

The Swargadeo's hunting excursion at Garamur.

The King then ordered the Barbarua to erect temporary quarters at Garamur where he proposed to stay for amusements and recreations. The Barbarua in obedience to the King's orders had camps erected by sending Kaliram Bara. Then in the month of Phalgun, 1707 *saka,* the King arrived at his Garamur camp. There the King amused himself by hunting elephants, tigers, buffaloes and deer. One day the King crossed the Lohit and proceeded to the monastery of the Narwa Mahanta. When the King reached the vicinity of the Satra, the Narwa Ata came out in a festive array, accompanied by singers, drummers and women to welcome and recieve His Majesty. The King asked,—'Whose marriage is this ?' Saying so he brought the Mahanta to him by sending the son of Bhumuk, who was a Bahua or comical actor, and Manjay. The two messengers upbraided the Mahanta very severely. The King had heard formerly that a prince had been living secretly in the Satra and for this reason the King now dishonoured the Mahanta severely. On enquiry it transpired that the man was not a prince, but a young Gohain of the Buragohain's family. Three days after the King crossed the Lohit to hunt buffaloes at Jengeraimukh. On the return journey, when the King was in a boat belonging to one Kathamia Naobaicha, there ensued a violent wind, and huge waves agitated the surface of the waters. The King unable to cross the river got upon a sand-deposit. The King immediately made a vow to offer the sacrifice of 10,000 buffaloes to the Goddess Kamakhya.

Then when six or seven *dandas* had elapsed at night the King crossed the river without fear and reached his camp. After four days the King proceeded to Khakandaguri in the North Bank, on reaching which he caused the firing of seven volleys. The villagers came to the King and complained loudly to him that they could not live peacefully on account of the oppression of the *Dafala-Bahatias*. The King ordered the Namtial Barbarua of the Sandikai family to enquire into the matter. The Barbarua also asked the complainants to come to him for purposes of enquiry. The King came back to his camp after having thus amused himself. After this the King's step-mother, who was a daughter of the Sandikai family, breathed her last. Her funeral rites were performed according to the Brahmanical code and His Majesty offered presents and charities. Then the King ordered the Na-phukan of the Duara family to square up the disturbances in the North Bank, and despatched him accordingly. 182.

Renewed influence of the Moamarias.

When there had remained only a day or two for the expiry of the month of Chaitra, the King left his Garamur camp and halted at his Sonai-nai residence. After celebrating there the Bihu festival he returned to Rangpur in Baisakh. The Na-phukan then intimated to the King in Sravan that he had suppressed the hostilities as commanded. Then the Saharia Barua posted at the main entrance to the Dafala hills communicated the following news to the Barbarua through one Sagar Bara,—'At Japaribhita, the Moamarias and the *Dafala-Bahatias* have erected houses of cloth or tents, and behaving as rebels they have recruited volunteers. They are parading with fans made of peacock feathers, and are causing a panic in the country by extortion and plunder.' Hearing this the Barbarua informed the King accordingly, who ordered the Barbarua to carefully enquire into the matter. In obedience to the King's order the Barbarua despatched the Bezbara to examine the situation. This officer went to the spot, and saw that the Moamarias acting in concert with the *Dafala-Bahatias* were perpetrating many misdeeds in the country and had also devastated a couple of villages; he informed the Barbarua of this, who in his turn communicated the news to the King, saying that the Moamarias and the *Dafala-Bahatias* were causing the dispersion of the people in the country. Having heard this the King summoned the three Dangarias, the Barbarua, the Phukans and the Rajkhowas, to a *Barmel* or grand conference, where he said,—'Reports have been received that there is an insurrection at Japaribhita. You should all confer and let me know whether the despatch of an expeditionary force to that place is desirable or not'. 183.

Conflict with the Moamarias in the North Bank.

Then the officers assembled had a consultation and submitted the following proposal to the King,—'Since Your Majesty's visit to Garamur, the people of the north have been frequently complaining to you that they are apprehending the necessity of leaving their villages. So it is advisable to give them courage by sending a commander with some soldiers. Yet, whatever Your Majesty may be pleased to command will be carried out.' The officers having thus advised the King, he despatched the Solal Gohain, the Marangi-khowa, the Dihingia Phukan of the Miri-Sandikai family and Lephera Chaodang Barua with their own men. The Marangi-khowa was supplied with the Majiu-Dayangias; and the Marangis of Naogaon accompanied the Solal Gohain. The three generals crossed the Lohit river and halted after erecting a fort. The Moamarias by a stratagem cajoled them to the bank of the Solmari Bil. The Solal Gohain, on the plea of a severe attack of diabetis, went to Kaliabar after he had informed the King of this.

The Moamarias paid a visit to the Marangi-khowa and the Dihingia Phukan on the pretext of offering them their surrender, saying that their hostility was due to the fact that God had wanted to destroy men. One day the Moamarias came to the Ahom fort with an armed force for the purpose of warfare. Thinking that the advent of the Moamarias was inspired by a motive of war, our men commanded the soldiers to come out of the fort. The Moamarias saw this manœuvre, pursued and attacked our men. Then there ensued an affray where men from both sides were killed. Then the Moamarias attacked the King's army from behind and began to massacre our men. Being unable to make a stand our men retreated and fell into quagmires and morasses. The Marangi-khowa Gohain and the Dihingia Phukan were both killed as well as other common men, and the remnant in the fort also fled. 184.

Fresh expedition against the Moamarias.

Having obtained a large quantity of provisions in this war, the Moamarias continued hostilities with redoubled strength. Kalia-bhomora, Bidur, Howha, Tamai, Parshad and Phofai were the leaders of the Moamarias, and there were also numerous other men. Then our fugitives from the war came and reported to the Barbarua of all that had happened,—'The Marangi-khowa and the Dihingia Phukan have both been killed, and their fort has also been demolished'. The Barbarua communicated the news to the King who became sad. Other persons also expressed sorrow. At this time the waters of the tanks and pools in the city were agitated, and the waves dashed against each other as if there was a naval engagement. A wild elephant entered the city and went away having crossed the walls. The image of Kesavrai in the Bardoul began to perspire, and there occurred also many other evil omens. At these inauspicious signs the three Dangarias and the Baruas and the Phukans removed their property from their houses. The King then convened a grand meeting of the three Dangarias, the Barbarua, the Phukans and the Rajkhowas, according to whose decision the Duara Na-phukan, the Dihingia Phukan of Gauhati and the Naobaicha Phukan were despatched against the rebels at the head of their personal contingents. They crossed the Lohit, and the Na-phukan and the Dihingia Phukan constructed a fort in the vicinity of the Somdiri river at Phukan-hat in the Miri *tangani* or sub-division, and they halted there. The Naobaicha Phukan erected a fort in the compound of Khara and encamped there.

Then at that time there occurred a great flood in the month of Ashar. The Phukans could not come out of their forts. The Moamarias nicknamed the Dihingia Phukan as *Muga-chungia, i.e.*, a rearer of muga silkworms. The Naobaicha Phukan fell ill, and the news was sent to the King who was also informed of the critical nature of the war. The King having heard it despatched the Kenduguria Barpatra Dangaria with his own men. The Dangaria, accompanied by an army composed of the Kowanr Hilaidaris or musketeers, the dowals of the three Abhaypurias and of the Namdayangia and Bacha, crossed the Lohit and erected a stockade where he stayed. Thence he proceeded to the Khararbari fort previously constructed by the Naobaicha Phukan. The Dangaria was the commander-in-chief, yet the Phukans did not intend to carry out his orders. The Dangaria gradually advanced, and constructed seven forts on the Garaimari Bil in the vicinity of the Moamarias. He stopped there within gun-shot distance of Japaribhita having gone there through Rani. 185.

The Battle of Garamur.

One day, there was an interchange of shots between the two parties, and in Kartik fighting commenced. A large number of soldiers belonging to the army of the three Abhaypurias fell in that battle, and the Dangaria's fort was also beleaguered by the enemy. The news was sent to the King through the Bahbaria Kataki Dhireswar, who delivered the message to His Majesty in his palace. The King appreciating the critical nature of the contest despatched the Rajneog Phukan of the Buragohain family with his men. The Phukan crossed the Dihing and stopped at Garamur after erecting a fort there. The King came to know that the Holongaguria Morans who were established at Rangdoichong had rebelled. He brought back the Neog-phukan and sent him to that place. A member of the Leba family held the post of the Jutakia Barua, while one Moi was the Changrung Barua. They were provided with an army of two thousand men and directed to remain at Garamur. In the meantime the chieftains of Rani, Luki and Topakuchi arrived from Gauhati. They were despatched to the war with a Bara of the Barbarua, and they halted at Pahumara. The Moamarias then left the Barpatra Dangaria and the two Phukans in their respective forts; and having crossed the river at Garamur they took in their company one Pitambar, the son of the Moamaria Mahanta's daughter, who had been previously established by the King at a place down Auniati Satra under proper guard. Then the Moamarias again crossed the Lohit and attacked Garamur Satra. There ensued a furious contest with the Bhakats or disciples, many of whom perished in the battle. Some Moamarias were also killed. The Gosain or the abbot of Garamur Satra made a narrow escape and reached the King's capital. The Moamarias set fire to the Satra. Having heard this the King despatched to the war the Mahamantri Buragohain of the Kuoigayan family with his own men. 186.

Death of the chieftains.

The Dangaria then halted at the fort erected on the bank of the Sonai river. In the meantime the Barpatra Dangaria retreated with his force, crossed the Lohit and remained at the Dakhinpat Satra. The Gosain of Dakhinpat crossed the Dihing on the day following and proceeded to Rangpur. The day after this the chieftains of Rani, Luki and Topakuchi stopped together at Pahumara, and they were attacked by the Moamarias. The chiefs of Rani, Luki and Topakuchi fell in that battle. 187.

Gaurisagar fort.

The Jutakia Barua and Moi Barua also perished in that fight. From this time the strength of the Moamarias became redoubled. Then the Barpatra Dangaria after having crossed the Dihing joined the Buragohain Dangaria. The King coming to know this directed the Barpatra Dangaria to garrison his forces at Dikhoumukh, and the Dangaria halted there that night. The next day the Moamarias erected a stockade at Dikhoumukh and halting there during the day crossed the Dihing in the evening; and proceeded to Rangdoichong to take the Morans settled at that place: and there they halted for the night. On that very day the King appointed a member of the

Bahgaria Buragohain family as Dekaphukan of Rangpur and despatched him to the company of the Buragohain. One Gathalu Medhi of the Tepartalia Gohain family was appointed Naobaicha Phukan and sent to join the Buragohain Dangaria. As ordered by the King the following officers halted at the stockade in Gaurisagar,—the Khargharia Phukan, who was a son of the Barbarua; the latter's nephew who was the Dulia Barua; Bhadari Choladhara Phukan of the Sandikai family; the Kath-katia Barua named Gangai; Ramnath; Domai Deka; and the Barsatola of the Bakatial family.

Meanwhile Basanta, Gayan and Karekar were reported to have harboured Moamarias in their houses; the three were taken out of the city and hewn to pieces with axes. One Lephera Dolakasharia Barua halted at a fort on the bank of the tank erected by the Magalu or Manipuri princess. In the meantime the King despatched a messenger to bring the Barpatra Dangaria from his garrison at Dikhoumukh. He was now placed at the parapet of the Barduar at Rangpur and charged with the offence of retreating from the North Bank without suppressing the Moamarias, and of having allowed the Moamarias to follow him. Having heard of these allegations the Dangaria begged the King to accept the following explanation,—'I, a paik or subject of Your Majesty, could not subdue the enemy for inferiority of strength, and I was fortunate that I could make a hairbreadth escape'. He offered the above excuse to the King with due submission. The King ordered the Dangaria to proceed to the court, where the following command was delivered to him,—'The Dangaria should again march post-haste with his men and join the Phukans and Baruas who are camping at Gaurisagar, where he should direct them by his advice with a view to attack and extirpate the Morans'. 188.

War at Sagunmuri.

Having received this order from the King the Dangaria proceeded to his town residence but did not enter the house. He called his mother to the gate-house and bowed down to her there, and then he marched with speed to the Gaurisagar fort. The day after this, the Premier Buragohain Dangaria encountered the Moamarias in a furious battle at the Sagunmuri field near the Sonai river. Some Moamarias perished in the battle; our Dekaphukan was also killed, as well as Bagai, the Tekela-Neog, and other common soldiers also fell in the engagement. Having found it difficult to continue the fight for the absence of a stockade the army retreated to Gaurisagar fort. 189.

War at Bhatiapar.

The next day the Moamarias burnt numerous villages. They advanced towards Gaurisagar fort near which they stopped for the night, and set fire to many villages on the morning of the next day. Our people were severely frightened at the sight of the fire. The Dangarias seeing the hostile attitude of the people retreated and joined the King at Rangpur. The Moamarias, having burnt a large number of villages halted that night at Bhatiapar, where they set fire to the residence of the Gahari-chowa Barua or master of the royal piggeries. They stopped there for the night. One Aka Bailung collected a number of villagers in Janji and attacked the enemy at Bhatiapar, where some Morans fell in the battle that ensued. The Moamarias first failed to kill Aka Bailung by any means, but at last they managed to surround him on all sides and speared him to death.

The Moamarias stopped there for three days. Meanwhile there was consternation in the city. Formerly the King had ordered the dismissal of the Dihingia Phukan, the Na-phukan and the Neog-phukan. At that time a young man belonging to the Labhabaria branch of the Duara family, who had been serving as Pachani or attendant, was appointed Neog-phukan; the younger brother of the Barsatola of the Bakatial family was made Na-phukan; while the Dihingia Phukan was retained in his former office. One Sarudeka of the Dihingia family was made Deka-phukan of Rangpur in place of the former incumbent. On the day of the Moamarias' arrival at Bhatiapar, the King ordered the Bargohain Dangaria to remain at Ouguri outpost, the Barpatra Dangaria at Barduar and the Buragohain Dangaria at Na-duar. The Nyaya-sodha Phukan of the Duara family, the Tamuli Phukan who was a Brahman, were posted at Na-duar, while the Changrung Phukan was placed at Pani-duar; and from the time that the war assumed a terrible shape all the young men who were closely related to the three Dangarias, and to the Phukans and Baruas, as well as the descendants of the several Ahom families were recruited, and ordered to remain in charge of the gates in a systematic manner. The King also offered the youths some money. The Mahanta of Dihing sent words to the King that he would extirpate the Moamarias, and the King agreed to this proposal. 190.

The Mahanta of Dihing collected all the disciples he could lay his hands on, and imprinted an identification mark of lime on the forehead of each. They were made to take an oath touching the Mahanta's body that they would not desert the field. The army composed of the disciples was nearly two thousand strong. The Mahanta was despatched with his Bhakat army by the route through Mathadang road; and a contingent of six hundred men composed of Deodhais and Bailungs was sent through Bargohain Pathar. Aka Bailung came through Jengera Pathar at the head of nearly two thousand villagers. The Moamarias went on setting fire to villages, at the sight of which the Dihing disciples advanced with the Na-phukan. At this the Moamarias rushed to encounter them. The Bhakats of Dihing were seized with scare and they took to their heels. The Moamarias then dashed towards the Deodhai-Bailung detachment commanded by the Phukan. There ensued a battle in which a large number of Deodhai and Bailung soldiers fell. 191.

Military coupês of the Dihingia Mahanta and his disciples.

The Deodhai Phukan and Barua also perished in the engagement. The Deodhais also retreated being defeated. The Moamarias pursued them, and appeared in the royal lands in front of the Na-duar. Our men then fired the guns from the bastions. The Moamarias hurried back towards the fort of Aka Bailung at Jengerai. Aka rushed forward into the thick of the Moamaria line and cut some of the enemy. Then a number of Moamarias surrounded Aka, clasped round his body and speared him to death. The army under Aka then took to their heels. At that time the Moamarias captured our chief mahut or elephant-driver and released him after having chopped off his hands. On the next day the King despatched the Dekaphukan through a field, the Dihingia Phukan through the Dubariani-ali, and the Nyaya-sodha Phukan of Rangpur was sent with the contingent raised from Bacha by the route through Bhatiapar-ali. Thus prepared they all proceeded to war. They fought only some petty skirmishes, and there was no serious encounter on either side. 192.

Aka Bailung.

At dusk they all came to the city. During this period the King used to be at the court-room both during day and night. Then the Moamarias having realised the impossibility of continuing the war by

Succour from Manipur solicited.

any means on account of their insufficient strength, retreated with their army to the bank of the Sonai river on the pretext of celebrating the Magh Bihu festival. The rural Moamarias who were capable of fighting joined the rebels in large numbers. When the Moamarias had reached the Majuli, the King despatched Ramdeo Bahbaria Kataki to bring the Barphukan from Gauhati. At that time the King also despatched Bishnuram Bahbaria Kataki to the Manipuri Raja's place. Letters were handed over to the envoy, and he was instructed to convey to the Raja an oral message to the following effect,—'The Moamarias have caused disturbances in our country. The Manipuri Raja should now come to help us in recollection of our old friendship; if not, he should send some warlike men.' The envoy was despatched with this mission, and the message was also embodied in the epistle.

On the retreat of the Moamarias to the Sonai river, the Premier Buragohain Dangaria, the Bargohain Dangaria, the Dihingia Phukan, and the Dola-kasharia Barua of the family of Lephera, proceeded to Gaurisagar where they halted after throwing off a stockade. In the meantime the Magh Bihu festival had come to an end, and the Moamarias again proceeded up the country by the road along the bank of the Janji river with the object of resuming war-operations. 193.

Lephera Barua.

Then the King sent an army to fall upon the Moamarias at Maskhowa-garh. Our men left the battle and fled. The Moamarias pursued them; and halting at Kakatipar for the night they resumed their march on the next day and encamped on the bank of the tank named Pajikata Pukhuri, situated on the south of the capital. On that day the Moamarias fought a battle with Lephera Barua at Jaysagar, where there was an interchange of gun-shots. The next day the Moamarias marched through the village Chekham; and after having burnt down the village they halted at Alikekuri. When there were four *dandas* of the day, the King posted a large army of cavalry at Uranar-choki, in the residence and compound of the Barbarua, and on the Meteka road. At the sight of our army the Moamarias rushed towards them; and our men, seized with dismay, took to their heels. The Moamarias set fire to the whole area between Meteka and the Pani-duar after which they came out through the *choki* or outpost at Pukhurichuk. A detachment of the Moamaries encamped at Jaysagar, while another came out to the Na-duar at eight *dandas* of the day. The Bargobain Dangaria had encamped at Ouguri-choki. At the Hatisal near the Na-duar there was an interchange of arrow-shots between the Moamarias and the soldiers of our fort recruited from the upper classes. Then night set in. There was a furious storm and rain that night. 194.

Proposal to go down to Gauhati.

The King in the meantime had consulted with the two Dangarias and the Barbarua, saying that it was not advisable to remain there any longer, and that they should go down to Gauhati. The ministers replied,—'O King, the attitude of the people here is hostile and dangerous, and we think it will be better if we go down to Gauhati'. Accordingly, the King appointed the Dihingia Sarudeka as Barbarua, and having made up his mind to go down he started in the middle of the fullmoon night by the river-gate, on Friday, the 8th Magh, 1709 *saka*. Having proceeded to the Barghat at Amguri, he entered into a boat belonging to one Naobaicha Kathamia serving under the Choladhara Phukan. The following persons accompanied the King,—the Na-gosain who was the preceptor of the King; the Choladhara Phukan Bhadari and his elder brother named Gangai; Bikai who was the Dulia Barua; the Bhitarual Phukan of the Lanmakharu family; his son the Tipamia Rajkhowa; the Chiring Phukan of Chiring; his uncle Gopal Tamuliligira; Phapari Tamuli-ligira; the Dhekial Phukan of the Changmai family, and a number of *ligiras* or attendants. With these persons the King proceeded down to his camp at Gauhati. On that very night the chief queen and the Parvatia queen accompanied by some female attendants and dancing girls proceeded up the country, as well as the Buragohain Dangaria and the Barbarua. The Barpatra-gohain entered into a boat at Lechang and proceeded down to Gauhati. The Bargohain Dangaria remained at the Ouguri-choki for three days, after which he left the fort at night and fled. The other Phukans and Baruas went to whatever place and direction they liked. 195.

King Gaurinath at Gauhati.

The Naphukial Raj-mao fell ill at that time, and stayed away at the capital being unable to go. The messengers who had been despatched before to bring up the Barphukan and the Pani-phukan, now proceeded up with these two officers; on their reaching the Latasil choki, the royal boat made its appearance on the river with the King. The Phukans were slightly frightened, not knowing who were in the boat. Then the King's men in the boat made a sign by waving clothes, and the royal boat in the meantime moved near them. The Barphukan and the Pani-phukan bowed down to His Majesty. The King and the two Phukans both expressed regrets at their plight. The Barphukan made an enclosure on the spot with the coverings of the boat where the King took his meal. The King had not bathed previously. A camp was erected at Dopdar or the Barphukan's council-chamber where the King was removed on horseback. The Barphukan made his obeisance to the King by offering him ornaments, provisions and other articles worthy of a sovereign. The King then sent Kaliman Rajkhowa of the Lanmakharu family, and Anandiram Dakar Kataki in a state-boat to fetch the queens. The Barpatra Dangaria then joined the King, and was followed a few days later by the Bargohain Dangaria also. 196.

Affairs at Gauhati.

The King then summoned a grand council of the Dangarias, the Barphukan, and other Phukans and Rajkhowas; and in accordance with the decision arrived at, the Pani-phukan and the Dhekial Phukan of the Changmai family were sent out to the war, at the head of an army raised from Rani, Luki, Naogaon and Kharangi and other men. The total strength of the army came up to nearly thirty thousand soldiers. The King exhorted the commanders as follows,—'You have seen the plight into which I have been thrown. Both of you should fight in a concerted manner; and do all that is necessary for the extirpation of the Moamarias'. On receiving this royal command, the Pani-phukan made the following prayer to the King,—'O Heavenly King, what will come out of my endeavours? Some good results may be achieved only through the divine might of Your Majesty. Specially, the forces of Gargaon and Gauhati have not been able to vanquish the Moamarias in war. Still, I, your slave, will kill the Moamarias, or will be killed myself.' Thus saying he bowed down to the King, who bade him farewell, and the Phukan started on his expedition. All this took place at Gauhati. 197.

Affairs at Rangpur.

Now to turn to the affairs at Rangpur. After the King had gone down, the Moamarias occupied the capital of Rangpur. Then the Saharias and Moamarias all met together, and called in the Mahajan of the Puranimatia

Satra by sending messengers. Then staying at Khutiapota for some time, the Puranimatia Mahanta quarrelled with the Na-mati Moamarias, quitted the place with his disciples and retired to his own Satra or monastery. Eight days after the downward journey of the King, the senior queen and the Parvatia queen went to Lechang and remained there in concealment. At that time Manjay, the son of Nyaya-sodha Phukan of the Bakatial family, was summoned and appointed Barbarua. The Khangia Phukan imparted the necessary instructions of appointment to the Barbarua, and he was then despatched with the three Abhaypurias to attack the Moamarias. With the villagers the contingent numbered some four thousand men, of which, Bhogai, a Dulia or a sedan-bearer of the *Purani-mel*, was appointed commander and was led into Gargaon. Then a princes' regiment two thousand strong, also came there and encamped with them after erecting a temporary thatched roof at Pani-choki. On the day of the arrival of Manjay Barbarua, a captain of the name of Merkai made his appearance in the south with some thousand men, and just when he was reaching the corner of the Jaysagar tank the Moamarias discovered them and began to slay them. Being unable to hold any longer they fled in all directions. 198.

Bhogai Senapati.

At that time the Buragohoin Dangaria, his elder brother the Neog-phukan, the Tamuli Phukan who was a Brahman by caste, his brother Khangia Phukan,—all joined the company of Manjay. On reaching Darika the Dihingia Barbarua then fought with the Moamarias at the head of some twenty thousand men. Some Moamarias fell in that engagement. The Moamarias being unable to stand any longer retreated and entered the city. The royal army also advanced and garrisoned at Sibsagar. A battle ensued there in which the Moamarias were beaten back, pursued and compelled to cross the Dikhou. The royal party passed one night on the bank of the Dikhou. The next day the Moamarias opened their batteries from the other side of the river, and the Dihingias also replied them with shots from the opposite bank. Just then a band of Moamarias crossed the river by the Hatikhokghat and began to slay our men from the rear. The other band attacked from the front, and thus a hand-to-hand fight took place accompanied by bloodshed and slaughter. There was a terrible massacre in the Dihingia regiment. Some Moamarias

were also killed. The Dihingias fled away. The deposed Naobaicha Phukan fell in the battle; also the Barbarua. Manjay Barbarua had stayed at Gargaon for eight days. Just at that time the Moamarias who went on setting fire to villages as they advanced, came to Alikekuri and there laid siege to the stockade of Senapati Bhogai. A hand-to-hand fight ensued accompanied by a general massacre. The Moamarias began to slay Bhogai's soldiers from behind. Yet the soldiers did not turn their face but they went on assiduously slaying the Moamarias. Then, however, Bhogai's followers took to their heels, and Bhogai too fell in the battle.
199.

Appointment of new commanders.

After this the Moamarias set fire to the villages and encircled them as if by a ring of fire. Seeing this Manjay Barbarua left Gargaon and fled to Bakata. His followers searched for treasures buried under the ground by goldsmiths and weavers and fled away after having extracted and acquired them. Manjay then went to the two queens and gave them detailed information. Just after the flight of Manjay, the Moamarias set fire to the capital, and destroyed everything that lay in the tract bounded by Uranar-chowki on one side and Doulguri on the other. Thenceforward the Moamarias began to bring the villages into submission; and the common people on the Ahom side also began to surrender themselves to the Moamarias in small numbers. After this the force from Gauhati advanced and reached Kaliabar. Just at this time the Buragohain Dangaria who was slowly going down with a view to meet the King arrived at Kajiranga. There the Pani-phukan met him and supplied him a fresh re-imbursement of recruits from Nam-Dayang; he then brought back the Buragohain. Then journeying up they all arrived at Dergaon. At this time the Namtial Barbarua went down to meet the King. Just then he received the news of the advance of the Pani-phukan and of the Buragohain Dangaria. On the other hand, the Pani-phukan hearing that the Barbarua was approaching invited him to the *namghar* of Bhagati Bapu and there received him. Then all four gave vent to a great deal of grief at seeing the unfortunate plight of the country and the people. Then the Barbarua said,—'Fighting with these same archers and shieldsmen our Kings had vanquished even the foreigners on numerous occasions, but the very same archers and shieldsmen become demoralised and terrified at the mere sight of the Moamarias and take to their heels. All this have taken place because God and the Goddess have so desired it. Therefore, the Wheel of Time being so powerful nothing can be presaged. So joining with the Buragohain Dangaria you should both go to the war to offer a united front. If you can subdue the Moamarias the Sandikai family will earn enduring fame, virtue and renown.' Hearing this the Pani-phukan said,—' You have said what is best. Besides, Swargadeo has bestowed on me these men and has commanded me to do the needful. What can be achieved by me alone ? All that will be achieved will be due to the prowess and virtue of the Swargadeo and by the mercy of God and the Goddess.' 200.

Fresh encounters with the Moamarias.

Thus the Barbarua instructed the three officers and said,—' Both of you should carry out the commands of the Dangaria'. To the Dhekial Phukan were attached the Bacha and Opar-Dayangia contingent; the Da-dharas or the bearers of the *dao*, and the Dola-kasharias or the attendants of the sedan were also attached to the Dhekial Phukan; the Majiu-Dayangias were made over to the Pani-phukan; and the Nam-Dayangias to the Buragohain. Then the Barbarua came to his own residence, and passing there the night he took his journey down to join the King's company. After the departure of the Swargadeo to Gauhati the villagers and the Moamarias made a common cause and burnt down houses and villages. At this time a *Kanri* of the Lukhurakhan family, named Min Senapati, recruited numerous villagers; and killing the Moamarias he obtained three elephants and two horses. With the rebels came the Morans who were established at Rangdoichong. Formerly these Morans once met together and burnt down the houses of several hundred families belonging to the regiment stationed at Dihing.

At this time three thousand men from Bacha assembled together and encountering the enemy beside the stream Charaipanikhati killed a great number of Moamarias. When the Moamarias, unable to hold any longer, were retreating, Min encountered them in the way and seized their horses and elephants. Then the Buragohain Dangaria arranged to bring Min with some men towards the east. At this time the Pani-phukan forcibly wrested away some men from the company of the Dhekial Phukan, arguing that they were his own men from Gauhati. Then the Dhekial

Phukan said thus about the Bailung Saikia of the Opar-Dayang,—'It is he who instigated the Pani-phukan to rob me of my men', and saying this he cut off the nose of the Bailung. 201.

The stockade at Mitangjan.

Then the Buragohain Dangaria, the Dhekial Phukan, Min Senapati, these three crossed the Janji and encamped there in three stockades thrown on the bank of the Mitangjan on the side of the tank of the Parvatia Phukan. Next the Pani-phukan proceeded along the Bar-ali and raised a stockade at Kapaukhat lying on the other side of the Chintamani-garh. On that very day when some four *dandas* of the night had elapsed, the Moamarias made a surprise attack on our soldiers and slew many of our men. Many others fled during the confusion that ensued. The Pani-phukan also emerged from the stockade and after receding a little he halted again, and on the same night despatched Srinarayan, the son of the Bahbaria Kataki Bachua, to relate to the Dangaria all that had taken place and to communicate this to him,—'Either let us be restored to his company, or let the Dangaria himself come to us, then only the King's mission will be accomplished.'

On hearing this the Buragohain Dangaria replied,—'Kataki, tell the Phukan to repair to this place.' Having received this information from the messenger, the Phukan retired and erected a stockade beside the Buragohain's. Next day the Tekela-Bara and the Dola-kasharia Bara were sent to bring back the fugitives. They met the fugitives at Gajpur, Kakila, Diha and Teok and returned them. At that time the inmates of all the stockades were allowed to come out to have a look at the Moamarias. Just then they espied near the stockade the returning fugitives, and mistaking,—as Fate would have it—their own men to be Moamarias, they were seized with dismay, and a few men were trampled to death. The Brahman Saikia also died by incurring a fall.

During that confusion the Dhekial Phukan's followers recruited from Bacha deserted the stockade and fled away; and the Phukan also accompanied them. The inmates of Min's stockade also dispersed and went to the villages. The Buragohain Dangaria found on enquiry that the approachers were not Moamarias and that the confusion was caused by the predominance of Fate to which we were subjected. He explained this to his men, and quieted them all. 202.

After this the Buragohain Dangaria summoned the Dhekial Phukan from the Janji stockade by despatching Bejia, a Kataki of the Dilihial family, and retained the Phukan in his own camp. At that time he caused the capture of numerous fugitives by deputing the Dola-kasharia Bara and the Da-dhara Bara. In the month of Phalgun all the men were collected and the camp was removed from Mitang, and re-erected by the Pani-phukan eastward at Bar-ali, extending as far as the bank of the river Namdang. Five stockades were thrown off at the following places within gun-shot distance from each other,—one near Kumargaon under Rupchand Gohain who was the Khargharia Barua, one near Namdang under the Premier Buragohain Dangaria, one at Pukhurichuk under the Gharphalias, one at Alikekuri under the Neog-phukan of Gauhati.

The stockade at Namdang.

After joint consultation they erected a bridge across the Namdang. The Moamarias crossed the river by that very bridge and attacked our army in the several forts. Our soldiers also followed suit, but our men were defeated. The Rajapowali or chieftain of Luki fought for some time. Some soldiers belonging to the Gharphalia stockade fell in the battle as well as a handful of Moamarias. The remaining soldiers then retired to their respective camps. 203.

His Majesty had despatched before one Kaliman Rajkhowa to fetch the queens and princesses. He had proceeded to his duties and come upon the chief queen, the Parvatia queen and the King's daughter at Abhaypur. He now conducted them through an out-of-the-way route and managed to escort them secretly with tact which he had to adopt for fear of the Moamarias. There was fear also from the Pat-kowanr. Kaliman Rajkhowa then reported on the arrival of the princesses to the Prime Minister the Buragohain Dangaria, who having received this intimation despatched provisions for the use of the ladies. They were then sent down to Gauhati to the company of the King under the careful escort of a number of men. With them there also went many Phukans and Baruas to join the King.

Succour of princesses.

In the meantime the Prime Minister the Kuoigayan Buragohain Dangaria sent for the ex-Dekaphukan whom he caused to erect a fort at Pepelaghat. The Chaodangs were sent over to the

Gharphalia stockade. The two forts at Dayang and Min were extended along the Bar-ali. 204.

Pat-kowanr.

In the meantime the Pat-kowanr, son of the late King Rajeswar Singha, who had been banished to Namrup, now obtained the support of Japara Gohain and many other Gohains. Being aided by them, as well as by Manjay Barbarua, the Landabi Barphukan, the Barpatra-gohain of the Kalugayan family, the Dimayal Bargohain, and the son of Nagamua of the family of the deposed Chaodang Barua. The prince in the company of these leaders, and having collected numerous followers proceeded to Panichoki where he erected stockades at twenty different places and halted there. Japara Gohain remained at a fort near Deobil with his men, near Athkhel and Hudupara. The Moamarias marched thither and attacked them there. Japara Gohain then issued out of his camp and encountered the enemy in an engagement at close quarters. The Moamarias were dispersed with the help of clods and throw-sticks. The enemy were pursued and slain. The Moamarias being thus repulsed returned to the capital. Japara Gohain then advanced and halted at Kharikatia-ali after erecting a fort there. The Prime Minister the Buragohain Dangaria proceeded along the Naga-ali above Gaurisagar; while the Pani-phukan, the Dhekial Phukan, the Neog-Gohain Phukan halted at Namdang after having raised seven forts at that place. All this took place in the month of Chaitra. 205.

Death of the Pat-kowanr.

Hostilities then continued from Baisakh, *saka* 1710, accompanied by minor casualties on the Moamarias' side as well as on ours. The Pat-kowanr also continued the contest for three months. In the meantime the Moamarias also were on the point of starvation being unable to move about in quest of food. The Pat-kowanr left a contingent at Panichoki and proceeded to erect a number of stockades at Sibsagar. In the month of Sravan the Moamarias destroyed the forts of the Pat-kowanr, and lay in ambuscade at Lechang. The Pat-kowanr was seized there and killed. The soldiers encamped at the forts of Panichoki dispersed on that night as well as two days after, and proceeded eastward. The fort of Japara Gohain at Kharikatia-ali was also broken open. The Buragohain Dangaria and the Pani-phukan continued to halt at the fort of Namdang as before, where they were fighting with the Moamarias till the month of Phalgun. During the selfsame month the King despatched the Barpatra Dangaria and the Bargohain Dangaria from Gauhati at the head of a large reinforcement of men and provisions. 206.

Pahar Senapati.

Previously to this the eastern Gharphalias assembled at Samaguri under one Pahar, one of their own clansmen, whom they had appointed their captain. The Moamarias attacked them whereupon the Gharphalias captured the raiders by a stratagem and after inflicting a severe defeat they acquired three elephants. The Moamarias being beaten came back to the capital. After this the two Dangarias went up to the bank of the Namti river where, in the company of the Barbarua, they threw off five forts at Barahibari, where they were joined by the Gharphalias under their leader Pahar Senapati. From there they erected forts near the Namti river to the south of Jengerai field. The Barpatra Dangaria left the place with his men with the object of erecting additional forts near the Kharghar. The strength of the army occupying the various forts became greatly diminished.

The Moamarias laid an attack to that place. Being unable to stand all our men took to their heels. The Dangaria had a hair-breadth escape after which he contrived to re-enter the fort which the Moamarias besieged for seven days. Japara Gohain acting in concert with the Gharphalias captured and killed a large number of Moamarias when they were reaping paddy. The Moamarias being thus beaten returned to the capital. The two Dangarias left their respective encampments and withdrew themselves to the fort at Pangera. 207.

Insurrection of the Lakhimpurias.

In the meantime the two Lakhimpuria brothers, adopting un-approved religious rites, made war at Rankham up the river Janji where they had collected a large number of men. They used to capture our men who went out to gather fuel from the forest; these men were incorporated in their army. Then there ensued a battle between the Lakhimpuria rebels and the Barpatra Dangaria in the vicinity of Janji. On the first encounter the two armies retired without having inflicted any loss on either side. The Lakhimpurias then collected a further reinforcement of villagers and waited together after having initiated themselves into an unapproved order. In the meantime the two Dangarias encamped themselves at Balihat. At that time the Moamarias laid siege to the fort of the Buragohain. The Bargohain Dangaria having advanced to take some men from the fort at Balihat halted at the temple at Dergaon. In the meantime the Barpatra Dangaria having exchanged greetings with the Buragohain Dangaria marched upward. The Bargohain Dangaria then left Dergaon and joined the Buragohain at the Namdang fort.

After this the Prime Minister despatched soldiers with instructions to seize the Lakhimpurias, but the two Lakhimpuria brothers escaped. Their leading followers were captured; their hands and feet were lopped off; they were then gagged into holes and thus killed after having allowed people to ease themselves upon them. Some were burnt to death being wrapped up with straw. Some were killed with axes and some were sawn alive. They were put to death with innumerable tortures in the month of Chaitra. 208.

Appearance of famine.

Then in the month of Baisakh, *saka* 1711, on the New Years' Day, the Moamarias besieged the fort of Gaurisagar. The eastern portion of the fort was kept open. Thus they laid siege for two months. Our ration-suppliers could not enter the fort, and so our soldiers suffered from all kinds of privations. The price of rice went up to one rupee per lime-pot. One mango cost one rupee. A bundle of arum used to be sold for one rupee or one rupee and eight annas. The sufferings of the people thus knew no bounds, and a large number of men died on that account. During that siege the following nobles died fighting in the fort,—the Madurial Bargohain Dangaria, the Sandikai Pani-phukan, the Naobaicha Phukan of the Lahan family named Das, the Bacha Rajkhowa of the Likchan family. Other people also perished in the contest in large numbers. The Prime Minister the Buragohain Dangaria seeing no means of salvation consulted with all, saying,—' We will not be able to save ourselves in this place, so we should retreat'. Thus saying they issued out of the fort and withdrew themselves to Taratali, where they halted for some days and collected followers. All men living in that tract were unnerved after the departure of the King to Gauhati. The Buragohain Dangaria, after having collected men at Taratali with great tact and effort and appointed one of them as commander, retreated to Dichoi, where he enlisted all men he could lay his hands on. A fort was erected there which was placed under the command of Japara

Gohain and the Parvatia Barua of the Brahman Kakati family. After this the Buragohain Dangaria marched to Kacharihatwhere he stopped and enlisted three hundred Dayangias, and erected a stockade.

In the meantime one Mukuta of the Chaodangs was captured in the camp of the Gharphalias. The Mahamantri Buragohain Dangaria accused him of joining the ranks of the Lakhimpurias as an officer and of defying the lawful authority of the land. He was put to various tortures and ultimately killed by being tied to a hook. The Dangaria then entered Bacha and pitched his camp at Rajankhat. From there he despatched Bejia Kataki to fetch the three regiments of Bacha, who in their turn replied through Bejia,—'We cannot go leaving our wives and children, nor can we fight with the Moamarias. Let him go back in the same way as he came. We cannot go.' Having heard this the Buragohain became angry and decided to first attack the Bachas; with this object he constructed a bridge at Kakadanga. The Bachas destroyed the bridge and having united themselves under the leadership of one Jabar Saikia, resolved to seize the Buragohain Dangaria. 209.

Disloyalty of the Bachas.

But by the grace of God a portion of the Bacha army came and joined the Dangaria. The Buragohain placed above them a member of his own family who was appointed Bacha Rajkhowa. From there the Prime Minister marched towards Kachajan where he raised a fort and halted. In the meantime the remaining portion of the Bacha army met together near the hills from where they as well as other men with Jabar Saikia and Tiktiki as their leaders joined Japara Gohain at Gajpur. Japara Gohain advanced with these men and halted at the *namghar* belonging to the Manipurias of Bacha where he collected an additional reinforcement and began to live in an independent manner. The Bachas also joined the camp of Japara. They brought one hundred and twenty men to the Deogaon camp. Thus the Bachas assumed independent authority. 210.

Japara Gohain.

The Buragohain Dangaria, the Prime Minister, entered into diplomatic friendship with Japara Gohain. Japara paid frequent visits to the Dangaria. One day the Premier had him captured by one Akhiranga Bara of Kharangi, the Chaodang Bara and other Baras. Then one Dolasharia of Kamalabari plucked out the eye of Japara; the other eye of Japara had been extracted before. All the rebels including

Jabar Saikia took to their heels. Jabar took shelter in the hills; he was, however, found in his concealment by the Kachari Saikia and he was killed. His sons were strangled to death with the hook. Tiktiki Neog, one of the accomplices, was pressed to death between wooden cylinders with his sons. The belongings of Jabar were confiscated, removed and subsequently distributed among the soldiers. The Prime Minister then left the place and remained in the camp at Chungighat, where a brother of Ghanasyam Kakati was hewn to death with an axe on the accusation that he had sold away his lands. He also executed several individuals by first cutting off their hands and feet, for adopting disloyal and heterodox rites. One Nerai Deka of the Betionia branch of the Sandikai family was appointed Na-phukan and placed at the head of the army raised by Min. 211.

Stockade at Jorhat.

After this they came away from that place in Magh and encamped at Charaibahi. While staying at that stockade, all parties of village musicians were invited to a celebration lasting for seven days; and in the month of Chaitra the Prime Minister advanced to Dichoi and stayed at Jorhat after raising a fort there.

After that, in the month of Baisakh, *saka* 1712, the Bacha Rajkhowa, the Gajpuria Rajkhowa of the Bargohain family, Taptalou Majiu-Dayangia Rajkhowa, Opar-Dayangia Rajkhowa, all these four Rajkhowas with their respective detachments were despatched to encamp at Meleng. A few days after this a member of the Lahan family was appointed Dekaphukan and was ordered to proceed to the Meleng stockade as commander over the four Rajkhowas. During that selfsame month of Baisakh, the four Rajkhowas quitted the stockade leaving behind the Phukan there. They then crossed the Meleng and proceeded to see the Moamarias. Just then the Moamarias made their appearance and attacked the enemy near the bank of the Meleng. But our soldiers could not long resist the attack and so they began to retreat. The Moamarias chased them and put the Bacha Rajkhowa and the Dayangia Rajkhowa to death. The fugitives all retired to the Dichoi stockade. The Premier intimated this news to the King by despatching Bejia Kataki. 212.

Burkendaz sepoys.

On hearing this the King commanded the Barphukan, the Dihingia Medhi, to march up at the head of four hundred Burkendaz sepoys. The Barphukan accompanied by the sepoys first made his obeisance to the King at his Dimou camp; and went up and joined the Buragohain at Dichoi. Then in the month of Jeth, the Buragohain took those sepoys with him and marching eastward halted at Teok erecting a fort there. But on account of the rains, the Dangaria again came back to the Dichoi camp. There was another stockade of the Gajpurias on the bank of the Kakila; this was besieged by the Moamarias in the month of Ahin. 213.

Atrocities of the Moamarias.

Hearing this the Mahamantri Buragohain Dangaria despatched the sepoys to the war. The Moamarias having noticed the approach of the sepoys left the stockade, and rushed to encounter the royalists. Many sepoys fell in that engagement. Being unable to hold any longer the sepoys retreated and came back to join the Dangaria. To the west of the Dichoi river, and near the Bar-ali there was another stockade composed of the inhabitants of numerous villages, under the command of a member of that contingent. The commander-in-chief of that fort was the Charingia Raja. The Moamarias then attacked the fort. Our soldiers killed some Moamarias by discharging shots from within the fort. After this the Moamarias again repaired to Rangpur. In this way the Moamarias overran the land repeatedly plundering and devastating the villages; sometimes they rowed upstream along the Kakadonga and the Dhansiri; and ravaging the villages they carried with them boat-loads of booty. The Buragohain Dangaria recruited soldiers in the villages and had stockades erected by them. Then ensued numerous encounters with the Morans followed by casualties in the camp of the Moamarias as well as in ours. 214.

The Buragohain, a saviour of his country.

Thus the Buragohain Dangaria staying at his camp at Dichoi adopted various means for restoring order in the country. He used to feed and clothe men and to send them to fight by giving them presents in the way of encouragement; he also subdued refractory people by threatening them with punishments, such as death by the axe, the saw and the hook. Thus he used to persuade people to fight. Day and night he thought of the best means of restoring peace and order in the country and prayed to God for the same. He devised methods and recalled the gentry who had deserted their country and taken refuge in foreign lands, and deliberating with them he waged war with the Moamarias.

Thus the Mahamantri Buragohain Dangaria regulated the affairs of the state by remaining at his encampment near the Dichoi. 215.

Local potentates assume independence.

At Japaribhita in the North Bank a body of Moamarias appointed one Tati as their chief and ruled over the territory as far as the Lohit river. At Majuli another batch of Moamarias exercised independent authority over the area extending up to the Dihing with Howha as their leader. At Rangpur another body of rebels, under the leadership of Pitambar Mahajan, was enjoying independent sway with Bharathi as their chief, and one Sukura as their Barbarua. At Bengmara in the east, the Hati-chungi Morans ruled the territory up to the Dihing with one Sarbananda as their chief and Godha as their Barbarua. The Khamtis ruled over the Sadiya tract with two chieftains, one known as Burha-raja and the other as Deka-raja. Thus independent rulers sprang up at various localities. 216.

The Buragohain attempts to save his country.

Our Prime Minister, the Buragohain Dangaria, marshalled the Bacha and Dayangi soldiers and procured by some means from Kaliabar fresh supplies of guns and gun-powder, with which he continued fighting with the Morans for some time. The people of Majuli, Abhaypur and Rangpur, as well as the religious leaders of those places deserted the country and took shelter in foreign lands being unable to stand the oppression of the Moamarias. Men were subjected to endless miseries. Half a seer of rice used to be sold for one tola of gold. People died of starvation by scores under trees. They deserted even their wives and children for want of food. With the greatest effort the Mahamantri Buragohain Dangaria saved the tract of Bacha and Dayang. The fugitives, being thrown into severe want and distress, took shelter at Bacha and Dayang; the Dangaria used to supply food-provisions to the refugees. Some of them were fed, maintained and then despatched to the company of the King. During that period of affliction and misery the Mahamantri Buragohain Dangaria protected the people like a mother-bird guarding her nestlings under her wings. The Moamaria revolt was also counteracted by him in various ways. Previously to this the Barpatra Dangaria had proceeded to fight in the east and had halted at Bengenabari encampment. In the meantime the Morans proceeded from Bengmara and attacked our forces in the stockade. Our men being unable to defend deserted the camp. The Barpatra Dangaria perished during this engagement. The Buragohain received this sad intelligence during his stay at Dichoi and communicated the same to His Majesty who expressed sorrow at the loss. 217.

The Manipuria high-priest in Assam.

Now to turn to the events at Gauhati. During the Swargadeo's stay at Gauhati the Bahbaria Kataki, Bisturam, was despatched to bring the Raja of Manipur. He now returned with the Dharmadhi, the spiritual preceptor of the Manipuri Raja, and with a number of Manipuris. The priest as well as his companions were left at Raha-choki, and the four Manipuri envoys Gauranga, Khagendra, Abhimanyu and Nimai were despatched to the presence of the King at Gauhati, with letters and presents. The King having heard of this commanded the Namtial Barbarua to receive the messengers. The Barbarua formally received the four Manipuri envoys at Sukreswar. The messengers were granted an interview with His Majesty. The King ordered them to the following effect,—'These men have been sent by the Raja of Manipur to fight with our enemy the Moamarias. So they should march up with the Dharmadhi and fight after joining the Mahamantri Buragohain Dangaria at Dichoi.' Having received this command of the Swargadeo the Manipuris said,—'O Heavenly King, our Manipuri Raja has deputed us with the mandate that we should fight in concert with the Barbarua after having intimated to you our arrival. So we have informed you.' The King then said that the Manipuris should proceed up and join the Buragohain. This command was communicated to the Dharmadhi by the Manipuris who came in the company of our Katakis. The Dharmadhi went down to Gauhati instead of proceeding up. He was received in the customary procedure by Jaynath Barbarua of the Bakatial family at Sukreswar and by the King personally at Nilachal. During the ceremony of reception the Dharmadhi sat on a white blanket before His Majesty. The Dharmadhi was commanded to proceed to Upper Assam to participate in the war. The priest spoke of the Barbarua. The King refused to place the Barbarua as his escort. On the other hand the Dharmadhi was sent up in the company of the Nibukial Rajkhowa of the Hati-Barbarua family who was appointed Na-phukan, and of one Gendhela, a Tamuli-ligira of the Sandikai family now appointed Opar-Dayangia

Rajkhowa. This contingent in their journey up plundered our villages and took with them the spoils. 218.

A new Barphukan.

Then the Manipurias left the company of our Phukans and Rajkhowas and returned all on a sudden to their country by the route through Raha, while our Phukans and Rajkhowas proceeded up and joined the Dangaria. In the month of Kartik, 1711 *saka*, the King intending to march upward halted at the emporium of gold and silver for four months, waiting for an auspicious day for starting. He then retired to the camp in the ancestral residence of the Gajpuria Rajkhowa. The King summoned to that place the Barbarua and the Barphukan and said,—'It is high time that we should return. Phukan, you seem to be in indifferent health and you are incapable of accompanying us on our return journey for which you should not be sorry. I have ordered that the Sologuria Rajkhowa, a brother-in-law of yours, should be appointed Barphukan'. Hearing this the Barphukan dashed out of the place, and mounting a litter at the Barduar started at once to his residence, where he remained in seclusion being offended with the King. After this the Sologuria Rajkhowa of the Dihingia family was appointed Barphukan and His Majesty's order was announced by the Tipamia Rajhowa and the Tamuli Phukan. The Kathkatia Barua was also in the company. The new Barphukan conducted His Majesty to the camp near the Naosal or boatshed. The King then said to the Barbarua and the Barphukan after having brought them to his presence,—'Please procure a detachment of up-country sepoys and escort me back to the camp of the Buragohain Dangaria'. 219.

A new Barbarua.

Hearing this the Namtial Barbarua replied,—'I, your servant, can neither arrange for Bangal soldiers, nor can I conduct His Majesty to Upper Assam as long as the Moamarias are alive. The person who will undertake to escort the King should be appointed Barbarua by His Majesty.' Saying this the Barbarua retired to his residence. The King then appointed Jaynath, the son of the Deka-Barbarua of the Bakatial family, to the office of the Barbarua. The appointment was formally announced by the Tipamia Rajkhowa, the Tamuli Phukan and the Kath Majindar. At that time the Gogoi Barphukan of the Sandikai family, being afraid of the consequences of his dismissal fled away from his residence and proceeded upwards. Having heard this the King ordered his belongings to be seized. His house was ransacked and the articles were removed to the King's residence. The Phukan then reached Dopgar up the river Janji. 220.

New officers.

The Chutia-kanris of Dopgar, seeing the large quantity of articles in possession of the Phukan, killed him. The Buragohain Dangaria heard this at Dichoi; he caused the arrest of the miscreants and put them to death for this crime. The King then appointed the Choladhara Phukan of the Sandikai family to the office of the Naobaicha Phukan and the Chiring Phukan was made Choladhara Phukan; the Tipamia Rajkhowa of the Lanmakharu family was made Khargharia Phukan, while his brother was appointed Senchowa Barua, and his son Tipamia Rajkhowa. The privilege of using a head-cover made of straw was conferred on the Tamuli Phukan, as well as the charge of one thousand Samdharias. Pijou, the brother of the Barbarua, was made Dhekial Phukan, and his brother, named Betmela, as Hati-Barua. One Bijoi Rajkhowa of the Lahan family was appointed Parvatia Phukan. 221.

Haradatta Chaudhuri.

After this the Deka-raja of Darang, and Phati a prince of Bhutan, and Haradatta Chaudhuri conspired to rebel against the authority of the King. The Swargadeo despatched soldiers who captured the Deka-raja and he was subsequently pressed to death. His fellow-conspirators took to their heels. The King, the Barbarua and the Barphukan consulted together and procured the services of Burkendaz Bangal sepoys in whose company they proceeded up to the camp at Dikhou, from where the King despatched the Dihingia Barphukan with the above sepoys to the Buragohain's camp. The Phukan proceeded accordingly and joined the Buragohain in his camp at Dichoi. 222.

Help solicited from the Manipuri Raja.

The King then advanced with an escort of sepoys and halted at the Hahchara camp in Naogaon from where he proceeded to Khurarmur. From his camp at the latter place the King despatched in Sravan three envoys, one Gauri Kataki of the Bahbaria family, one Baneswar of Niraha, and one Krisnahari of Gajpur, with letters and presents to fetch the Raja of Manipur. They proceeded by the route through Raha and arrived at the capital of the Manipuri Raja, who accorded them a reception according to the approved procedure. The Manipuri Burha-raja realised the situation from the letters and from the oral statements of the envoys. They returned in the month of Pous of that very year with the old chief of Manipur accompanied by a detachment of four thousand soldiers. The Manipuri Raja was accommodated in temporary quarters erected near the Swargadeo's camp at Khutarmur, and he stayed there. Sometime after the Dhekial Phukan of the Bakatial family said one day to the Manipuri Raja,—'His Majesty has commanded the Manipuri Raja to proceed up to join the company of the Buragohain Dangaria.' 223.

The Manipuri Raja Jai Singha is offended.

Having heard this the Manipuri Raja said,—'How can I go without meeting and exchanging greetings with the Swargadeo?' Thus saying the Raja dashed out of his house, and reached Hatipara beyond Khagarijan. The Swargadeo deputed the Khargharia Phukan, the Tamuli Phukan, and the Dhekial Phukan to bring back the offended chief. They proceeded and succeeded in bringing him back. 224.

Men of Nowgong harassed by King's officers.

After this the King interviewed the chief of Manipur sitting on his sedan at the entrance of the Barduar and despatched the latter to the company of the Prime Minister the Buragohain in Upper Assam. In the month of Magh the Swargadeo proceeded to bathe in the Brahmaputra at Leterimukh and waited for that occasion in his camp. The men of Naogaon intending to rebel against the King left His Majesty in his camp there and assembled in their respective villages after having destroyed the bridge over the Rupahi. The next day the King returned to his Naogaon camp. After this the Nagayans came out with *daos* and spears in their hands and began to yell round the King's residence and shouted out in an insolent tone,—'The King should go away from this place. If he does not quit this place, let him replace the present set of Phukans and Baruas including the Barbarua and the Barphukan. We, your slaves, have been compelled to approach Your Majesty having found no other means of redress.' During the King's stay at Naogaon, the Baruas and the Phukans used to remove the betel-nuts and betel-leaves from the trees in the orchards of the Nagayans; they further caused the capture of virgins and distributed them among themselves. Most of them acquired lands and established regular *khats* or estates. It is for these acts of harassment that the Nagayans supplicated the King for substitution of the old officers by new ones. The King asked as to whom they wanted to nominate for the offices of the Barbarua and the Barphukan. The Nagayans reiterated their demand saying,—'There are many families from which Barbaruas and Barphukans were selected before; the King should now select such new officers from among these families who are likely to give us protection and safety.' 225.

The Duara Barphukan.

The King appointed the Na-phukan of the Duara family as Barphukan after having ascertained the intention of the Nagayans. One Bhadari of the Sandikais was made Barbarua. Nine days after this incident the Nagayans prayed for the reinstatement of the old Barbarua and Barphukan who were accordingly restored to their old offices. At this time the King appointed a member of the Bartamuli Patra family as Barpatra-gohain. 226.

The Bairagi Raja.

After this at Panisangal in the North Bank several villages combined in attacking the Moamarias, having appointed one Bairagi or itinerant hermit as their Raja, and one Deka of the Lahans as their Barbarua. This Barbarua proceeded to Biswanath with a number of men. From there he united with the Kharangis of Naogaon with the consent of Helimeli Solal Gohain. He now crossed the river at Kaliabar and proceeded to capture the King in his Naogaon camp. Having heard this the Swargadeo asked the Bakatial Barbarua to despatch some soldiers to encounter the rebels. The Barbarua then deputed some Kharangis of Naogaon to the engagement after having administered oaths to them. Some of the soldiers marched up, but they halted on their way at Michamukh from where they despatched men to negotiate with the Lahan Barbarua. They became friends with him and admitted him to their company. He now marched with the Kharangis of Naogaon and besieged the King's camp during the night. 227.

The King leaves Nowgong.

When there were only two *dandas* for the termination of the night the King came out with the Barua and the Phukan through the river-gate and proceeded downward. The Lahan Barbarua joined the Nagayans with whom he confronted the King in his march. The King then said to one Nathusing Jemadar,—'Well, open fire at the enemy.' The rebels came back out of fear, but they plundered the goods in the residence of the King. On Saturday, the last day of the month of Ashara, 1714 *saka*, the King moved away from Naogaon and reached the Auniati Satra, where he said to the senior Deka-gosain,—'Well, Deka-Bapu, you should remain in your Satra, and if possible, you should collect our wives and children and give them shelter in your monastery'. Having said this the King abandoned the main road but proceeded along the marshes and ultimately reached the monastery of the Dakhinpat Gosain situated near Kachari villages. He then proceeded in a boat in the company of the Dakhinpatia Deka-gosain and finally reached Gauhati. 228.

Jai Singha at Dichoi.

Then the Baskatia Barbarua entered into the King's camp and having seized the goods of that place went back to Baskata. Now to turn to the affairs at the Dichoi encampment.—In 1713 *saka*, the Burha-raja of Manipur came with his son Madhuchandra and joined the Prime Minister Buragohain at Dichoi. The Dangaria had some quarters erected for the Manipuri Raja near the Dichoi and supplied him with provisions according to the prevailing custom. The Prime Minister with a view to please the chief of Manipur erected a big shed with a dais where he took his seat under a red canopy. The Marangi-khowa, the Barphukan, the Naobaicha Phukan, the Na-phukan, the Neog-phukan, the Duara Nyaya-sodha Phukan, took their seats in the assembly with due pomp and array according to their respective ranks. Bejia and Kamdeo, the messengers who had accompanied the Manipuri chief, introduced the Raja in that pavilion where he was given a seat under an overhanging canopy. Screens were also set up. 229.

Reception of Jai Singha.

After this the Mahamantri Buragohain Dangaria said to the chief of Manipur,—'O Manipuria Raja, at the time of your departure from Manipur, were the cows and the Brahmans as well the people of your country enjoying happiness and prosperity?' Hearing this the Raja replied,—'By the grace of God and the Goddess they were all well. We also pray that you may also enjoy bliss and happiness.' The Dangaria questioned the chief regarding the privations he might have experienced during his journey, and the Raja related all the particulars. The Dangaria then said to the

Raja,—'The predecessors of our present sovereign had been enjoying the friendship of the former chiefs of Manipur. Our Swargadeo, being unable to withstand the growing influence of the enemy, and in recollection of that time-honoured friendship intimated the facts about the plight of the country to you. If the Raja succeeds in extirpating the enemy then his triumph, virtue, and renown will increase and the old friendship will be further strengthened, specially it is said,—

'The pious are ever the agents
To relieve the virtuous of their calamities;
Of elephants that are stuck fast in the mud,
An elephant is the only extricator.'

Having heard this the Manipuria Raja said,—'O Mahamantri Dangaria, being informed of the disturbances in the kingdom of the Heavenly King from the lips of your ambassadors I was filled with extreme regret. I came quickly and had an audience with your King at Naogaon where he commanded saying,—'The Raja of Manipur should go up, and by acting in concert with the Prime Minister, the Buragohain Dangaria, should suppress our enemy the Moamarias.' So I have come here at the instance of His Majesty and met you presently. So Dangaria, I shall be able to fight only if you make arrangements for the same.'

At this the Dangaria asked the Raja regarding the numerical position of the army that accompanied him. The Raja informed that he had four hundred men with horses, and another four hundred with guns; while the carriers and labourers would come up to a few thousands. This statement was confirmed by the Marangi-khowa as well as by the Barphukan; but the Naobaicha Phukan of the Lahan family could not say anything. Then the Raja was bidden farewell whereupon he retired to his camp; the Dangaria also entered the fort. The Buragohain Dangaria presented to the Raja of Manipur ornaments and robes as well as a pair of gold bangles worthy of a monarch: he also supplied the Raja with food-provisions, utensils and other necessaries. Similar gifts were made to the Raja's son the Juvaraj. 230.

Jai Singha proceeds to fight.

After this the Mahamantri Buragohain Dangaria appointed men to erect two stockades in the vicinity of the Teok river whereto he marched with the Raja of Manipur in 1713 *saka*. It was from this camp that the Mahamantri Buragohain Dangaria despatched the Manipuria Raja with a large force to Rangpur, in the company of the Marangi-khowa Na-phukan, the Opar-Dayangia Rajkhowa of the Sandikais, and the Majiu-Dayangia Rajkhowa. The Raja chased the Moamarias with his army, and halted at some distance down Gaurisagar. In the next morning Madhuchandra Juvaraj marched towards Rangpur with a detachment of warriors, and was followed by the old Raja with his army. The Moamarias, divided into several batches, had been cunningly lying in wait along the road concealing themselves in the woods. When the Deka-raja had reached Ouguri-choki, the Moamarias came out from their coverts in several groups and fell upon the Manipurias. 231.

The Manipuris in action.

The Manipuris then fought for some time but being unable to stand they dispersed in numerous directions. The Moamarias then attacked the Burha-raja who alighted from his litter and mounted a horse named Hoiraj. His followers also mounted their respective ponies. The Burha-raja as well as his son fought a long fight on horseback with the Moamarias; but being unable to hold any longer they retreated with their face towards the enemy. A large number of Manipuris fell in the engagement; and the Moamarias seized all the goods of the Raja. The Manipuria Raja met the Mahamantri Buragohain Dangaria at Teok and communicated to him all the particulars. They all then withdrew themselves to the Dichoi camp. The Raja of Manipur returned to his own kingdom by the way through the mouths of the two rivers after having left a force of one thousand soldiers with the Dangaria. After this the Moamarias attacked our men on the other side of the Dichoi, and the Manipuri soldiers were despatched to that engagement. They went out; but instead of going to fight they returned abruptly to their own country by the mouths of the two rivers. 232.

The Moamarias ravage the kingdom.

The Moamarias thus devastated the country by acts of plunder and rapine. The Mahamantri Buragohain Dangaria enlisted the inhabitants of several villages, caused stockades to be erected by them, and thus protected the locality of Bacha and Dayang. On the North Bank also the Moamarias ravaged the people of all grades including the spiritual leaders, belonging to Majuli, Rangpur and Abhaypur; they devastated their territory and compelled them to desert their homesteads. Hosts of people died for want of food. Those who came to Bacha were given food and raiment by the Dangaria; and some of them were sent up to the company of the King. During that period the Mahamantri Buragohain Dangaria saved the destitute people just as a mother-bird guards her young ones with her wings. In the meantime the Kenduguria Barpatra Dangaria who had encamped at Bengenabari was seized by the Morans of Bengmara and put to death; and his fort was also destroyed. This sad event was communicated to the King by the Dangaria through some Katakis. Soon after the Moamarias entered by the Dhansiri river and attacked the three stockades at Kacharihat set up by the three Dayangias; and our men took to their heels being unable to stand. 233.

A rampart of earth-work.

The Morans killed a large number of our men. The Rajkhowas escaped with great difficulty. In *saka* 1713, the Mahamantri Buragohain Dangaria constructed an earthen rampart at Bacha extending up to the Naga hills, with the Dichoi fort inside its walls; and on the other side, it extended outside the Cheuni-ali and reached the precincts of the Kalioni hills of Marangi. The rampart was strongly barricaded with wooden posts. Soldiers were posted to watch day and night, and it was from here that the war operations against the Moamarias were conducted. At this time the Captain sent two Chota-bardars or lieutenants to enquire into the condition of the country. They were received by the Buragohain Dangaria near Tarajan. The above rampart was also penetrated through by the rebels who entered our territory and devastated the land. This time they entered by the Dhansiri and captured Alan Kakati Bara of the Chaliha family and put him to death. The Moamarias also plundered Marangi during this attack. 234.

Disturbances in the North Bank.

After this, the Baskatia Barua came from Baskata with a large force of Miris, Dafalas, and others, and halted at Dergaon. He then went to Dichoi and interviewed the Buragohain Dangaria to whom he said,—'O Prime Minister, give us a commander. The Baragi commander who led our force has died'. As requested the Dangaria made presents to their Barbarua and their Barsenapati including a pair of bangles, and said,—'Move at once and collect all the men of the North Bank and remain in preparedness for proceeding to Rangpur. I will give you a commander'. Saying this he despatched them to the north. Sometime after their departure, the Charingia Raja who had been living in a fort to the east of Dichoi holding absolute charge of the same was now despatched to the camp of the Barbarua in the North Bank.

The Charing Raja having crossed over to the north the Baskatias refused to obey him, nor did they join his forces; so he came back to his own fort at Dichoi. The Charing Raja then communicated all the details of the situation in the North Bank to the Mahamantri Buragohain. After this, the Moamarias broke open the stockade at Jorbari in Dergaon, and put to death on the spot the Na-phukan of the Hati-Barua family, and also the Sologuria Rajkhowa of the Lahans. The Tekela-Neog and Govinda Maharia Senapati fell in that affray, and a large number of His Majesty's soldiers. 235.

Further Moamaria ravages.

The Moamarias penetrated further into the country and after having devastated Bacha and Dayang they searched for men in the Naga forest and put them to death; from this they returned in the month of Chaitra, *saka* 1714, and laid siege to the fort at Dichoi which continued for three fortnights. Then as luck would have it, in the month of Baisakh the Dichoi was swept over with a heavy flood which inundated its banks. With the waters came a large quantity of fuel and dilennia; and soldiers from inside the fort were sent out to fight with the besiegers, with the result that there were occasionally minor casualties in the Moamarias' camp as well as in ours. The Mahamantri Buragohain Dangaria tactfully manœuvred to send out a force one morning; they attacked the Moamarias in the mouth of the Tokolai. There were heavy casualties on the side of the Morans. Being afraid the Moamarias retired to Rangpur after having plundered Bacha and Dayang. Thus the Buragohain Dangaria encountered the Moamarias with various tactics and protected the country up to the limits of Ladoigarh, by capturing and killing the Morans. 236.

Intervention of the East India Company solicited.

From Nagaon the Swargadeo proceeded to Gauhati where he halted for sometime. In the meantime, a few hundred Doms or fishermen of Pakariguri and Chelenghat under the leadership of Hoidhan of the Lukhurakhun family had made a Bairagi their Raja; they now went down to Gauhati and set fire to the King's house at the main gate. The King, seized with fear in apprehension of a battle, crossed the stockade and proceeded down in a boat by the Brahmaputra to Nagarbera. One Rausch Saheb used to live at Bangalhat. The King had despatched to him Bika the Majindar of Gauhati, and Bhaba Kataki, with the request to arrange for the deputation of a contingent of sepoys from Calicata. They approached the Barsaheb, and now came back with a detachment of seven companies of sepoys, and met the King at Nagarbera. The Swargadeo sent up two companies of sepoys under the command of a Saheb. The Khargharia Phukan and the Kathbarua were also despatched with this force. At that time the Bairagi went on falsely proclaiming around the town to the following effect,—'I am the nephew of the Swargadeo; the citizens should not disperse.' In this way he obtained possession of the city for seven days. At this stage the Saheb arrived with the sepoys. 237.

Battle between the Bairagi and the Company's troops.

The Bairagi then fell upon the sepoys and the latter opened fire at his army. Some Doms fell in that engagement. The Bairagi took to his heels being unable to stand. Some twenty Doms were captured as well as Hoidhan and the rest fled away. This intelligence was communicated to the King. Having heard this His Majesty came up to Gauhati with the Captain and put to death the captive Doms, and Hoidhan was strangled to death by the hook. The Bairagi was hacked and subsequently transfixed to a spear. The Swargadeo continued at Gauhati for a couple of months, and offered his obeisance to all the shrines by personally visiting them. During this period the Captain's grocer used to slaughter cows and sell them. 238.

The Captain in Assam.

The Swargadeo having heard this prohibited the slaughter of cows and it was accordingly discontinued. The Captain then seized the persons of Jaynath, the Bakatial Barbarua and the Chiring Choladhara Phukan, and sent them to Calicata after informing the King,—'Why should His Majesty retain with him wicked and untrustworthy ministers?' The Captain further advised the Swargadeo that an elderly personage should be selected for the office of the Barphukan. Having heard this the King dismissed Medhi Barphukan of the Dihingia family, and appointed in his place the Na-phukan of the Duara family who was now living in exile. This noble had been previously appointed Barphukan at Nagaon, in which office he had served only for three days. He was known by the name

Haliram Phukan; but he died after enjoying office only for a year. There was one Chetia Phukan. He was a Kachari-kumar by caste, but he assumed the title Chetia. He implored the Captain to procure him the office. The Captain accordingly advised the King to appoint this Chetia as Barphukan. The Swargadeo being unable to disoblige the Captain appointed his nominee as Barphukan. 239.

Lieutenant MacGregor.

In *saka* 1716, the Swargadeo, accompanied by the Captain, proceeded upstream and arrived at Kaliabar. From there he despatched the two Sahebs, Mihnagar Saheb and the Chota Saheb with a detachment of sepoys, to the camp of the Buragohain, who had been fighting with the Moamarias at Dichoi for full seven years. The Dangaria had also been maintaining the celebrations connected with the Durgotsav, the Phalgutsav and other festivals in his place and elsewhere. The Moamarias then attacked the fort of the Dangaria, but fortunately the Sahebs now joined the Mahamantri Buragohain at Dichoi. The Dangaria engaged the sepoys in the fight and it resulted in his victory. This intelligence was communicated to the Captain by Mihnagar Saheb and the Chota Saheb; and the Dangaria sent a similar message to the Swargadeo through his own men. The Dangaria supplied the two Sahebs with provisions and kept them in due style. 240.

The Buragohain's interview with the Captain.

During the Swargadeo's stay at Kaliabar, he reinstated the deposed Bargohain of the Madurial family in his former office. At this time the Chetia Barphukan acting in concert with Helimeli Solal Gohain, collected all the princes together with unlawful intentions against His Majesty. Having heard this the Captain dissuaded them from doing so as it implied hostility towards His Majesty. The Captain purchased rice to the value of one thousand rupees and deposited it in two granaries erected for the purpose at Kaliabar. In the meantime intelligence was received from the Dangaria at Dichoi, whereupon the Swargadeo soon proceeded upstream with the Captain by boats and reached the mouth of the Dichoi where they halted. The Mahamantri Buragohain Dangaria proceeded to the same place. The King secretly advised the Dangaria to see the Captain first, and the Dangaria went first to the Captain accordingly. The Captain was pleased to see the Dangaria and offered him a chair to sit. The

Captain then said,—'I thought the Buragohain to be a Burha or old man; I now see that he is young.' The Saheb continued,—'Buragohain, at the instance of our Barsaheb, we have come in the company of the Swargadeo to recover the garrison of Rangpur.' The Dangaria then replied,—'Captain Saheb, you have come with a large force of sepoys, and so you shall be able to take possession of Rangpur.' Having said so the Dangaria came and offered his obeisance to the King who at the sight of the minister expressed many regrets. The Dangaria gave vent to his sorrow as well. The Dangaria then took leave of the Swargadeo and returned to his camp. 241.

The Captain recovers Rangpur.

The next day he joined His Majesty at the Sonai river. From there the King despatched two Sahebs with a detachment of fifty sepoys to re-occupy Rangpur. Some of our soldiers were also sent with this force. The Moamarias fell upon them when they reached the tank of the Magalu princess. But the Moamarias were defeated. This news was communicated to the King. The Captain having heard this proceeded with twelve sepoys and joined the force previously despatched. There was also some fighting at Bhatiapar in which too the Moamarias were discomfited, and they, left Rangpur and dispersed to the east. The Captain then occupied Rangpur and communicated the news to the Swargadeo. The Moamarias fled, crossed over the Dikhou and halted on the other side of that river. Hearing of the flight of the Moamarias the King was delighted, which was shared by other people as well. 242.

The Swargadeo re-enters Rangpur.

Then the King marched quickly and occupied the capital of Rangpur, on the twenty-second day of Chaitra, *saka* 1715. The Kenduguria Barpatra and the Madurial Bargohain proceeded by land and joined the King a few days after. The Lahan Barbarua came with the Baskatias and joined the King at the Sonai river. The Swargadeo condoned the former offences of the Baskatias and re-appointed him Barbarua. The Moamarias having fled were staying in the vicinity of Lechang. From there they brought the Bengmarias and marched with hostile intentions towards Rangpur, and reached Darika. The Captain and the Chota Saheb marched with their sepoys and attacked the rebels. The Moamarias and the Morans rushed at the sepoys and surrounded them from all sides. The sepoys began to fire from within which resulted in the death of a large number of Moamarias. Unable to stand the Moamarias fled away eastward. The Chota Saheb returned with the sepoys to the company of the King. 243.

The Captain leaves Assam.

In the meantime the Barsaheb despatched a letter from Calicata by post asking the Captain not to stay any longer in Assam. He also wrote many other things in that letter. The Captain having received that note resolved to return. The Bangals removed to their boats the articles belonging to the King which were found in the capital of Rangpur. The list of the articles is as follows,—400,000 pieces of gold ornaments, 400,000 pieces of silver ornaments, gold to the value of 20,000,000 rupees; and who will be able to finish counting the quantity of copper, bellmetal, brass, cloths and ornaments taken by them? They also took 2,000 boats, one tusker, one she-elephant, 4,000 guns. With these all the Sahebs proceeded down to Calicata with the sepoys in the month of Jaistha, 1716 *saka*. Previously to this the King had despatched the Chetia Barphukan to Gauhati with Kamdeo Kataki of the Dilihial family. The Mahamantri Buragohain Dangaria of Kuoigaon manipulated the detention of two sepoys belonging to the Captain's force, named Dina and Phakirchand. 244.

The King at Dichoi.

Then the King went to Dichoi in that very month of Jaistha, leaving the following officers at Rangpur,—the Kenduguria Barpatra Dangaria, the Madurial Bargohain Dangaria, the Baskatia Barua of the Lahans, the Dekaphukan of the Buragohain family, the Dekaphukan attached to the establishment of Gauhati who was by caste a Lukhurakhun of the Barpatra's *khel*, the Dihingia Phukan of the Chayania Gohain family, Manjay Naobaicha Phukan of the Bakatial family, the Rajneog Phukan of the Buragohain family, the Changrun Phukan of the family of Okanimaria Chetia. The Dangaria erected a camp for the King who lived there. A thousand or so of Moamaria fugitives from war assembled and attacked Rangpur. Our soldiers seeing the inadequacy of their number came out without offering any fight and joined the King at Dichoi. 245.

Assamese troops trained on Company's lines.

At this time tigers devoured a large number of men at Dichoi. The Dangaria killed the tigers by blockading them with crossly woven bamboo fencing; and by bringing and slaying wild buffaloes he used to afford amusement to the King. The Captain after reaching Calicata sent back the Bakatial Barbarua and the Chiring Choladhara Phukan to the company of the King, and they met His Majesty at Dichoi. At this time the King celebrated the festivals of Durgotsav and Phalgutsav. He also went to Titabarhat to survey the condition of the country. The Swargadeo thus resided at Dichoi amusing himself with pastimes and recreations. The Mahamantri Buragohain Dangaria of Kuoigaon arranged for the training of the soldiers of Bacha and Dayang by the two sepoys, by drilling them with flint-guns. For want of regular guns the soldiers had to be instructed with the help of bamboo clubs and shoulder-pieces in their hands. The Dangaria also sent Bejia Kataki and Datta Bairagi with money to Calicata to fetch therefrom guns and gunpowder. The Parvatia queen was living at Gauhati with her daughter. It was from this time that flint-guns were introduced in our country. The King conferred upon the Chetia Barphukan the privilege of using a golden knob on his *Japi* or straw umbrella and a canopy, as well as the distinction of sitting in the same row with the Dangarias on a single-folded seat-cover. 246.

Revolt of the Chetia Barphukan.

Having received this distinction the Phukan became blind of his power, and proceeded to Gauhati where he procured the services of the Jamadar Hazara Sing Bangal and of some sepoys intending to rebel against the authority of the King. Having lost his senses the Barphukan plotted with Kamdeo Kataki of the Dilihial family, Helimeli Solal Gohain of the Madurial family and Badal Rajkhowa, and fetched one Bapi Gohain of the Tungkhungia family whom they proclaimed Raja at Gauhati. But the Sandikai Pani-phukan and the Lanmakharu Phukan and other Phukans and Rajkhowas of Gauhati declined to accept the impostor as their Raja. The Chetia Barphukan then extorted money from the second in rank of the Pahumuria Na-gosains who happend to be the *guru* of the Swargadeo. The Gosain and the officers of Gauhati communicated the whole affair to the King who consulted with the Dangarias and despatched the following officers to seize the person of the Chetia Barphukan,—The Dekaphukan of the Lukhurakhun family, the Khargharia Phukan of the Lanmakharu family, the Brahman Tamuli Phukan, who were also given secret instruction as follows,—'After reaching Gauhati, you should capture the Phukan by fair means or foul, and bring him to my presence.' 247.

The Dekaphukan of the Buragohain family was summoned to the presence of the King who commanded him to proceed to Kaliabar with his allotted contingent to capture the Solal Gohain by tact or stratagem. With this commission the King despatched the four officers. The Dekaphukan halted at Kaliabar while the three others proceeded to Gauhati. The Barphukan knowing that emissaries had come to arrest him resolved to capture them first. Hearing this the two Phukans decamped, and the Barphukan captured the Tamuli Phukan but spared his life as the latter was a Brahman. He was simply kept in confinement. The Dekaphukan also was turned out of Kaliabar by the Solal Gohain. Having heard this the King despatched Dhireswar Kataki of the Bahbaria family to the Phukans and Rajkhowas of Gauhati on the pretext of conveying a message. The officers were commanded to capture and make over the Chetia Phukan, and they all agreed to execute the King's wishes. 248.

Attempts to capture the Barphukan.

At this juncture, the second one of the Na-gosains informed Jati Rajkhowa of the Buragohain family by sending men as follows,—'You should promise to pay Hazara Sing Bangal some money if you want to capture the Barphukan. He is a Bangal and is therefore avaricious; and he alone will be able to seize the person of the Phukan.' The Rajkhowa promised to give the Bangal ten thousand rupees, and had the Barphukan captured and imprisoned by him. This Jati Rajkhowa was placed in the office of the Barphukan by common consent but he continued in that office only for three days. At this stage the son of the Senapati Phukan of the Duara family promised to give Hazara Sing Bangal the sum of sixty thousand rupees according to which the Bangal appointed the son of the Senapati Phukan as Barphukan. The new Barphukan consulted with the Phukans and Rajkhowas of Gauhati and extracted the eyes of the Chetia Barphukan. The Bangal then demanded the payment of the promised sum, and the Barphukan finding no money to pay proceeded to the temples including those of Kamakhya and Madhava, and seized the *Koshas* and *Arghas* of gold and other vessels of gold and silver used in worship; those were melted whereby the Bangal was paid the sum of sixty thousand rupees. 249.

Hazara Sing Bangal.

In the meantime the Phukans and Rajkhowas of Gauhati

despatched Katakis to the King with the following message,—'We, your slaves, have managed to capture the Chetia Phukan and the prince. They are now kept under guard. They will be dealt with according to the command of His Majesty.' The messengers marched day and night in full speed and informed the King accordingly. The King was extremely pleased at the news as well as the Dangarias, the Baruas and the Phukans. The Swargadeo then despatched Lambo Dola-sharia Barua of the Lahans to fetch the Chetia Phukan. The Dola-sharia Barua reached Gauhati, and in obedience to the King's order he plucked out the eyes of Kamdeo Kataki and imprinted on his forehead the customary distinctive mark of a Hāri. The hukkah-bearer of the Lakhurakhun family was hacked to pieces. The Barphukan, Badal, the *Pachani* or attendant and the prince were taken up. On reaching Dichoi, the Dola-sharia Barua made over to the King all the accused, the Barphukan being the principal. With them there was also the Lanmakharu Dihingia Phukan. The King then ordered that the Phukan should be charged of his misdemeanour and tried near the Dola-sharia gate-house in the presence of the Mahamantri Buragohain Dangaria of Kuoigaon. As commanded by the King the Phukan was brought thither and thus questioned in the presence of the Dangaria,—'The King has commanded that the Phukan should be asked as follows,—'What have I done to him? More specially the Phukan is a Kachari-kumar by caste, and I should not have appointed him Phukan. I made him Phukan because the Captain importuned me strongly in his favour. Now why did you set up a bogus Raja, and what did you yourself want to be?' Having heard this the Barphukan admitted all his guilt. 250.

Trial of the Chetia Phukan.

The Swargadeo caused severe abuses to be hurled at the Phukan. He was cut to pieces with a hoe and his head was transfixed to a spear. His attendant had his eyes and knee-caps extracted, after which he was thrown into a field, where he died a few days after. The prince was punished and exiled. Kamdeo Kataki was made a priest of the Hāris and had to perform their religious rites. 251.

The punishment of the Chetia Phukan.

After this a Bangal named Jogangiri accompanied by some sepoys occupied Gauhati. The Barphukan unable to stand retreated to Kajali. Having heard this the Swargadeo despatched the

Jogangiri occupies Gauhati.

Marangi-khowa Gohain of the Buragohain family and the Opar-Dayangia Rajkhowa of the Sandikais, named Kalia-bhomora, with their personal forces. The King further commanded them as follows,—'The Solal Gohain has repeatedly attempted to rebel against our authority. In violation of our order he turned out the Dekaphukan; so on your way you should first capture the Solal Gohain by stratagem or tact and then proceed to Gauhati.' The Marangi-khowa and the Opar-Dayangia Rajkhowa knelt down before the King and proceeded down to Kaliabar; and encamping at the sandbank belonging to the Akrohi Bhattacharyya they sent Katakis who fetched the Solal Gohain to that place.

Then the Bahbaria Kataki Gauri delivered a false message to the Solal Gohain,—'The Swargadeo has deputed the Marangi-khowa and the Rajkhowa to fight with the Bangals at Gauhati. The Solal Gohain has been commanded to stay at Kaliabar and supply these commanders with men, provisions, gun-powder, and rice.' Helimeli Solal Gohain undertook to carry out this order. He then retired to his camp. The next day the Marangi-khowa and the Rajkhowa proceeded down to Michamukh where they halted for three days, after which they sent the Bahbaria Kataki Rameswar to bring the Solal Gohain to the temple of Madhava at Saubhagi. While travelling to the temple a projecting handle of the mace belonging to the Solal Gohain gave way. He, however, arrived at Madhava. The Marangi-khowa and the Rajkhowa also reached Madhava in the meantime. According to the command of the King the Bahbaria Kataki Gauri announced the royal mandate effecting the dismissal and arrest of the Gohain. The Dola-sharia Bara, the Chaodang Bara and the Da-dhara Bara then captured the Gohain. Of his followers those whose arrest was deemed necessary were captured. 252.

Helimeli Solal Gohain punished.

The Gohain was brought to Michamukh where he was made to put on iron shackles and impounded. On the next day his eyes were taken out. Of his adherents some were executed. In the meantime Lambo Dola-kasharia Barua of the Lahans arrived at that place. The officers handed over the Gohain to the Barua and continued their journey downwards. The Barua escorted up the Gohain with him and had him cudgelled to death in the vicinity of the Dewar Satra as ordered by the King. His house was plundered and the belongings removed to the royal store. The

Marangi-khowa and the Rajkhowa on reaching Nagaon fetched the Dualia Gohain of the Madurial family from Kacharipar and appointed him Solal Gohain at the sandbank adjoining the Auniati Satra in obedience to royal orders which were delivered by the Bahbaria Kataki Gauri. The new Gohain was sent up to Kaliabar in the company of Dhireswar Kataki of the Bahbaria family. The others proceeded down to Kajalimukh and halted there in a stockade. 253.

Recovery of Gauhati by Niamat-ulla.

In the meantime, the two Katakis, Bejia and Dutta who had been despatched to Calicata, came back with Niamat-ulla Subedar with a contingent of sepoys. These soldiers now occupied Gauhati and Hazara Sing Bangal fell in that engagement as well as numerous other Bangals. The Barphukan also went to Gauhati from Kajali. The Marangi-khowa and the Opar-Dayangia Rajkhowa went up and bowed to the King at Dichoi. Then Bejia Kataki and Datta Bairagi placed Niamat-ulla Subedar and his force with the Barphukan at Gauhati. With the guns and gunpowder they proceeded up and joined the King at Dichoi. The Mahamantri Buragohain Dangaria distributed the guns and powder to the recruits trained at Bacha and Dayang and made them regular soldiers by giving them frock-coats and caps. 254.

Death of Gaurinath Singha.

After this, in the month of Sravan, *saka* 1717, the attack of dysentery from which His Majesty had been suffering took a serious turn. Then he summoned the Mahamantri Buragohain Dangaria of Kuoigaon to his presence and said as follows,—' O Dangaria, I do not deem my physical condition to be so very hopeful this time. So I ask you to protect my kingdom and my subjects. The Baskatia Barbarua has done me severe wrong; and I ask you, if possible, to put an end to his life and thereby remove the anguish of my mind.' On that very day the Dangaria fetched the Barbarua, and after admitting him into his presence had him imprisoned under royal orders. On the following day Swargadeo Gaurinath Singha breathed his last, in the month of Sravan, *saka* 1717, his reign having lasted for sixteen years including the period of flight. The remains of the deceased king were cremated near the river down the encampment at Dichoi. The bones were removed to Charaideo and a mound erected over them. The Dihingia

Phukan of the Miri-Sandikai family and the Chetia-patar Barua escorted the bones. 255.

Half-anna silver tokens.

During the stay of King Gaurinath Singha at Dichoi he was compelled to mint half-anna silver pieces for convenience in giving away charities on account of paucity of cowries. Half-anna pieces were introduced from that time. The funeral obsequies of the deceased monarch were performed according to the Brahmanical code; gifts were made and a festive congregation was held to which the Mahantas were invited and fetched. 256.

CHAPTER X.

SWARGADEO KAMALESWAR SINGHA.

Accession.

On the death of Gaurinath Singha, the nobles including the Prime Minister Kuoigayan Buragohain Dangaria, the Bargohain Dangaria of the Madurial family, the Kenduguria Barpatra Dangaria and the Baruas and Phukans conferred together and brought Kamaleswar Singha, son of the Charingia Raja, who was in his turn the grandson of King Rudra Singha's brother named Lechai. He was placed on the throne at the Dichoi camp in the selfsame month of the same year. The name 'Kamaleswar Singha' was sent down to Calicata for being impressed on the coins. 257.

A new Barbarua.

The Swargadeo after assuming his kingly office at the Dichoi camp held the trial of the Panisalia Barbarua in the presence of the Dangarias and accused him of an offence. The guilt being proved the Barbarua confessed it. Then the Barbarua was cudgelled to death sometime in the month of Sravan. The body was interred in a *maidam* constructed by the Gharphalias. In the same month of Sravan of the same *saka* the deposed Bhadari Barbarua of the Sandikai family was made Barbarua by the King. On that very day the Nyaya-sodha Phukan of the Duara family was made Bhitarual Phukan. The former Dulia Barua, a Nara-Kowanr of the Charniga branch, who was living without any office, was now made Naphukan. 258.

Kalia-bhomora Barphukan.

One Bhomora-kalia of the Sandikais was serving as Opar-Dayangia Rajkhowa. He undertook to pay the last unpaid monthly salaries of the Bangal troops; and the King appointed him Barphukan. In that period the Dafalas were ravaging villages in the North Bank; and during the general flight of the people from their homes a large number of His Majesty's subjects took shelter in foreign lands. The King consulted the Mahamantri Kuoigayan Buragohain Dangaria as a result of which the Swargadeo commanded the Sandikai Barbarua and his nephew the Barphukan, to suppress the disturbances and pacify the country. The Tamuli Phukan who was a Brahman was despatched along with them. The Barbarua and the Barphukan bowed to the King and proceeded down by boat with a contingent of sepoys. Reaching Kaliabar the Barbarua threw off a stockade in the vicinity of Silabandhabil, from where the Barphukan left for Gauhati. In the meantime the Dundia Bangals of the Lengta denomination murdered the Firinghee merchant Rausch Saheb at Darang while engaged in a trading excursion, and carried off two of his boats. The Barphukan during his halt at Gauhati captured Haradatta Chaudhuri and put him to death. His son and his brother had their eyes extracted and were then sent up to the presence of the Swargadeo. 259.

Suppression of the Dundias.

The Barbarua then despatched the Bahbaria Kataki Ramdeo to fetch from Gauhati, with the permission of the Barphukan, Niamat-ulla Subedar along with some sepoys. The Barbarua retained the reinforcement with him. By this time the Dundia Bangals had occupied the north bank of Gauhati. Seeing that the two Jamadars Bajusing and Alosing with their forces had crossed over to the Southern Bank, the Barphukan encountered them on the river bank at Kamakhya in which the Dundias were defeated resulting in the death of a large number of Bangals. Having received this intelligence the King was delighted and presented to the Barphukan a *japi* or a wicker hat-umbrella with a peak of gold. The King also conferred upon him the title of *Pratap-ballabh*, literally, 'one whose friend is valour'. The Sandikai Pani-phukan was removed from office and the King attached the responsibilities of the said post to the Dekaphukan of the Doulchetia family. 260.

During the Barbarua's halt at Silabandha, the King despatched Phedela the Sitalial Kataki and Lakhiram Bara with letters and presents to Krishnachandra Narayan, the Kachari Raja. The letter ran as follows :—

Letter to the Kachari Raja.

Hail! To Raja Sri-sri Krishnachandra, Lord of Heramba, one who depends upon the prowess of his own self, gladdened by the drinking of the honey flowing from the two lotus-like feet of the daughter of the Lord of Mountains, adored by the host of the denizens of heaven, including the glorious Purandara, this letter is addressed. We always solicit the welfare of both ourselves and yourself.

This is our special message :—During the disruption of our country our subjects, out of fear for the enemies, deserted the land, and Barmura, the fugitives as well as the Moamarias took refuge in your territories. Now we have recovered possession of our kingdom through the favour of God after suppressing the enemies ; and so we desire that in remembrance of your sacred promises of old our subjects who have taken shelter in your land should be sent back to us in the company of Phedela Kataki and Lakhiram Bara. It is only by this action that our old relationship as father and son can be maintained as well as the demands of virtue and religion. If Barmura, the fugitives and the Moamarias are not restored the consequences will be seen with your own eyes. And we are sending the following presents as tokens of the authenticity of our letter which will reach you in due course,—two knives with ivory hafts embroidered with gold ; two others with similar hafts inlaid with silver; four knives with brazen handles ; twenty plain knives with hafts of buffalo-horn; four crimson-coloured silk *dhutis*. *Saka* 1717, the month of Aghran, the fifth day. 261.

With this letter and gifts the Katakis left the presence of the Barbarua and proceeded towards Khaspur. During the Barbarua's stay at Silabandha, the *Dafala-Bahatias* and fugitives of the North Bank, having met together crossed the Brahmaputra at Duimuni-sil and attacked our forces. Having received this news the Barbarua

Insurrection of the Dafalas.

sent out three companies of sepoys to oppose the insurgents. They opened fire on the Dafalas on the river bank, and the Dafalas being unable to stand hastened to get into their boats, and in the consequent scare and confusion many of them fell into the river and were drowned. Many lost their lives by hostile bullets. A few others of the rebels were captured alive; they were subsequently beheaded by the Barbarua and their heads were transfixed to spears near the two celebrated rocks or Duimuni-sil. The Barbarua then communicated the tidings of victory to His Majesty. 262.

Contributions from the Mahantas.

The same Kataki was asked to intimate to the King that there was no money for paying the Bangals their pay. The messenger informed the Buragohain Dangaria accordingly, who communicated it to His Majesty. The King became delighted at the news of victory. He then conferred with the Mahamantri Buragohoin Dangaria and directed the latter to pay up the Bangals by raising donations from the Mahantas or spiritual leaders. The Barbarua summoned the Khataniars or representatives of the various Mahantas including the four principal pontiffs and caused them to contribute according to the following scale,—rupees 4,000 from every principal monastery; rupees 400 from a Satra of intermediate rank; rupees 100 from each of the minor Satras; and rupees 50 each from still smaller Satras. With the sum thus raised the sepoys were paid their arrear monthly dues. 263.

Letter from the Kachari Raja.

Then the King deputed the Dihingia Phukan to the company of the Barbarua; and the Phukan accordingly joined the Barbarua at Kaliabar. After this the Barbarua, the Solal Gohain, the Dihingia Phukan, the Tamuli Phukan jointly deliberated as a result of which they crossed the Lohit at Kaliabar and encamped on the Northern Bank in the Dulingial sand-bank. There the Dafalas of the Naduaria and Chaiduaria *khels* offered their submission. In the meantime our Kataki Phedela, accompanied by the two envoys of the Kachari Raja Krishnachandra Narayan, named Sagarpha and Phela, arrived at the Barbarua's camp there. The Barbarua made arrangements for the stay of the two Kachari ambassadors and supplied them with provisions and food. They were then formally received in audience by the Barbarua where he listened to the contents of their letter.

The following is the text of the letter brought from the Kachari Raja by Sagarpha and Phela :—

Hail! to the minister Srijukta Bhadrakanta Barbarua, one who adheres to the path of precedents and customs, one who delights in the science of polity, one whose heart is like that of a black-bee maddened with delight by listlessly drinking the honey flowing from the lotus-like stainless feet of Sri-sri Radha and Govinda, whose abode is situated in the sacred Brindavana, the place of their Rāsa or divine sport. Here we pray day and night for your welfare and advancement by the grace of God. May you be blessed with happiness.

Thus runs our message :—From the moment when King Rudra Singha established paternal relationship, attended by all the solemnity of a sacred covenant, by seating Siva Singha Raja on his right thigh, and Tamradhwaja Raja on his left, at the holy site of Viswanath, after having rescued Tamradhwaja from among his enemies who were no other than his own kith and kin, the uninterrupted friendship between the two kingdoms flowed, as it were, in the majestic pace of the Ganges. We still cherish in our heart the same old feelings of amity, though the condition of our respective kingdoms is not what it was in previous years, which has occasioned slight violation of the friendly terms in which we were placed before. Still amicable relationship should be re-established by interchanging letters by meeting the circumstances of the time; and this is the desire of my heart. Let it be said that some of my subjects living at Dharmapur did what they ought not to have done out of greed for wealth. But my commands became powerful and the old relationship of father and son became revived, and the two countries have now become as if they are one. I have not the audacity to discuss the rightness or wrongness of this action. I am sending herewith my letter. I hope you will place the facts before the Swargadeo and remove any slur which I might have acquired by my vaingloriousness, I being an insect among mortals. This letter is addressed to one who is regarded as the most learned. 264.

Barbarua's reply.

Having heard the contents of the epistle the Barbarua said to the Kachari envoys,—'We have understood what your Raja means to say in his letter. Please deliver to us now his oral message.' To this the messengers made the following reply,—'Our chief Raja Krishnachandra Narayan has asked us to say that he cherishes still the old feelings of friendship and goodwill'. The Barbarua then replied,—'Go and tell your Raja that as evidence of his assertion implying his continuance in terms of friendliness, he should take immediate steps to trace out our subjects who have taken shelter in his territories and repatriate them to their own kingdom'. The messengers were then given leave and permitted to return to their country, *saka* 1717, the month of Phalgun, dated the tenth day.

The Barbarua then went up to Viswanath, from where he came down to Gauhati being accompanied by the sepoy detachment under Niamat-ulla Subedar. The Barbarua then proceeded upstream and encamped at the mouth of the Selem. The Swargadeo then directed the Mahamantri Buragohain Dangaria to proceed towards the south who accordingly set out for Kuruabahi where he halted after having erected a stockade there. The rains then set in and there was no possibility of action with the Dafalas. The Barbarua crossed the river and returned to the South Bank. The Mahamantri Buragohain Dangaria marched to Dichoi with the Barbarua where both paid their obeisance to His Majesty. 265.

Phofai Senapati.

In *saka* 1718, a road was constructed from the main entrance of the Dichoi camp to Bacha. At this time the *Dafala-Bahatias* and fugitives in the North Bank united themselves at Baskata under one Phofai, a Bahatia. They then despatched one Madhuram Bairagi to Bangal to fetch a detachment of Barkandari sepoys. After this they ravaged numerous villages in a spirit of hostility with the aid of these mercenaries. Having received this intelligence the King despatched a messenger to Gauhati to fetch the Dekaphukan with a force of sepoys. On reaching the Bharali in the north the Phukan was attacked by the Baskatia sepoys in the vicinity of the Bharari. The Phukan sent out his sepoys to resist the rebels, and the sepoys opened fire accordingly. Then ensued a terrible contest, where the Baskatias being unable to stand took to their heels, after which they assembled again at Baskata. The Phukan then returned to Gauhati at the instance of the Swargadeo.

10

The King then commanded the Mahamantri Buragohain Dangaria of the Kuoigayan family to quell the disturbances in the North Bank. The Dangaria crossed the Dihing and halted at his camp at Garamur, from where he despatched a force against Phofai Barsenapati and others of the North Bank, and asked them not to take up arms against the King. The rebels did not pay any heed to this order. The Dangaria then crossed the Lohit, on which Phofai Senapati attended by a number of followers entered into the forest with the object of fighting. The Dhekial Phukan who was the elder brother of the Baskatia Barbarua fled away. The Dangaria after arriving in the North Bank captured Lahar of Lakhimpur and his nephew, both of whom had been living in an unapproved manner. They were then sent up to the King being chained and put in cages. The Swargadeo tried them in which their guilt was proved. They were then hacked into seven pieces, and their heads were transfixed to spears. 266.

Suppression of Phofai's revolt.

The Dangaria then sent some men with six companies of sepoys to seize the person of Phofai Senapati. The royal army came upon the rebels in the forest. Seeing them Phofai came out and rushed at the King's forces saying,—'I will eat them up'. The sepoys then fired at the rebel leader. Phofai was struck with a bullet and he lost his life. His followers deserted the field of battle. Some of them were captured by the sepoys and handed over to the Dangaria, who tried them; their crimes being proved they were hooked or pressed to death. The Dhekial Phukan was eventually found and captured, but he committed suicide on the way by swallowing poison. The other people all came and offered their submission to the Dangaria. The houses of the Barsenapati and of the Dhekial Phukan were searched and pillaged. On that occasion a large number of buffaloes, cows, ornaments and other articles were recovered and confiscated to the state. After having quieted the Uttarkol, the Buragohain paid his obeisance to the King, and submitted the booty to the royal treasury. 267.

Moamaria insurrection at Chokihat.

After this a number of Moamaria fugitives went up and assembled in a body at Chokihat and Soaluguri. The King commanded the Kuoigayan Mahamantri Buragohain Dangaria to march against these rebels. The Dangaria provided himself with the necessary quota of men and provisions and saluted the

King, after which he proceeded by land and water, and fell upon the Moamarias at Chokihat, where fighting took place with the Moamarias. Being unable to hold their ground the Moamarias fled and dispersed by land and water towards the east. One Pitambar Thakur of the Moamarias was seized in the affray. Many Moamarias being famished offered their submission to the Dangaria who settled them at Khutiapota. Bharathi Raja proceeded up with some of his followers; and he alone could not be found. 268.

Khamti insurrection.

Almost at that time the Burha-raja of the Khamtis came down with a large army, and waited with hostile intentions at an encampment at Nibok in the North Bank. The Dangaria then despatched a force who after having vanquished the Burha-raja in an engagement captured him with his followers. The Dangaria obtained a large quantity of booty by defeating those Moamarias. 269.

Reception of the Munkang ambassador.

At that time the chief of Munkang despatched his ambassador Panchamru with letters and presents. He, coming by the route through Mahang, arrived at the Dichoi camp in time. He was kept according to the approved custom being supplied with the necessary provisions and articles. The King himself received him in audience at the Ranghar as dictated by the custom of the country. His Majesty sat at the Ranghar wearing a turban and a cloak. The King's father, the Charing Raja, also sat in the assembly. Two platforms were erected on the two sides of the hall, one of which was occupied by the two Dangarias and the other by the Barbarua and the Phukans. The Swargadeo took his seat being surrounded by the imposing congregation of Katakis, Kakatis, Dolois, Deodhais, Bailungs and other men including the sepoys. Towards evening the Choladhara Phukan of the Chiring family presented the Munkang envoy Panchamru before the court with his letters and gifts. The King then commanded the Choladhara Phukan to make the necessary inquiries. As commanded by the King the Phukan asked the envoy regarding the condition of his Raja's territories and the object of his mission: and the Kataki communicated the desired information with respect to their happiness and weal. Having heard the letter the King said,—'The reply to the Raja's queries will be submitted to the messenger at the time of his departure. In the meantime he should wait at his camp'. After sitting at the court for sometime the messenger retired to his camp and the King to his palace. The presents brought by the ambassador were as follows,—one horse, two pieces of yellow broadcloth, one red broadcloth, one black. The Swargadeo handed over to the Kataki the letter and presents, and sent him to the Buragohain in the company of our envoy Ramdeo of the Gharpora family. The Dangaria granted him the usual interview and permitted him to go back to Munkang. 270.

Purnananda restores peace and order.

After having re-established peace in the eastern region, the Mahamantri Buragohain Dangaria came and paid his respects to His Majesty. All the goods obtained during the operations in which he was engaged were made over to the royal store after being embodied in a list. The Dangaria then settled the captive Moamarias at Khutiapota, Dhali, Jankhana and Uttar-Gahpur. The Burha-raja of Khamti was kept under guard near the royal camp to the east of the Dichoi. The Khamtis who were his followers were settled at the Tokolai forest to the south of the camp. Those Khamtis were attached to the two Hatimurs, Lebang and Lalim, forming part of the Buragohain's *khel*. The King conferred upon the Buragohain as marks of distinction,—one silver dish with tripod and three silver cups with gold linings. 271.

Dismissal of officers at the instance of the paiks.

After this, complaints were lodged against the Madurial Bargohain by his servitors who thereby caused his dismissal from office. The King then appointed the deposed Bargohain of the Madurial family to the vacant office. The newly deposed Bargohain was settled in the vicinity of Kakadonga under the surveillance of twenty Dola-sharias in charge of one Dola-sharia Bara. After this the Barpatra Dangaria of the Kenduguria family was dismissed from office on complaints being made before the King by the constituent members of his *khel*. He was also made to reside near Kakadonga. The son of the Kenduguria Barpatra Dangaria who had fallen in the eastern campaign was now appointed Barpatra by the King. Manjay Naobaicha Phukan of the Bakatial family was fined and dismissed from office, being charged with the offence of destroying royal stores and granaries. The son of the deposed Barpatra was appointed Naobaicha Phukan. 272.

Female jugglers from Bangal.

After this the King brought a party of female jugglers from Bangal. The King went to the Ranghar and made the jugglers perform their feats. The following tricks were shown,—a dish was placed on a small platform supported by four posts below which there was another dish on a pitcher on the head of a man. A woman stood up on the upper dish with a shield and a sword. The man below went on spinning breadthwise like a top. Another woman, similarly armed with shield and sword, danced on the top of a bamboo post from where she jumped on to the earth, being caught by a man below with his hands. The Swargadeo became pleased with the performance and gave the jugglers a reward of rupees four hundred. They were subsequently taken to the interior of the palace where also they performed their feats. 273.

Death of Kadamdighala.

In the month of Bhadra, *saka* 1721, the Charingia Raja's mother who was known as 'Murar-Deuta' breathed her last. On the twentieth of Aswin, the day when the purificatory rites were performed after the lapse of a month, the King's father the Charing Raja also passed away. The funeral rites occurring a month after were performed according to the Brahmanical code, where largesses were distributed, and the Mahantas or religious leaders were brought to perform congregational recital of religious music attended by the usual festivities. The bones were removed to Charaideo Hill under the escort of the Dihingia Phukan and the Chetia-patra Barua of the Doijania Bargohain family. 274.

The Darangi Raja pays homage to the Swargadeo.

The Swargadeo had been formally crowned before the death of his father the Charingia Raja. The custom demanded that the Rajas of Darang should personally bow before the King at the time of his coronation. According to this custom, Krishnanaran the Darangi Raja, and Hayanaran the Saru-raja of Darang, bowed down to the King during the Phalgutsav festival. The procedure adopted in salutation was as follows,—after His Majesty had taken his seat in the court-chamber, the Dangarias seated themselves in the eastern side of the hall leaning against their respective pillars. The Rajas advanced to the court and took their seats below those of the Dangarias in the centre of the hall being permitted to use the distinctive marks assigned to the Dangarias. Then Bhadari Barbarua of the Sandikai family presented the Rajas to the King from their seats. The Rajas bowed down to the Swargadeo seven times at the end of which they resumed their respective seats. The ex-Raja sat on a blanket. The following were the presents offered by the two Rajas at the time of salutation,—forty tolas of gold; two horses, eighty yaktails, eighty pieces sal-cloth; eighty blankets; eighty pieces of cloth each ten cubits long; another set of eighty pieces each twelve cubits long; eighty more pieces each having five colours. When the time came for the court to disperse the King distributed betel-nut and leaf placed in a *bata*. The Rajas then retired to their camps. 275.

Srinath Barbarua of the Duara family.

After this the Sandikai Barbarua died in *saka* 1722. The Bhitarual Phukan of the Duara family was appointed Barbarua by the Swargadeo, while a member of the Bakatial family was made Bhitarual Phukan. 276.

Moran-Singphou encounter.

In 1723 *saka*, the Swargadeo commanded the Dekaphukan of the Buragohain family to quell disturbances in Upper Assam. The Phukan was provided with five companies of sepoys. He saluted the King after which he marched to Bengmara where he surrounded the Moamarias. There ensued an engagement with the Moamarias who being unable to stand took to their heels and proceeded eastward to Namrup where they waited in conjunction with the Singphous in the Matak country. They were besieged again by our army, and there followed a terrible contest with the Morans and Singphous. We lost fifteen sepoys, and our soldiers renewed their attacks with greater vigour. The Morans and the Singphous formed themselves into two separate groups and dispersed in opposite directions. The spoils obtained in this warfare consisted of men, provisions, buffaloes, cows, copper, brass and cloths. The Singphous appeared on this occasion as tame and submissive. The Phukan then came back and bowed to the King. The articles seized in the war were removed to the royal treasury. 277.

The death of Bharathi Raja.

Then the King commanded the Dekaphukan to start for the eastern campaign. The Dekaphukan went with six companies of sepoys to chase the Morans; the rebels were attacked near the

Dangari. The Morans then deserted their homes and entered into the forest. Looking for them our men found them out in that very forest. Our sepoys besieged the Morans. Then Bharathi, the Raja of the Marans, accompanied by five Morans rushed at and attacked the company commanded by Nasipsing, and pierced a sepoy through with a spear. In this opportune moment one Jogising Sepahi fired on; and the ball struck the thigh of Bharathi. Still the chief without turning his face back rushed forward and caught hold of the gun. In the meantime two sepoys pierced Bharathi to death with their bayonets.

Having seen the fall of Bharathi the Morans dispersed into the forest. Our people came out and joined the Phukan near the Dangari. Thirty Morans fell in that battle. Then the Phukan sent by boat the corpse of Bharathi to the King under the charge of the Bahbaria Kataki. By order of the King the corpse was transfixed to a spear in the midst of the newly settled Moamaria village at Khutiapota. The Phukan too halted at his encampment by the side of the Dangari. 278.

Origin of the name 'Bhogdoi'.

The Morans were forced by starvation to offer their submission by coming to that camp. Some men, buffaloes, cows, copper and brass were obtained. At that time, Sivanath Nam-Dayangia Rajkhowa, the youngar brother of the Kuoigayan Mahamantri Buragohain Dangaria, was commanded by the King to trace out the fugitives who had taken refuge in the Kachar country. Some sepoys were also given with him. After bowing to the King the Rajkhowa went down by boat and stayed at Raha-choki where he had thrown off a stockade. At that time the Mahamantri Buragohain Dangaria excavated a canal named 'Bhogdoi' extending from the Dichoi to the Kalioni. During the excavation of that stream the *Adhikars* or the heads of the religious institutions fed the people with rice and cakes, one *khel* after another; and the King, the Dangaria and the Barbarua also supplied refreshments to the labourers. The name 'Bhogdoi', literally food-offering, was thus given to the canal. The King went to see that stream. He was honoured with gifts on a *sarai* and a *taoban*. The queen-mother also went thereto. Largesses were given on that day to women on the way. 279.

In *saka* 1723, the Purbaparia Chaudhari Brahman named Pankaj, and the Lekharu of Kharang named Kapchiga, were despatched by the Sandikai Phukan to the presence of the Deva-Dharma Raja, the ruler of Bhutan. The Raja Deva-Dharma then sent with them to the Swargadeo the four *jinkaps* or envoys named Jiva, Dindu, Khupa and Barukdewa, with letters and gifts. The Barphukan sent them up to the presence of the Swargadeo. They were kept at Sarbaibandha.

The embassy from the Deva-Dharma Raja of Bhutan.

The four *jinkaps* were received in audience by the Kuoigayan Mahamantri Buragohain Dangaria when he was witnessing the flight of the birds from the aviary at Domjan, down Tarajan. The Dangaria rode on an elephant and was attended by an imposing assemblage of elephants, horses, retinue and sepoys. The envoys were introduced by the Jakaichukia Tekela-Bara of the Dangaria's constituency or *mel*. The Dangaria then directed Biswambhar Bahbaria Kataki to make the necessary enquiries on his behalf in the native dialect of the ambassadors,—'Kataki, please ask the messengers Jiva, Dindu, Khupa and Burukdewa, whether at the time of their departure, their lord the Deva-Dharma Raja was in the enjoyment of peace and happiness exercising his protection over his subjects living in the plains as well as in the hills, with his Lemas, Jongpungs, Jadungs, Tangchur-subhas and Gelans.'

Having heard this the *jinkaps* replied,—'Our Deva-Dharma Raja was living in happiness by the grace of Kali-Thakurani when we left our country. We are not in a position to say what has transpired in the meantime'. The Dangaria then said,—'It is also our desire that the Deva-Dharma Raja should be enjoying prosperity and happiness. Please ask them in which month they left their country. When did they reach Gauhati? How long it was since they arrived at this place? Had they to face any danger or difficulty in their journey?' Having heard this they said,—'We started from our country in the month of Pous, and arrived here in Chaitra, and we had no misfortune in our travel'. Having heard the contents of the letter the Dangaria said,—'I have understood what the Deva-Dharma Raja communicates in his letter. Please tell us now what he has communicated through you orally'. The messengers then stated,—'The Deva-Dharma Raja has commanded us to say that seven hundred Gelans had previously solicited the permission of the Swargadeo to settle in the area bounded by the Gohain-Kamala Ali, for the purpose of rearing betel-nut trees and leaves *i.e.*, for earning their livelihood. The permission was granted by the Swargadeo and the Gelans accordingly settled at the place prayed for. But the people living on the other side of the road have transgressed the line of demarcation, and have captured our men after crossing that road. Our King solicits the favour of the Swargadeo's protecting the former boundaries'. To this the Dangaria replied,—'All right, the messengers will be given a reply to the message of their Raja communicated in his letter and also orally at the time of their departure. If they are fortunate they may be favoured with the opportunity of personally paying their respects at the feet of the Swargadeo'. The messengers were allowed leave to retire to their camps, after which they were presented with the customary offering of flowers and sandal-paste. The Dangaria also went to his camp. The following were the gifts brought for the Dangaria,—One *than* or long piece of *gomcheng* or China silk; one *than* of Kilmij; four pieces of *dwaraka* cloth; one piece of white sandal-wood; one piece of red sandal-wood; four chamars of musk-deer. 280.

The Bhutan envoys at the royal court.

The four *jinkaps* were presented to the Swargadeo by the Choladhara Phukan of the Chiring family in the front portico of the Barchora during the Durgotsav celebrations. The King then directed the Majindar Barua, who was a Ganak by caste, to put the necessary questions on behalf of His Majesty, and he said,—'I have been commanded by His Majesty to enquire of Jiva, Dindu, Khupa and Burukdewa, whether at the time of their departure the Deva-Dharma Raja was living in peace and prosperity, by protecting his subjects along with his Lemas, Jongpungs, Jadungs, Tangchur-subhas and Gelans'. Having heard this the messengers replied,—'At the time of our departure the Deva-Dharma Raja was living in peace and plenty through the favour of Kali-Thakurani. We cannot say what has transpired in the meantime.' The King then said,—'It is also our desire that the Deva-Dharma Raja should live in happiness and prosperity'. He directed to further enquire as follows,—'In which month did they leave their country? When did they reach Gauhati? How long it was since they arrived at this place?' Having heard this they said,—'We started from our country in the month of Pous; in the month of Phalgun we reached the place in the jurisdiction of the Barpani Raja of Gauhati, and we arrived here in the month of Chaitra. We did not experience any danger or fright in our journey'. The Majindar then read out the letter, after which the King said,—'I have understood the purport of the message as communicated by the Raja in his letter. Please tell me now what he intends to inform in his oral message'. Having heard this the messengers said,—'The true intent of the Raja's message is what he has communicated in his epistle. But in addition to this he has directed us to say that seven hundred Gelans had previously prayed for and obtained permission from the Swargadeo through the Barpani Raja to settle in the area bordering on the Gohain-Kamala Ali, for the purpose of taking betel-nut and leaf, by singing religious songs. But the subjects of the Swargadeo have now violated the boundary line, ravaged the villages and committed many oppressions. Our Raja prays for the restitution and protection of the old limits'. After the messengers had submitted their prayer the King said,—'The Mahamantri Buragohain Dangaria will communicate his reply to this prayer at the time of the messengers' departure. They should now wait at their camp'. After this they were given flowers and sandal-paste and allowed to retire. They continued in the court for some time and then retired to their camp. 281.

Presents from the Bhutan Raja to the Swargadeo.

The following articles were sent as presents by the Deva-Dharma Raja to the Swargadeo,—one silver pot containing smaller caskets inside; one steel sword; a sheath to match the above, with silver linings, occasionally interspersed with gold and set with precious stones; one waist-belt of *kocha* cloth; one red frock-coat of *kuchi*; one red *than* of *gomcheng-mechi*; three pieces of red *dwaraka* for wearing on the body; one white piece; one piece of red *gomcheng*; one piece of black *gomcheng*; one piece of light-red *gomcheng*; another piece of Feringhee *gomcheng* of light-red colour; one *satranj*; one *namdang*; with four broad laces; one piece of *kilmij* cloth; one *dinga* blanket; twelve *khulu* blankets; fifteen red blankets; nine *pipranga* blankets; sixty yaktails from Kariapar; one black mithan; two *toka gumuni* cows; one horse; two red Tangon ponies; one blackish piebald pony harnessed with saddles, bridles, and other fittings. From Tangchur-subha,—one piebald pony; one piece of golden red *gomcheng*; two pieces of red *dwaraka*; one blanket; one soft red blanket; one blanket for sitting; one *dinga-kheh* or Chinese blanket; one rug made of furs, but so smooth that one would think it is not made of furs at all having stripes like those of a tiger; three whitish straw-coloured yaktails. From Jadung, one Tangana pony; one piece of *namdang* cloth. From the two messengers Jiva and Dindu,—two pieces of golden *gomcheng* cloth; nine blankets; one red piece of *dwaraka*. From Khupa and Burukdewa,—three pieces of *namdang*; four blankets. For the recreation of the Bhutanese ambassadors a pair of *Banaprasthi* Bangals danced in mid-air with lights on their backs; while another pair walked on a rope with a stick with buffalo-horns fastened at its lower end. They also exhibited numerous other feats for amusement. 282.

Joint insurrection of the Kacharis and the Moamarias.

The Rajkhowa staying at Raha-choki fetched one Saranamati of the Kacharis as well as the Laskars and asked them to produce our fugitives. They were then put under watch and guard. In the meantime, the Kacharis, the Moamarias and the fugitives, accompanied by a person who was given out to be a prince, assembled in one place with motives of revolt. One day the Rajkhowa despatched a contingent of his army, who crossed the Kalang, and dispersed the rebels who had assembled at Jamunamukh. The so-called prince, and the Barbarua of the Dihingia family as well as a number of fugitives were captured; the prince, the Barbarua and Saranamati were sent under Durga Kataki of the Bahbaria family, and the Tekela-Bara Gunai of Candahar-choki, to the presence of the Swargadeo accompanied by the escort of a force of sepoys. After a journey of two days the Barbarua effected his escape at night from Bharaligaon. The prince and Saranamati were made over to the King at his Dichoi camp. In the trial that followed it was found that the so-called prince was an impostor, and he was beheaded, while Saranamati was kept in confinement. The Kacharis, the Moamarias and the fugitives managed to assemble again taking with them a son of the Barmura Gohain. Apprehending a conflict the Rajkhowa reported the matter to the King, who accordingly ordered the Dekaphukan of Gauhati to march to the outpost at Raha in the company of a number of sepoys. The Phukan after his arrival at Raha-choki collected men for united action. The Moamarias then issued out of the route through Potani and burnt a number of villages of the men of Nagaon. The Phukan gave the Nagayans a contingent of sepoys, and arranged for the erection of a stockade at Potani, where they were afterwards attacked by the Morans. The Nagayans came out of their camp and joined the Moamarias; and they also killed some sepoys. The latter came back and joined the camp of the Phukan and the Rajkhowa. The Moamarias became powerful again. After this our Phukan, Rajkhowa and the Rohial Barua, came out one day with their army; and after having crossed the Kalang and the Kapili they attacked the Moamarias who also resisted by a counter-attack. There ensued a severe contest between the two parties. There being no stockade our men could not continue their stand, and so they had to disperse. 283.

Victory of the rebels.

In this engagement we lost the Dualia Rajkhowa of Ghiladhari, the Rohial Barua of the Duara family, the Nagayan Hajarika named Ranjay, the Kharangi Hajarikia named Chengkali, the Bahbaria Kataki named Gauri, 240 sepoys, and 300 other men. Being defeated in this battle, the Dekaphukan went to Gauhati, and the Rajkhowa joined His Majesty. After this the Moamarias came out and compelled the people to offer submission to them in the area bounded by the Kajali, the Brahmaputra and the mouth of the Micha river. Dhireswar, the Kataki of the Bahbaria family, came from Upper Assam to report to the King the particulars of the war. 284.

Fresh army despatched to suppress the Kacharis.

Having received the intelligence of our defeat in the Kachari war, the King commanded the Kataki Dhireswar to bring up the Dekaphukan and the Captain. The Kataki proceeding in a boat by day and night came back with the Captain Gohain and three companies of sepoys. Before the arrival of the Captain, the King sent down the Bacha Rajkhowa of the Buragohain family with three companies of sepoys to proceed downstream and continue the fight. The Tekela-neog was also given in his company. The Bacha Rajkhowa proceeded down and erected a stockade at Michamukh and halted there. In the meantime the Captain Gohain joined the King who despatched the said Captain Gohain to war with three companies of sepoys; Hao-Sagar Bara was also sent with 400 Baskatias whose weapons consisted of *daos*, spears, bows and arrows. Dhireswar Kataki was also allowed to accompany them. 285.

The Bhogdoi canal.

The Captain proceeded down by boat and joined the Bacha Rajkhowa at Naogaon. At this time, the Deka-phukan paid his obeisance to His Majesty after having posted a small force at Namchang consisting of the three Abhayapuria units together with thirty sepoys. The articles seized by him were made over to the King accompanied by a descriptive list. The Kuoigayan Buragohain Dangaria then excavated a canal from the Dichoi to the Kalioni, during which the *Adhikars* or religious heads supplied refreshments to the labourers, from which the canal was known as Bhogdoi. 286.

Fresh hostilities with the Moamarias.

Then the Captain and the Bacha Rajkhowa halted at their camp above Khagarijan in the north bank of the Kalang. The Kacharis, the Nagayans, the fugitives and the Moamarias attended by a regular force and accompanied by the bogus prince, made their appearance near the encampment of the royalists. The Moamarias having crossed the Kalang had set fire to the villages during their march. Our men also issued out with the sepoys and the Baskatias and fell upon the Moamarias. The Bangals had with them Dhireswar Kataki and Jagannath Baragi, while the Baskatias had Sagar-Bara Hao. Then ensued a severe contest with the Moamarias. 287.

Victory of the royalists.

During this engagement the Bajupuri Bangals hurled a missile of fire at the sight of which the Moamarias fled in terror and dismay. The Baskatias pursued them and cut them off. The entire force took to their heels and entered again the Kachari country. Our men halted at the camp at Raha-choki. The Moamarias lost in this war one Hanumanta, a *Bar-yoga-dhari* or one who was renowned for his staunch *yoga* austerities, and 120 other men. Dhireswar Bahbaria Kataki was despatched to the capital to communicate the news of this victory to the King. The Kataki delivered the message to His Majesty in his palace, who on hearing it became delighted and rewarded the messenger with presents. 288.

Fresh preparations.

The Swargadeo sent back Saranamati to the Raha-choki camp under the escort of one Hahchowa Tekela-Bara. After this, the King placed at the disposal of the Dekaphukan of the Buragohain family five companies of sepoys, and commanded him to proceed to the Kachari-Moamaria war. The Phukan saluted the King, and proceeded down by land and water to Raha-choki where he joined the Captain and the Bacha Rajkhowa, and halted there by erecting a big stockade. Anticipating a severe engagement the King commanded the transfer of a portion of the army stationed at Gauhati to the main theatre of war. Messengers were despatched and they brought up the soldiers. The two Rajas of Darang with their two thousand soldiers of the Chutia-kowanr unit, the bearded Brahmachari with five companies of sepoys, the Dekaphukan who had deserted the army before, and the chief *Tamol-kata* of the Barphukan, they all came up to Jagi-choki and halted at the camp erected by them. In the meantime the Solal Gohain died at Kaliabar; and the Dekaphukan was placed in charge of the Solals till the appointment of a new Gohain. As commanded by the King, the Dekaphukan assembled the Solals, the Chai-duarias, the Deuries, the Ghiladharias, the Samdharias, the Nagayans, the Kharangis, the Panchrajias and the Satrajias, and remained ready for action with this large force. 289.

Reception of Jayantia Katakis.

Previously to this the Namdangia Rajkhowa had, at the instance of His Majesty, despatched the Jayantia envoy Ramchandra to the Jayantia chieftain Ram Singha. He now came back with an epistle and presents from the chief of Jayantia. The Phukan sent the messenger Ramchandra to the presence of the Swargadeo. The Kataki was placed down Sarbaibandha where he was supplied with provisons and other necessaries. The ambassador was received at the official residence of the Barbarua of the Duara family, in the presence of a large assembly of Katakis, Kakatis, Dolois, Deodhais, Baras, Baruks and sepoys, attended by elephants and horses. The officers were attired in turbans and cloaks. An elevated place was also constructed for the occasion. In the evening the envoy was received according to the customary procedure. He was introduced by the Namdangia Bara named Nartam. The envoy placed the letter on a *sarai* and sat on a plaintain leaf at the end of the court. The seat was given to him owing to his insistent request, specially as he was a Brahman. The Barbarua directed the Bahbaria Kataki Jaydeo to put the usual questions in the following words,—'Kataki, ask Ramchandra, whether his lord Ram Singha was enjoying peace and happiness at the time of his departure, ruling over his cows and Brahmans, Baras, Baruks, and his subjects living in the plains as well as in the hills.' On hearing this the envoy replied,—'At the time of our departure from Jayantiapur, our chief was in happiness and safety ruling over his territories and people. We do not know what has happened afterwards.'

The Barbarua then replied,—'It is our desire that your chief should be in the enjoyment of peace and prosperity.' He ordered fresh queries to be made on the following lines,—'In what month did he leave his nativeland? When did he reach the outpost of Jagi? How many days have elapsed since his arrival here? Did he encounter any fright or trouble in his journey?' Hearing this the messenger replied,—'We started from Jayantiapur in the month of Phalgun and reached Jagi-choki in Baisakh and arrived at this place in the month of Jaishtha. We did not encounter any fear or trouble on our way.' The Majindar Barua then read aloud the letter on hearing which the Barbarua said,—'We have understood what the chief has communicated through the letter. Now please let him say what message has been conveyed orally.' The messenger then said,—'The message is nothing but what has been communicated in the letter. Yet the Raja has asked us to say that he has been continuing in the same old terms of friendship which had been established long before, and that he has not forgotten them in his heart.' The Barbarua said,—'The Raja has expressed his desire for the enhancement of our mutual friendship. This desire is also shared by us. Further message will be delivered to the envoy at the time of his departure. If he is fortunate he may also be blessed with the sight of His Majesty's feet. Let him now retire to his camp.' The Kataki was then allowed leave after being offered flowers and sandal-paste. He then returned to his quarters after waiting at the court for sometime more. The Barbarua then caused the distribution of betel-nut and leaf to the Katakis and Kakatis of the court in an earthen pot. These officers had also been offered seats. Some articles of food were sent to the Jayatia envoy on that day. 290.

Letter from the Jayantia chief.

The following letter from the Jayantia chief to the Swargadeo was brought by the aforesaid envoy Ramchandra :—

Hail! To the glorious Swargadeo, King and Paramount Sovereign, who like a black-bee drinks the honey-drops flowing gently from the lotus-feet of his tutelary deity, illumined by the sun-like effulgence emitted by the jewels set amidst the Mandara flowers on the heads of gods led by Brahma and Indra, here shines the epistle despatched by the Lord of Jayantipur, who is gladdened by the all-absorbing adoration of the feet of his own deity, one who is blessed with abundant prosperity and wealth, one who is a sun to the lilies in the shape of his enemies, but who shines in the company of his lotus-like powerful allies, one who has suppressed the misery of the indigent. First of all we solicit your uninterrupted prosperity.

Thus runs our message:—I have received your news from your confidential letter. What you have said regarding our old friendship is just and proper. I have been highly delighted to receive intelligence of the suppression of your powerful enemies. Besides, you have written that Jayantiapur is Rangpur, and Rangpur is Jayantiapur, and that both are one and the same. I am not unconscious of our indissoluble friendship. As fate decreed, no interchange of embassies could take place on account of the disturbances near Raha. A number of Garos who are my subjects conspired in secret and caused the disruption. The frontier chiefs have now become submissive being placed out of the line of mutual communication. After a short while those not yet quelled would be brought to submission by the grace of the Goddess. We shall see the termination of their hostility in some way or other. I communicate to you this news as we are inseparable in friendship. You have also written about the fugitives and I shall see to the necessary arrangements for bringing them round. I am now attempting to open up the ways which will lead to the removal of the disturbances in my territories. I have heard from others that you have transgressed the boundaries and taken away some men who were sheltered in my territories. Yet I have not done anything in the way of reprisal or retaliation in remembrance of our old friendship. These acts are not justifiable. I write again that nothing is impossible if the Goddess is favourably disposed. I wish that messages and embassies should come and go as before which will lead to the increase of our friendly relations. The rest you will learn from the lips of Ramchandra and Bhudev. *Saka* 1723, the month of Magh. Here ends the epistle. I send the following presents as tokens of the genuineness of this letter,—One scarlet-coloured *sari*, one *than* of white cloth, four nutmegs, and some quantity of cloves'.

On that occasion a letter only was brought to the Swargadeo. The Barbarua gave two pieces of *tao* or broadcloth and two rugs, with which the envoy paid his respects to the Swargadeo. 291.

Moamaria reverses.

After this the Dekaphukan, with the object of capturing the Kacharis and the Moamarias, crossed the Kalang river and entered the Kachari territory where he halted after erecting a stockade. He continued his advance after having sent Dhireswar Kataki of the Bahbaria family by the route through Jagi at the head of a Gauhati contingent. The Kacharis then expressed their intention to expatriate our fugitives but the Moamarias being powerful withstood this proposal. The Moamarias attacked the Phukan when he arrived at Chang-choki, where the insurgents were routed with the loss of some men. The news of this battle was communicated to the King by Dhireswar Bahbaria Kataki whom the Phukan had despatched for the purpose. The Kataki informed the Barbarua. The King admitted the messenger to his chamber and asked him the details of the campaign. His Majesty became pleased to receive intelligence of the victory of the royalist force. The Phukan in the meantime searched for the Moamarias as far as Barthal. He set fire to the villages and captured some Kachari Laskars, Kacharis, Moamarias and fugitives whom he brought out after which he halted at his fort at Raha-choki. The detachment which had proceeded through Jagi now returned with four frontier chieftains or Raja-powalis as captives, and they now halted at the stockade at Jagi-choki. Some of the Moamarias and refugees escaped into Khaspur and Jayantiapur. The Barmura Gohain could not also be found. 292.

Punishment of Nagayan rebels.

At that time the Phukan charged seven Saikias of Nagaon and four Raja-powalis of Satrajia and Pachrajia grades with the offence of being in league with the Moamarias, and put them to death by pressing them between wooden cylinders or by hooking them like fish. He also caught some elephants there. In the meantime, Doloi Rupai and Hari Ligira, envoys of Raja Ram Singha of Jayantia, reached the Phukan's camp, who sent them up to the presence of His Majesty, and they in time arrived at the Dichoi encampment. They were kept at Sarbaibandha where they were supplied with provisions. The Duara Barbarua had, before the arrival of these envoys, received Ramchandra at his residence and given him leave after delivering to him the message as stated above. 293.

Barbarua's message to Jayanta.

The Barbarua said,—'Jaydeo, tell Ramchandra that I have allowed him leave to-day to go back to his own country. He will rest at his camp to-day and start for Jayantiapur tomorrow. We have given a written reply to the message sent by the Raja in his letter. The Raja will know our reply by looking at our letter; besides, his Kataki will also tell him orally as follows,—'The Raja always informed us of his continued friendship. The Moamarias had previously set fire to the Singari-ghar and raised the standard of revolt. His Majesty commanded that the Moamarias should be captured and put to death in all places. Out of fear for death the Moamarias escaped into the territories of the Raja after having looted the money and treasures from the villages and stores belonging to His Majesty. At that juncture our men stationed at the chokis or outposts warned the Raja's subjects saying that the Moamarias should not be given shelter as they were hostile to the Swargadeo and that they had removed large quantities of articles by destroying His Majesty's emporiums. Some of the Jayantia Raja's subjects ignored this warning and harboured the rebels coveting the goods in their possession. They further said that they were prepared to face any complication that might arise therefrom. Thus were the fugitives sheltered. Now, many of our men have taken shelter in the Raja's country owing to the disturbed condition of our kingdom and the scarcity of food-grains. The Moamarias, the fugitives and the Kacharis united themselves and raised an insurrection near Raha and destroyed a large number of His Majesty's subjects as well as provisions. The Jayantia Raja might have heard of the consequences which have been experienced by the Kacharis after our victory in that war. They have also been witnessed by those present here. If the Raja be intent upon the progressive advancement of our mutual friendship then he should send back the Moamarias and our other subjects who had taken refuge in his territories. They should be sent back with our envoys Jaydeo and Jay Bara after they are safely escorted to Jagi-choki.'

Having heard this Ramchandra Kataki said,—'We shall tell our Raja all that we have been commanded to say. Things will happen according to the wishes of the Raja. The four frontier Raja-powalis who have been detained at Raha-choki should be released and handed over to us.' After the Jayantia envoy had thus informed the Barbarua, the latter said,—'All right, I permit the four Raja-powalis to accompany the messenger; and we also have deputed our own Katakis Jaydeo and Jay Bara with a letter and presents to the Raja. Ramchandra should proceed to his country and arrange the speedy return of our messengers after they are granted audience with the Raja.' He was then allowed to retire to his camp. 294.

The Barbarua's letter to the Jayantia Raja.

The following is the text of the letter addressed by the Duara Barbarua to the Jayantia Raja Ram Singha and sent in the custody of our messengers Jaydeo and Jay Bara.

Hail! To Ram Singha, whose abode is the intense delight in the unctuous honey flowing gently from the lotus-feet of Sri-Govinda, which are worshipped by the host of the adorables headed by the glorious Indra, one whose body is embraced by the nymph of polity, one who is Lord of Jayantipur, resplendent with glory resembling the foam oozing out of the exude of the tree of Indra, which has been humiliated by the Monarch's distribution of largesses. Hail! Here shines the epistle of the glorious Barbarua, the peak of ministers, and the protector of the bridge of traditions, one whose intelligence is inspired by Vrihaspati himself, one whose heart is fully devoted to the feet of the glorious Visweswar. We who solicit your uninterrupted welfare are in enjoyment of prosperity.

Thus runs our special message :—The letter which you despatched to the Swargadeo with Ramchandra Kataki has reached our hands. Receiving the news through this letter and also through the oral message His Majesty has become greatly pleased. The King granted personal interview to your envoy as a special favour, and the envoy has learnt all that was told in the conversation which followed. You have, besides, written about the safe continuance of our old friendly terms which had recently assumed a different shape. Now measures should be adopted which will lead to the safeguarding of your friendly relations with His Majesty. You have also said that you are extremely delighted to hear of the suppression of our powerful enemies. It is meet and proper for a trusted ally to desire for the welfare of his friend. Your representative has further said that the amicable relations between the two countries should never be lost sight of; this message of yours is certainly true. You have further stated that you have put a stop to the obstructions of the route by some Garos of Narthang which were caused by God and Goddess as it were, and that the settlement of this matter is nearing completion and that you intend to see the termination of these disloyal activities within a short time. You have also assured us of your indissoluble friendship. We are perfectly aware of all these matters. We shall both be immune from future troubles and our friendship will increase henceforward leading to the interchange of embassies between the two territories, if the Raja will kindly complete his task of subduing the unruly elements in his state and remove all obstructions now impeding the route to Raha, by living in the previously trodden path of righteousness. His promise of enduring friendliness will then come to fruition. As to your promise to settle up the matter relating to our fugitive subjects, this is only just that you should do as you have said. But actions have belied this statement. At the time when we were engaged in the suppression of the Mayamarias, many of our subjects took shelter in the frontiers of the Raja's territory. Our men warned the Raja's subjects against harbouring and feeding the refugees pointing out to the possibilities of complications emanating from hostile quarters which may lead to the destruction of the friendly relations existing between the two states. Still then the Raja-powalis of the place, the borderers and the Garos, out of greed for their goods, sheltered the fugitives on their own responsibility, saying,—'Nothing untoward will take place, and if anything unexpected happens, we will shoulder the blame.' Now the Raja-powalis of the frontiers, the Garos and the Kacharis have all united with the Mayamarias and committed misdeeds, from the nature of which we imagine they are themselves incapable of these daring acts. We have rather been surprised as we hold that these ordinary people could not perpetrate these acts if they were not secretly aided by some powerful ally behind the scene. His Majesty will deal with the party at whose instigation these acts have been committed, according to the exigency of the situation. We expect that the Raja will command his subjects in those places where our fugitives and Mayamarias have taken shelter, to release and repatriate the refugees, in recollection of our old friendship. If instead of acting in consonance with our desire he deviates from the sacred obligations of the past and refrains from carrying out his expressions of friendship the consequences will be patent to him in no time. Later on it will be beyond his power to retain our subjects and the Mayamarias, and so we are writing this in time. The Raja has further written that he has received a report alleging the transgression of his territories by His Majesty's subjects and the removal of the Raja's people, adding that this procedure which is in contravention of old terms is certainly objectionable. What the Raja has said is unwarranted. You should know for certain that we are acting up to the terms of our old covenant; if we had violated them, so many of our subjects would not have remained there so long. We have received the Mayamarias and the refugees which have been sent back by your officers under your command. These officers and the Raja-powalis have gone back after making promises to send the remainder as well. They have not as yet fulfilled their promises, nor are we in a position to recover them by violating the territorial limits; and so we expect that you will not pay heed to the machinations of wicked people. Now we hope that you will see to the speedy restoration of the fugitives. If you do not return them listening to the counsel of wicked people, His Majesty is the best judge of the consequences thereof, and not I. I send herewith some tokens testifying to the genuineness of this epistle, and I hope they will reach your hands. You will be apprised of further messages from our envoys Jaydeo Kataki and our Tekela-Bara Sri Jaydas and your Ramchandra Kataki and others. We hope you will delight us by sending us the news of your welfare after you have received our message. *Saka* 1725, dated Magh 28. 295.

Articles presented to the Jayantia Raja.

The following is an inventory of the articles presented,—one kerchief with a tuft of gold in the centre; one pair of cloth with embroidered borders breadthwise and lengthwise spotted with flowers and stripes woven into the texture; one *cheleng* or single sheet with decorated fringes; one waist-cloth made of the same stuff; one sheet of white broadcloth; one frock-coat made of satin; one silk *dhuti*; four knives with gilt handles, six knives with brass hafts, and six plain ones. 296.

Articles presented to the Jayantia envoys.

The following articles were presented to the envoys,—to Ramchandra Kataki, a turban made of yellow-coloured stuff; one cloak of greenish colour; and also two-fold pieces, one piece of *patuka* or head-wear, earrings, and a pair of bangles worked with gold in three places; he was also given as his pocket money thirty rupees and one gold mohar. His two fellow-envoys of the junior rank were presented with cloaks, turbans, two-fold sheets and girdles all made of cotton; they were also given earrings. The same set of articles were also presented to a Garo. The above three were given rupees thirty-six for their joint expenses. The following were the presents given to our Kataki Jaydeo,—one yellow-coloured turban; one cloak used by bridegrooms in Lower Assam; one two-fold piece made of yellow texture; one piece of cotton *patuka*; plain bangles; earrings; and for his expenses twenty-four rupees and one gold mohar. The two junior Katakis were given *dhutis*, *chelengs*, turbans, earrings and rupees twenty-four. The Tekela-Bara was given a reddish turban, one two-fold sheet, one cotton cloak, one *keru* or ear-ornament and twenty rupees for expenses. The Bartekela was given a *dhuti*, a *cheleng*, a turban, earring, and rupees twenty-four for all the Tekelas. The Chokia Bara, or the officer attached to the frontier outpost, was given rupees eight. After offering these presents and money they were despatched to the court of Ram Singha, Raja of Jayantia. 297.

Leave to Jayantia envoys.

The four Raja-powalis of Khala, Gobha, Neli and Sahari, who were detained as captives under watch and guard were taken in their company from Raha. In the meantime the Jayantia Raja had despatched his ambassadors, Doloi Rupai and Hari Ligira, with letter and presents to the charge of Ramchandra Kataki. They were formally received by the Duara Barbarua in his official residence after they had been kept for sometime being supplied with provisions and necessaries. They were now granted leave to depart. They now returned post-haste and went to Jayantia in the company of Ramchandra. 298.

Return of the Bhutia envoys.

After this the Dekaphukan halted at Raha-choki, while the Captain, the Bacha Rajkhowa and others joined the King. The Prime Minister Buragohain Dangaria of the Kuoigayan family sailed up the Bhogdoi in his barge and escorted the Bhutia envoys whom he subsequently granted leave to depart after having delivered to them the following message:—'Well, Jiva, Dindu, Khupa and Burukdewa, I now grant you permission to return to your country. You should stay at your camp this night and start homeward to-morrow. We have given our reply in our epistle to the message communicated by Raja Deva-Dharma in his letter. The Raja will know everything from our letter; and in reply to his verbal message we would like to say that the Nawab of Barpani stationed at Gauhati has been commanded to square up the matter. I have sent our Kataki Anai of the Haramia family to speak to the Barphukan along with you. He will proceed to Gauhati with the foreign envoys. After interviewing the Barphukan they will then start on their journey to their own kingdom.' Having thus bidden them farewell with these words the Premier Buragohain Dangaria retired to his residence. 299.

Presents to the Bhutanese envoys.

The following articles were presented to the messengers,—to Jiva, one yellow turban, one cloak of white *patuka*, one two-fold piece of yellow colour, one girdle, one earring containing two and a half tolas of gold, one pair of bangles with gold work in three places. The same presents were also given to Dindu. The following presents were made to Khupa and Burukdewa each,—one turban of yellow colour, one cotton cloak, one sheet of yellow-coloured two-fold piece, one cotton *patuka*, one earring made of one and a half tola of gold, a pair of silver bangles measuring ten tolas. The same set were given to Burukdewa. For their expenses Jiva was given thirty rupees and two gold mohars; the same to Dindu. Khupa was given rupees twenty and one gold mohar; the same to Burukdewa. Letters and presents to Raja Deva-Dharma were handed over to the messengers. It was in the month of Sravan, *saka* 1724, that the Bhutia envoys departed from the headquarters at Dichoi or Jorhat. The Haramia Kataki Anai was attached to the envoys to escort them as far as Gauhati. 300.

Presents to Raja Deva-Dharma of Bhutan.

The following articles were presented by the Swargadeo to Raja Deva-Dharma:—One lime-pot made of five tolas of gold with jewels inset; one receptacle for tobacco made of four tolas of gold; one peak of three tolas of gold used in *japis*, along with a sunshade; one *Ahom-jara* or casket made of one hundred and six and a half tolas of gold; one silver betel-pot weighing seventy-two and one-fourth tolas; one silver *khadaban* weighing thirty-four tolas; one silver cup pinned on a conical support weighing twenty-seven tolas; one copper *sarai* inlaid with silver; one plain brass dish with support; one knife set with gems; fifteen knives with ivory handles inlaid with brass; fifteen knives with handles of buffalo-horn inlaid with silver; two fans made of peacock feathers; one ivory box; four bags of poppy seeds and four wreaths of ivory. Of cloths,—one turban made of very fine texture; one *cheleng* with embroideries in the four margins; one *satin* cloak made of *laljang* stuff of the colour of the leaves of sugarcane; one cotton girdle with embroidered lines; one *dhuti* of fine silk; one *japi* with gold points and flowered at places. In another set were given one cotton kerchief, one embroidered *patding*; one pair of double-folded cloth with embroideries running through the length and breadth; one piece of *baswal* or loin-cloth; one piece of embroidered *tangali* or girdle; one silk *dhuti*; one *satin* frock-coat of the colour of sugarcane leaves; one flowered cotton napkin. The following articles were presented on behalf of the Buragohain Dangaria,—one turban sixteen cubits long made of *bara-ania* or very fine yarn; one large double sheet embroidered on the corners and lengthwise, lined with stripes woven at regular intervals; one *boswal*; one embroidered *tangali*; one spotted napkin; one silk *dhuti* ; one *satin* frock-coat with sewn flower-work at intervals ; three knives with ivory handles and the blunt portion inlaid with brass ; four knives with plain horn handles ; one *japi* made of palm leaves with a silver point and embroidered trimmings ; two ivory wreaths ; two ivory pots of poppy seeds ; and one ivory box. 301.

Panimuar Khabar or plot.

In the month of Phalgun, 1724 *saka*, one Jabar of Lakshimpur assumed a hostile attitude towards the King, and putting himself at the head of some followers attempted to rebel against the authority of His Majesty. His accomplices in this plot were the following,—the Dola-sharia Barua of the Miri-Sandikai family ; the Chaodang Barua of the house of Lephera belonging to the Chaodang *khel* ; the Tipamia Phukan of the Moran-Barua family ; his brother Oja-ligira or head attendant ; one Bakali who was a Jaradhara Barua of the Jaradhara *khel* ; one Khutikhowa who was a Changmai or cook of the Changmai *khel* ; his son ; one Halowa who was an Oja-ligira or chief servitor attached to the temple of Hara-Gauri ; one Kalita Hazarika ; one Lutum who was a ligira or attendant of the Malakhu-bacha brigade ; the Hazarika of Khaman ; one Lebang who was a Hatimuria ; one Kataki Bara ; one Krishnai who was a Likchan Bara of the Barbarua's *khel*, and five hundred other men. There was one Panimua belonging to the Gajpuria *khel*. Being reckless of the consequences he proceeded to set fire to the residence of the Swargadeo. He was captured and being interrogated he confessed everything. He also delivered a written document containing particulars of the conspiracy. The rebels as mentioned in the document were captured, and were subsequently put to death by being pressed or hooked. Some were let off after their eyes had been extracted, or their noses or ears chopped off, according to the nature of their guilt. Among the rebels there was one Brahman Mahanta or religious head of Katanipar named Sunanda. He was turned out of the state having been placed on the back of an ass accompanied by the downpour of liquor upon his head. In that connection the King commanded the Duara Barbarua to summon the Medhis living in villages as representatives of Mahantas, in order to urge upon them to remain aloof from all disloyal activities. The Barbarua accordingly called in all the Medhis and asked them to surrender all the rebels that would be found among them, saying,—'If any rebel is found amongst you you will have to pay one hundred rupees'. The Medhis also undertook to act accordingly. The names of all the Medhis were taken down. 302.

Envoys of the Kachari Raja.

After this, during the stay of the Dekaphukan at Raha, in the month of Baisakh, 1724 *saka*, Chenakhumdang, the envoy of the Kachari Raja Krishnachandra Narayan, arrived at the camp with letters and presents. The Phukan erected a big house at the stockade at Raha where the Ukil or envoy was formally received in the midst of a large assembly. The Phukan listened to the contents of the letter addressed to him. Then in the month of Jaistha the Phukan sailed upstream and paid his obeisance to the Swargadeo at the Dichoi encampment. He sent to the royal residence the goods seized during the war after having drawn up a descriptive list of the articles. He also took with him the envoy Chenakhumdang. Besides he took the following captives in war,—one person known as Baragi Raja, one Barphetia Khumdang of Kachari, and his four sons who were Laskars. These were kept at Sarbaibandha. The Ukil Chenakhumdang was also given quarters at Sarbaibandha where he was supplied with provisions and necessaries. 303.

Reception of the Kachari envoy.

Then in the year 1725 *saka*, at the court attached to the official residence of the Duara Barbarua, the Kachari ambassador Chenakhumdang was introduced by the Hahchowa Bara in the midst of a gorgeous assemblage of Katakis, Kakatis, Dolois, Deodhais, the Majindar Barua and three companies of sepoys, attended by elephants and horses, where the officers appeared wearing turbans and cloaks. An elevated ground or dais was also constructed for the purpose. The Kataki sat on the ground after having placed his letter on a *sarai*. The Barbarua then directed the Dilihia, Kataki Narayan to put the usual questions,—'Ask the envoy Chenkhumdang whether at the time of his departure from Khaspuri Raja Krishnachandra Narayan was in the enjoyment of peace and prosperity, protecting cows and Brahmans, Baras and Baruks and his subjects living in the plains and hills'. The Katak resumed his seat after making the above queries when the Kachari envoy replied,—'At the time of our departure our Raja was living in health and happiness ruling over his state'. After the above message was conveyed the Barbarua said,—'It is equally our desire that the Raja should live in peace and happiness. But may I ask in which month did they leave their own country, and when again they reached Raha-choki? How long ago have they arrived at this place? Did they encounter any fright or trouble during their journey?'

On hearing this the envoy replied,—'We started from our country in the month of Phalgun, '24 *saka*. In Chaitra of the same year we reached the outpost at Raha. We waited there for some time after which we had interviews with the Deka-phukan; we sailed upstream with the Phukan and arrived here in Jaishtha of the year '25 *saka*. We have not met with any danger in our travel.' After they had thus replied the Majindar Barua read out the letter, hearing which the Barbarua said,—'Well, tell the messenger Chenakhumdang that we have learnt what his chief has communicated in the letter; now let him say what the Raja has communicated to us in his oral message'. Having heard this the envoy replied,—'The oral message is materially the same as that transmitted by our Raja in his epistle. In addition to this the Raja informs that he is not forgetful of the old friendship; he has further made the request that the war-captives, Barphetia Khumdang and the four Laskars, should be released and sent back with us'. The Barbarua replied,—'All right, the reply to the Raja's message will be delivered at the time of the envoy's departure. If he is fortunate he may also have a sight of His Majesty's feet. Let him wait at his camp for the present'. Saying this he caused the presentation of flower and sandal-paste, betel-nut and leaf to the envoy. At that time the Barbarua accused Barphetia Khumdang and the four Laskars, who were captured in war, and said,—'The Raja has intimated that he is continuing the old terms of friendship; then with whose permission have these men taken up arms against us? Why do they not restore our fugitives who have taken shelter in their territory? Let these men answer these questions'. Being thus asked the captives admitted their guilt. They were then sent to their camp in the company of Chenakhumdang. The Barbarua then caused the distribution of betel-nut and leaf to the Katakis and Kakatis in earthen pots. 304.

Kachari Raja's letter to the Barbarua. The following is the text of the letter brought by Chenakhumdang to the name of the Duara Deka-Barbarua,—

'Hail! To Srijut Barbarua, endowed with a liberal disposition, who is like a black-bee having his heart gladdened by drinking at the stream of honey dropping from the two lotus-feet of the glorious daughter of the Lord of Mountains, one who is like a Panchanan among the exterminators of his elephant-like foes, one who with the blessings of the Brahmans has shattered the banner of the enemy. We, through the favour of your friendship and goodwill, which is ever an object of solicitude on our part, are in enjoyment of prosperity and happiness.

Here runs our special message :—We have learnt everything from your epistle despatched with Sarnamati who is an intelligent man. You have made references to Barmuria Gohain and other fugitives in your letter. During the unsettled state of the Swargadeo's country he introduced himself as a descendant of His Majesty's family. We were not aware of the real facts and so we kept him after arranging for his livelihood here. After this, during the visit of Jai Singha Raja of Manipur to your country he was found to be on friendly terms with the Manipuri prince Juvaraj Anupananda. As an offshoot of this relationship he was taken to Manipur as soon as he made a request in a letter. But somehow or other he suddenly entered into a conspiracy against the authority of the Swargadeo, having intrigued with the subjects of this country, the Purania Bhakats or Moamarias and other common people. On receiving intelligence of his intention we deputed Sri Phergakhunglang to arrest and bring him to our presence. Having heard this he insulted our Sri Phergakhunglang and killed Natua Laskar and some other people. But he was ultimately defeated in action; and having had to starve for want of food he left this country and took shelter in a foreign land. *Saka* 1725, Jaistha.' 305.

The Barbarua's oral instructions.

(One folio is missing here, and what follows next is the conclusion of the Duara Barbarua's oral instructions delivered to the Kachari messengers for communication to Raja Krishnachandra Narayan.) '..Our sepoy forces were destroyed, our provisions were looted and squandered and we were put to serious annoyance and discomfiture. Chenakhumdang has an accurate recollection of all that took place. But subsequently, through the power of His Majesty, Barmura was defeated in an engagement and put to flight. The Raja procured the flight of Barmura by employing his men, and then gave him shelter in the Raja's own country. Yet we are wrongly informed that Barmura is at large outside the Raja's territory. We have been subjected to these gross misdeeds and misrepresentations. The remedy is in our hands, but we have refrained from adopting counter-measures in remembrance of our sacred promises. We have also desisted from inflicting punishments on the captive Laskars proportional to their crime. The Raja remembering all that is needful should send out to Raha under the escort of his own men and in the custody of our Katakis,—Barmura, our fugitive subjects, and the Moamarias together with their children and relations. Then the imprisoned Laskars will be released, and our old friendly relations will be maintained. If acting contrary to our expectations the Raja continues indulging in false statements he will know the consequences which the Swargadeo will mete out to him.'

Being thus instructed the messengers were given leave to depart. The Laskars captured during the war were sent with them to Raha-choki, to be detained there under proper watch.

306.

Barbarua's letter to Raja Krishnachandra.

The following is the text of the letter addressed by the Deka-Barbarua of the Duara family to the Kachari Raja Krishnachandra Narayan, conveyed by Dhireswar Kataki of the Bahbaria family.—

Hail! To Sri-Sri Raja Krishnachandra, whose heart like a black-bee has been tinted by the pollens of the feet-like lotus of the Goddess (Sakti), adored by the host of the adorables headed by Brahma, here shines the epistle of the glorious Barbarua, a chief minister, sprung from the Duara family, who is an ocean of all good qualities, and whose chakora-like heart has been enlightened by tasting the beams of the full moons in the nails of the feet of Sri-Gopala.

Here runs our special message :—We have received your message communicated in your letter through Sri-Chenakhumdang. The letter which you have sent to the Swargadeo along with the customary tribute of horses and elephants has been delivered at the feet of His Majesty, and

Sri-Chenakhumdang has also been granted an audience with the King. You will know of the conversation that took place on that occasion from the lips of Sri-Chenakhumdang. You have written in your letter,—'About Barmura Gohain and other fugitives, I first sent the news in a letter through our Kataki Phedela'. You also referred to the matter in your letter conveyed by the Katakis Phelai, Sagarpha and Phedela and in the oral message delivered by them:—'During the disturbed condition of the Swargadeo's country Barmura Gohain visited our place, and not knowing the real facts we kept him here and provided him with means of livelihood. In the meantime, Anupananda son of the Manipuri Raja, being friends with him took him away to Manipur having given him a written assurance. If ever he returns to Khaspur he will be seized and sent back'. This was written in a letter and also transmitted in your oral message. Now you have acted contrary to these assurances and written in your letter,—'Barmura Gohain, after his return from Manipur conspired with the Purania Bhakats of this place and other common men, and raised the standard of revolt against the Swargadeo. Hearing this we despatched Phergakhumdang to seize the person of the Gohain and bring him to us. Coming to know this he insulted Phergakhumdang, and killed many of our men including Natua Laskar. Afterwards, meeting reverses in fight and being pressed for food he deserted this territory'. The above statement which you have made concealing your own guilt is unworthy of you. We know very well how Barmura killed Natua Laskar and others, and how he took to his heels after his defeat in the battle! We forbear to mention in a letter the wrong which you have perpetrated against the Swargadeo, when being oblivious of your former promises, and severing the relations of a father and a son and the sacred assurances made to the Swargadeo, you organised a confederacy of Barmura who is the son of a maid-servant, with the Moamarias, the fugitives and the Kacharis, and instigated them to wage war against our forces. Yet, remaining in our old relations of a father and a son as bound by ancient promises we do not intend to avenge the wrong done to us. If you are intent upon respecting the old and sacred terms, you should act in a manner which will lead to the repatriation, at an early date, of Barmura, the refugees and the Moamarias with their wives and children. If you do not pay any heed to these demands, what the gods will direct will certainly take place and you will understand it. 'You will know the real situation if you properly enquire in consultation with Srijut Barasaheb of Calicata. The wheel of fate is really very powerful, and its movement can never be checked by anybody'. With reference to what you have said as reproduced above every corporeal being is subject to fate. What is decreed by fate is the only thing that happens; and man has no hand in its operation. Still the man walking in the path of righteousness is never deserted by virtue. If you admit your guilt the father-and-son relationship which was established by the Swargadeo in that sacred place is no longer maintained. 'So the Swargadeo is in the position of our father. If the son commits some offence against his father, it is desirable for the father to forgive the transgression'. You have written like this, and we on our part have not taken your guilt seriously into our heart. If we had done so, vengeance would have been inevitably accorded by His Majesty. So it is evident that we have continued in the terms of the sacred promises of old and in the old relationship of a father and a son and have never done anything in contravention of the laws of righteousness. If you desert the sacred ordinance of virtue, virtue will as well cease to protect you. So you should act in a manner that will lead to the preservation and continuance of our old friendship. *Saka*, Chaitra. 307.

Presents to the envoys deputed to the Kachari court.

The following articles were presented,—two pairs of silk *dhutis*, two knives with gilt handles and two with silver hafts. The letter placed in their hands by the Kuoigayan Mahamantri Buragohain Dangaria was the same as the one reproduced above. The articles presented were,—one turban of fine linen, one pair of double sheets with embroideries on all four borders and stripes and flowers, one cloak of malmal, one embroidered waistband and one silk *dhuti*. The following amounts were also paid to them in cash for their expenses,—to Chenakhumdang, one gold mohar, and thirty-two rupees; to the two Katakis of the middle rank, thirty-two rupees; forty rupees were given in all to the Sarkar, the hostler, the elephant-driver and to the letter-carrier, at the rate of ten rupees each; while a sum of rupees fifty-two was given to the thirteen attendants, at the rate of rupees four per head. Our chief Kataki Dhireswar was given one gold mohar and twenty-eight rupees; the two Majalia Katakis were given twelve rupees each, making altogether a sum of rupees twenty-four; the Hahchowa Bara was given sixteen rupees; the four Tekelas were given a sum of rupees sixteen in all, at the rate of rupees four per head; the Chokial Bara was given six rupees, and the Bartekela seven rupees. Other presents were also given:—To Chenakhum, one pair of earrings made of two tolas of gold, one pair of silver bangles of twelve tolas inlaid with gold, one double embroidered piece, one turban made of fine linen, one head-wear, one cloak of *atlas* or green texture, one waist-band or girdle; to the two Majalia Katakis, two pairs of earrings each made of two tolas of gold, two big turbans, two pieces of black wrappers, two cloaks made of cotton manufactured at Marangi. The Sarkar, the elephant-driver, the hostler and the letter-carrier were given four pairs of earrings each made of three-fourth tola of gold, four turbans, four *tengchols*, four cloaks, and four girdles. The thirteen carriers were given thirteen turbans and thirteen *chelengs*; the Hahchowa Tekela-Bara was given a pair of gold earrings, one turban, one cloak, one *patuka*, one *barkapor* with black borders; the four Tekelas were given four turbans, and four *chelengs*; the Chokial Bara was given one black *barkapor*, one turban, another spotted turban; our Barkataki Dhireswar was given one pair of earring made of one and one-fourth tola of gold; one pair of bangles made of twelve tolas of silver; one embroidered doubled piece; one coloured turban, one cloak used by Dhekeri bridegrooms and one cotton *patuka*. The Majalia Katakis were given two yellow-coloured plain pieces, two coloured turbans, two *bhunis* or *dhutis*. The Bartekela was given a pair of earring made of three-fourth tola of gold, one piece of black *barkapor*, one spotted piece and one coloured turban. 308.

Kanak Sing punished.

At that time the Duara Barbarua tried Kanak Sing in open court and found him guilty of ravaging villages with rebellious intentions. He also admitted his guilt. Then Kanak Sing was blown off by a cannon-shot. His two followers who were Bangals were settled at Amguri-khat, their names being enlisted in regular records. 309.

Kamaleswar Singha at Auniati.

After this, on Thursday the sixteenth of Chaitra, 1726 *saka*, His Majesty proceeded to Auniati to bow down before the image of Govinda-Thakur, being accompanied by the Kuoigayan Mahamantri Buragohain Dangaria, the Barpatra Dangaria, the Duara Barbarua, as well as other Phukans and Rajkhowas. The Bargohain could not join the royal party being laid up with loss of eyesight. The Gosain made the following gifts to the Swargadeo,—two sets of copper and brass vessels, and three sets of dress, twelve rupees and two gold mohars, all placed in a *sarai*. The King returned these articles to the Gosain. His Majesty presented two gold mohars and thirty rupees; the Buragohain Dangaria gave twelve rupees, the Barpatra Dangaria ten rupees, and the Barbarua eight rupees, according to their respective rank and distinction. The Gosain entertained his visitors with refreshments; and supplied food articles for His Majesty's meals. 310.

The King's reception by the Duara Barbarua.

The King retired to his camp in the evening. On the twenty-fourth of Chaitra the King paid a visit to Dakshinpat. On that day the Duara Barbarua received the King in the vicinity of Darika-duar, and offered him for ride an elephant, named Tilak, duly decorated and caparisoned. The elephant was attired with the following ornaments,—six pairs of silver bangles inlaid with gold were put on the tusks; eighty-nine silver knives were inserted on the borders of a velvet cushion; sixty-six mirrors; three tufts of white chowries with silver handles; one silver girdle; one pair of silver bridles; one silver goad with tufts of velvet at four places; one pair of *nupurs* or tinkling bells made of bell-metal; two *chal-ghuguras* or bells; one pair of *talacha* or sheet-cover, one of them being an embroidered cushion with *kingkhap* background. On that occasion the King presented to the Barbarua gifts worthy of his rank and position. 311.

The King at Dakshinpat.

The Swargadeo then crossed the Dihing and paid his adoration to the image of Jadavrai. The Gosain presented to the King two sets of copper and brass utensils; and he also gave him three sets of cloth, twelve rupees and two gold mohars, all placed in a *sarai*. The King returned these gifts, and presented to the Gosain two gold mohars and sixty rupees; the Buragohain gave twelve rupees; the Barpatra Dangaria ten rupees; the Barbarua eight rupees; thus all according to their rank and position. The Swargadeo retraced his steps and reached Khaji-khowa. Provisions and foodstuffs were all supplied by the Gosain, and the followers of the Swargadeo were given a sumptuous refreshment. The arrangements for food and amusements at Dakshinpat were more splendid than at Auniati. The King retired to his camp in the evening. 312.

The Dekaphukan's victory over the Morans.

In the month of Magh of the same '26 *saka*, the Dekaphukan of the Buragohain family was despatched to suppress the Moamaria disturbances in Upper Assam. He was attended by the Bhiturual Phukan, the Captain Gohain, the Bacha Rajkhowa, Hao-sagar Bara of Mechaghar, five companies of sepoys, consisting of men recruited from the three Dayangias and the three Abhaypurias; the soldiery allotted to the two Phukans consisted of one regiment of Chutia-kanris, one regiment of Kamalabarias, one regiment of Moran-kanris, one regiment of Chekeratalias, one regiment of Bhitarual or household retainers, one regiment of Khargharias. The Phukan departed having paid his homage to the King, crossed the Dibru, pursued and fell upon the Morans at Bhutiating. The Morans took to their heels and concealed themselves at Holongaguri. The rains then set in in a heavy form; and nearly one thousand Morans died of fever, dysentery and scarcity of food. The Morans having starved for want of food came and offered their submission. The Phukan crossed the Dibru with these Morans and settled them at Ghilamara, where he posted one company of sepoys to watch the captives. In the month of Bhadra, *saka* 1727, the Phukan came and saluted His Majesty. An inventory was made of the articles seized, and then they were made over to the royal household. 313.

Return of the envoys to Jayantia.

On the twenty-ninth of Aswin, 1727 *saka*, our Bahbaria Kataki Jaydeo and Jay Bara who were deputed to Jayantia, returned. They also brought with them the Jayantia Katakis Ramchandra and Sarkar Hari. Ramchandra Kataki was encamped at Sarbaibandha where he was supplied with provisions and necessaries. The Jayantia Raja presented the following articles to Jaydeo Kataki,—

one pair of gold bangles, two pairs of earrings. The two Majalia Katakis were each given a pair of silver bangles and gold pendants. Jay Bara was given a pair of gold earrings and a pair of silver bangles. The Kataki was also given a cloak and a turban, one doubled piece, and one waist-band; the Majalia Kataki was presented with a *dhuti*, one cotton wrapper and a turban; the Bara was given a cloak, a *cheleng* or single sheet and a turban. The Bartekela, the Chokial Bara and the minor Tekelas were also presented proportionate to their rank and dignity. The Kataki was also given one gold mohar and 40 rupees. The two Majalia Katakis were given 40 rupees, and the Bara 30 rupees. The Bartekela, the Chokial Bara and the ordinary Tekelas received cash presents proportionately. 314.

The King rides on a Chandra-chilimi horse.

In the same '27 *saka*, on Monday the 22nd of Aswin, on the occasion of Bijaya-Dasami, the Duara Barbarua received His Majesty at the extremity of the Dolasharia-chora with a horse of the species Chandra-chilimi, i.e., brown ponies, which was gaily decorated and harnessed. The King riding on that horse proceeded from there to the Barchora or royal court. 315.

Punishment of the Darangi chiefs.

In the selfsame *saka* '27, on Thursday, the 2nd of Kartik, the Majindar Barua told the Duara Barbarua at the instance of the King at the *Biali-mel* or evening conference,—'His Majesty has deposed Krishnanarayan the Bar-raja of Darang and Haynarayan the Saru-raja, after having found them guilty. Their sedans and maces are to be taken away from them and deposited at Hatisal'. Then in the presence of the Barbarua, Ramdeo Kataki of the Bahbaria family was despatched with an order to carry out the above instructions. The Kataki was accompanied by Mitha, a Kukura-chowa Bara, and Haripada, a Tekela-Bara. The Kataki proceeded to the encampment of the two Rajas at the spot where the Kalioni branches off. The chiefs were brought together and made to sit on a mat. The Kataki then accused them of grave charges and deposed them with the following words,—'Thus stands the command of His Majesty, according to which we have been instructed by the Barbarua to accuse the two Rajas of Darang as follows,—In days gone by the Darangi Raja Balinarayan sought refuge with the Swargadeo who placed the fugitive as head of the province of Darang. His descendants have been enjoying the lordship of Darang uptill now. Taking advantage of the disruption of our country Hangsanarayan proceeded to Gauhati; and in spite of the presence of his own uncle he attempted to assume hostilities. The Swargadeo pardoned him and placed his son on the throne. The son also in his turn joined the rebel forces of the Baragi and roamed about with hostile intentions. His services were, however, procured for the operations against the Kacharis; but he refrained from taking any part; on the other hand he entered into a league with Barmura and returned to his own territory. For these reasons the King has deposed the two Rajas'. Having deposed them with these words he took from them one hundred and twenty rupees as perquisite. Then the Kukura-chowa Bara and the Tekela-Bara took from the Rajas the *dolas* or sedans, the *arwans* or maces, their princely ornaments as well as their retinues, which were all kept at Hatisal in front of the Na-daur. After this, on Sunday the 5th of Kartik, according to royal command issued at the time of supper, the Majindar Barua, the Tamuli Phukan, the Khargharia Phukan and the Naosalia Phukan came out and despatched a messenger to fetch the Darangi prince Samudranarayan from Sarbaibandha. They then appointed Samudranarayan as the Raja of Darang on both sides of the portico of the Barchora, somewhat towards the west. 316.

Counsel to the Darangi Raja.

Having been appointed Raja, Samudranarayan sat on a piece of cloth. The Majindar and the Phukans took their seats in due order and precedence, while the Majindar communicated the following advice to the newly appointed chief,—'I have been commanded by His Majesty to tell the Raja that the position which has now been conferred upon the chief as a token of royal favour is not due to any services rendered in recent times. During the time of the Swargadeo's predecessors the ancestors of the Raja had offered their homages to our kings in an earnest fashion. The present honour has been bestowed on the chief looking upon him as a descendant of the long line of loyal adherents of the Swargadeo. If the chief continues loyal to the throne the rank and honour now conferred upon him will increase during the regime of his descendants. The chief has witnessed and has also heard of the consequences following upon dereliction of duties. The King also desires that the chief will look into the weal and woe of His Majesty's subjects residing in the Raja's territories instead of indulging in personal gratification. The Swargadeo has also received reports of people who have deserted their original homes during the disturbances in the country, and of the Bhutias transgressing our boundaries and occupation of a portion of our territories; His Majesty desires that the chief on his return to his own country will restore them all to their former places. If he fails in any attempt he will devise means to carry out the royal mandate in consultation and communication with the Barphukan and the Barbarua. 317.

The Darangi Raja's reply.

Having heard this the Raja replied,—'Nothing untoward will happen to me if I can with a pure heart carry out the instructions of His Majesty which have accompanied the favour now conferred upon me. Still we are in the position of matter whereas the Swargadeo is spirit, and we should act as guided by him. At the same time I would say that we shall be useful only if we are properly trained and instructed and our manifold offences pardoned'. Having thus offered his submission he took his seat on the embroidered carpet, a few steps further from the post which is occupied by the Bacha Rajkhowa. Then a sum of rupees three hundred was placed in the hands of the Barbarua for distribution as largesses to the Katakis and others in the assembly. The Raja then retired to his camp being conducted to the spot on a pony belonging to the royal stable. 318.

Reception of the Munkang envoy.

On Tuesday, the fourteenth of Kartik, '27 *saka*, there was an assembly at a big pavilion erected near the Ranghar. A dais was constructed there of earth which was covered by a mat, over which was placed a piece of *banat* or velvet. On the cloth was placed a *Narapira* or wooden seat which was draped by an embroidered cushion with pillows; the legs were decorated with pieces of yellow-coloured mica. On the dais overhang two layers of white canopy. Then in the evening the Katakis, the Kakatis, the Dolois, the Deodhais, the Bailungs, the Chamuas, the Baruas, the Phukans, the Baras, the Buruks, the Kanris, the Baruatis or shieldsman and the five companies of sepoys, with elephants, horses and cannon, took their seats in order being attired in their turbans and cloaks.

Just then the Ahom ambassador presented Hing-mungkang, Hing-lipmungha and Hing-ha, the three envoys who brought letters and presents from the Nati-Raja of Munkang and his consort. They lowered the letters from their necks and after having placed them on the *sarai* took their seats on leaves of plantain at the extremity of the court. The Mahamantri Buragohain Dangaria of the Kuoigayan family directed the Ahom Kataki to put the usual questions in the diplomatic style, whereupon the Kataki resumed his seat and asked,—'Well, Hing-mungkang, Hing-lipmungha and Hing-ha, the Mahamantri Buragohain Dangaria desires me to ask you if at the time of your departure, the Nati-Raja of Munkang with his consort, had been enjoying peace and happiness with his ministers and counsellors, having duly administered his territories and subjects'. Having heard this they said,—'Yes, he was in peace and plenty. We are not aware if anything has transpired in the meantime'. Thus informed the Dangaria said,—'It is also our desire that the Raja should live in prosperity and happiness. But, may I know when the envoys started from their country, and when they reached Sadiya, how long ago they reached this place and if they encountered any fright or danger in their journey?' Having heard this they said,—'We left our country in the Phalgun of '26, and reached Sadiya in the Baisakh of *saka* '27. From there we came to this place in the company of the Ahom Kataki in the month of Ashar. Through the mercy of God we did not face any danger on our way'. 319.

Munkang affairs.

The Chiring Phukan then read the letter whereupon the Dangaria said,—'We have understood what the Raja has communicated in his letter; now, tell us what he has transmitted orally'. Having heard this they said,—'The purport of our message is what the Raja has recorded in the letter. Still we have been instructed to say,—'The King of Burma has detained me in his territories after having defeated me in battle. It is also surmised that the Raja has fled from that kingdom and he is now living as a fugitive in China. It is also reported that a chief minister of Munglungia is governing the country and people as lord having indented a large number of up-country sepoys. Now, in accordance with our old relationship we pray you should place with us some soldiers and regain for us the country of Munkang'. The Buragohain then said,—'The envoys will receive a reply to their chief's message at the time of their departure. If they are fortunate they may also have an opportunity of paying their respects to His Majesty. Let them go and stay at their camp for the present'. They were then granted leave after being presented with flowers and sandal-paste. The Dangaria too retired to his residence in the stockade.

On the twenty-sixth of Kartik, the Barpatra Dangaria similarly received the Munkang envoys in the audience-hall of his residence. The Dangaria gave the Katakis two loads of rice, four hens, one pig and some quantity of salt and oil. The Bargohain Dangaria of the Madurial family received the Munkang envoys at the inner court of his residence and gave them two loads of rice, four hens, one pig and some quantity of salt and oil. As the Bargohain Dangaria could not see properly with his eyes, he had to receive the envoys in his inner apartments. 320.

Majiu Aideo's marriage.

On Tuesday, the nineteenth of Aghon of the same *saka*, the younger sister of the Swargadeo was married to the second son of the Kuoigayan Buragohain Dangaria according to the *Chaklang* rites. In that marriage the purificatory water was raised for nine consecutive days, and singers and musicians were brought from all monasteries and villages. On the day of handing over the bride to her husband the Dangarias, the Barbarua and the Phukans sat in the audience-chamber. The Buragohain Dangaria made presents to the Chamuas, Baruas and Phukans, and to selected Katakis, Kakatis and tenants. 321.

The King hunts buffaloes.

On the fourth day of Pous of the same *saka* the King proceeded to the mouth of the Dilsiri to hunt buffaloes. The elephants flung out a buffalo from the stockade. The buffalo in its turn made good his escape after having killed three men. Having hunted buffaloes the King retired to his camp in the evening. 322.

The King receives the Munkang envoys.

After this in the evening of Friday, the fourteenth of Pous, the King received the Katakis of Munkang at Ranghar. Two temporary sheds were erected near Ranghar, which were covered with cloth. The two Dangarias sat on one platform, while on the other were seated the Barbarua, the Phukans, the Rajkhowas, the Katakis, the Kakatis, the Dolois, the Deodhais and the Bailungs. The Munkangia Katakis were allowed to sit in a pavilion on the lawn. The Chiring Phukan presented the Katakis to the assembly and gave them a silver *sarai* for placing their letter which they had brought in a casket tied down to their neck.

They then placed the letter on the *sarai*, and after having bowed down seven times they took their seat in their allotted shed. The King directed the Chiring Phukan to put the usual questions in the diplomatic style. The Phukan enquired of them of the welfare of their Raja and communicated the same to His Majesty. The Chiring Phukan read aloud the letter to the King, whereupon the Swargadeo said,—'Tell them that the reply to the Raja's message will be delivered to them at the time of their departure. For the present they should wait at their camp'. After this flowers and sandal-paste were given to the envoys, who after sitting in the assembly for some time retired to their camp. The King also returned to his palace. On the occasion of the reception of the envoys the Ranghar was draped with cloth on the fringes of which were suspended silver hangings. A piece of *banat* or velvet was spread over the platform. The King, attired in his turban and cloak, had sat on the platform under an overhanging canopy. The others in the assembly had also worn their turbans and cloaks. The gathering was a gorgeous and magnificent one. 323.

Juggleries and entertainments.

A variety of amusements were arranged for the entertainment of the Munkangia Katakis,—scintillators and wheels of light were displayed, and guns were fired from under water, as well as other fireworks. Sheep came out and knocked their heads against each other. There was also the blossoming of *Aparajita* flowers. They also arranged to have a tiger killed by an elephant. No sooner did the elephant place his head in the proper position the tiger as well as the elephant broke open the net and escaped. The tiger mauled a sepoy, whereupon the other sepoys assembled together, and pierced and hacked the tiger to death with their bayonets and swords. A Neog of the Dayangia clan fell down while bringing a torch for burning the whiskers of the tiger and died. 324.

Presents from Munkang.

The following articles were brought by the Munkang Katakis as presents for the Swargadeo,—two pairs of bangles made of seventy-nine tolas of gold with stones inset; ten sheets of *jara-pata* made of sixteen tolas of gold; two pairs of embroidered footwear made of black velvet which had twelve stones inset; one piece of silk cloth eighteen cubits long, with a mixture of three colours, green, white and crimson, with embroideries sewn lengthwise, but plain at the ends; one piece of bi-coloured silk cloth coloured red and white, seventeen cubits long with embroideries sewn lengthwise; one piece coloured red, white and green, six cubits long, with embroideries inserted lengthwise; another piece, six cubits long, coloured red, white and green, with black patches inserted here and there; one black makhmal piece thirteen cubits long; another piece eleven cubits in length; one cotton sheet thirty cubits long; another piece twenty-seven cubits in length; four cups made of glass; two pairs of *jangphai* earrings; one piece of *dukharia*; another broken at the end; two musks; one piece of vermillion; eight packets of needles in two hollows of *kāka* bamboos; one red chowri; one white chowri; two big dishes inlaid with gold; one earthen pot or *bhabuki* containing a peculiar glue or paste known as *Ahom-etha*, and some more quantity in the hollow of a bamboo; two hundred sheets of paper; two cane chests coated with Ahom glue containing the cloths brought by the envoys; two horses with their saddles and bridles. 325.

The King's hunting excursions.

After this the men of Bacha were engaged in opposing the advance of a powerful elephant in Panibebejia. The King proceeded to witness it on Tuesday, the twenty-fifth of Pous, being accompanied by the Buragohain Dangaria, the Barpatra Dangaria, the Duara Barbarua, the Marangi-khowa, the Bhitarual Phukan and the Dihingia Phukan. Being blind the Bargohain Dangaria remained at his own residence. The Swargadeo returned to his camp in the evening. On the twenty-seventh of Pous, the King went to Khutiapota to hunt buffaloes. The Moamarias captured twelve young buffaloes alive. The King returned to his residence at eve. 326.

Death of the Darangi Raja.

On Tuesday, the first of Phalgun of the same *saka*, the deposed chief Krishnanarayan Bar-raja of Darang breathed his last at his camp situated at the mouth of the Kalioni. The remains of the Raja were cremated on the bank of the river Brahmaputra. 327.

Royal camp at Bacha.

In the same year, on the twenty-eighth day of Magh, the Swargadeo paid a visit to the Amgurikhat, where he witnessed the fighting of buffaloes and the flight of hawks; after this he retired to his camp. On Saturday, the twentieth of Phalgun of the same *saka*, the King went to the small camp at Jabar in Bacha, where he used to live during his princehood. He had erected a residence there after he assumed sovereignty. He now went to see that place. On that occasion the King gave a feast to the Dangarias, the Baruas and Phukans, and returned to his camp in the evening. He had also visited that place once before in 1723 *saka*. 328.

Rukmini-haran Bhawana.

After this on the eighteenth Phalgun, 1727 *saka*, the Baregharia Mahanta, at the instance of the King, enacted the play *Rukmini-haran* on the model of the *Ankia* drama, lasting for four days, near the Dolasharia-chora. The two brothers of the Mahanta sat on that occasion on a plantain leaf in the eastern corner. They displayed one cobra, one bear, and a pair of elephants. The other parts were also properly acted. The Swargadeo presented forty rupees, the Buragohain Dangaria thirty rupees, the Barbarua eight rupees, and the Phukans and the Rajkhowas also gave according to their rank and position. The Mahanta then stood up and offered blessings to the Swargadeo. The Buragohain Dangaria and the Barbarua were also blessed. 329.

Presents to Samudranarayan.

After twenty-eight days had elapsed of the year '27 *saka*, the Dilihial Kataki named Narayan, and the Barbarua's Bara named Agni, were deputed at the command of the King, and offered the following presents to the Darangi Raja at his camp at Sarbaibandha,—one pair of earrings made of two-and-a-half tolas of gold; one pair of bangles of twelve tolas; a lime-pot of three tolas; one casket for tooth-pickers made of two tolas; one betel-nut of two tolas; one napkin; one scarlet-coloured turban and cloak; one waist-band; one piece of golden lace; one large sheet of flowered cloth. The Raja presented to the Kataki carrying the presents, ten rupees, and two blankets. The Majalia Kataki was given five rupees and two blankets; and the Bara, five rupees and two blankets. As commanded by the King, Narayan Kataki invited the Raja to pay his respects to His Majesty on the following day. 330.

Fresh counsel to Darangi Raja.

In the early morning of the next day, Samudranarayan, the Raja of Darang, was fetched by Narayan Kataki to the presence of the King at the audience-hall attached to the temple where Phalgutsav was celebrated. After having knelt down to His Majesty, the Raja took his seat with all the dignity of a Dangaria, a little further down the place reserved for the Dangarias below the central rafter of the roof. Narayan Kataki placed some flowers and sandal-paste on a dish and gave them to the Raja. The Jalbhari Phukan took in his lap the flower offerings of the Swargadeo and distributed them to the Buragohain Dangaria, the Barpatra Dangaria, the Barbarua, the Darangi Raja and the Phukans in the order of precedence. The Duara Barbarua then introduced the Raja saying,—'Samudranarayan, the Raja of Darang, has presented himself at the feet of the King and knelt down before His Majesty'. The articles presented were,—one *sarai* containing velvet pieces; two plain sheets of cloth; one wagtail with the handle inlaid with gold and silver; one *langar* or anchor; twenty blankets; twenty chamars or chowries of *latha* deer. The Raja knelt down before His Majesty seven times, each time standing up from his seat; after this he resumed his seat. As commanded by the King the Majindar addressed the Raja in the diplomatic style,—'His Majesty has permitted the Darangi Raja to return to his own territories. I have been further instructed by the King to tell him that all necessary advice had been imparted to the Raja on the day of appointment. If the Raja remembers the counsel and acts accordingly his honour and prestige will be ever on the increase during the days of his sons and grandsons. The Raja has witnessed with his own eyes the consequences meted out to those who violate the commands of His Majesty. The Swargadeo has further desired me to say that he has received reports of his subjects of Darang migrating to other territories, and of the Bhutias' occupation of some portion of His Majesty's dominions by transgressing the old boundaries. The Buragohain Dangaria and the Barbarua deputed men to trace the fugitives and having procured their return settled them in Darang. It is desired that the Raja should make a search for them and restore them to their former places, and push back the Bhutias to their original limits. If the Raja fails in any attempt he will try to effect his object in consultation with the Phukan who is the governor of the place, the Rajmantri Buragohain Dangaria and the Barbarua.'

Having heard this the Raja submitted,—'What will not be gained by me if I succeed in carrying out the royal command communicated to me by the Majindar? Still, what can be expected to come out of me alone? I shall be useful only if the Swargadeo trains me up on proper lines.' The above prayer of the Raja was communicated to the Swargadeo by the Majindar.

Similar counsel was imparted to the Raja by the Mahamantri Buragohain Dangaria and the Barbarua. The Kataki Narayan handed over betel-nut and leaf to the Raja in a *bata*. The Raja bowed to the King and retired to his camp. 331.

Akruragaman Bhawana.

After this, on the third day of Chaitra of the same year, the Namatia Mahanta of Dihing, arranged the enactment of the play *Akruragaman* lasting for three days under the command of the King. The performance took place near the Dolasharia-chora. The Mahanta sat on a plantain leaf. There was no *Bahua* or comic character, and the parts were not well executed. The Swargadeo gave forty rupees, the Buragohain Dangaria thirty rupees, the Barbarua ten rupees, and the rest gave ten or eight rupees according to their rank and position. 332.

Jayantia Kataki at the Swargadeo's court.

In the evening of Monday, the fourteenth of Phalgun of the year '27 *saka*, the Deka-Barbarua of the Duara family sat in the parlour of his town residence attired in a cloak and turban. There was a gorgeous assemblage of persons consisting of the Katakis, the Kakatis, the Dolois, the Deodhais, the court Pandits, the Baragis, the Baras, the Buruks, elephants and horses as well as three companies of sepoys. Jay Bara of Namdang introduced Ramchandra Kataki and Hari Sarkar who came with messages and presents from the Jayantia Raja Ram Singha. Ramchandra Kataki took his seat after having placed the letter on a *sarai*. The Barbarua then directed Biswambhar Kataki of the Bahbaria family to make the usual enquiries in the diplomatic language,—'Well, Biswambhar Kataki, ask Ramchandra if at the time of his departure Raja Ram Singha was enjoying peace and happiness by offering protection to cows and Brahmans, the Baras and the Baruks, as well as his subjects in the plains and the hills'. The Kataki returned to his seat and put the questions, to which they replied,—'When we came, the Raja was in the enjoyment of health and peace'. Having received this reply the Barbarua said, —'It is also our desire that their lord should be enjoying health and happiness. But may I know when they left their country, when they reached the outpost at Jagi, when they reached this place, and whether they encountered any danger or fright in their journey?' Being thus interrogated by the Kataki they said,—'In the month of Baisakh, '26 *saka*, we left Jayantipur, and reached

Jagi-choki in Sravan of the same year. We proceeded up from there in Bhadra and reached this place on the twenty-eighth of Aswin. Owing to the mercy of Jayanti Thakurani we did not meet any fright or danger on our way'.

The Kataki reported the conversation to the Barbaura who said,—'Well Kataki, please tell them that we shall understand what their Raja has intimated in his letter; now let them say what the Raja has commanded them to tell orally'. The Kataki asked them accordingly and they said,—'The drift of the Raja's message is the same as that communicated in his letter. Yet the Raja's verbal message runs to the effect that he is acting according to the old terms and promises of friendship'. This was reported to the Barbarua who said,—'Well Kataki, tell them, they have said that their Raja is acting in accordance with the old terms of friendship; but how shall we know it? Specially, this very Ramchandra Kataki assured us in his last visit that acting up to the advice of his chief he would expatriate the Moamarias and the fugitives on his way back, as well our subjects taking shelter in Jayantipur, in the custody of the Kataki Bara. We despatched with him Jaydeo Kataki and Jay Bara with letters and presents. He also took away on his own responsibility the chieftains who were detained as captives here. But subsequent acts belied all expectations. Besides, from the way in which the Raja greeted our Kataki Bara and others by causing them to sit in the reception ceremony in a manner unapproved by former precedents, has he been able to make us realise by his action that he still remembers the old friendship? From this we have realised that in the court of the Raja there is no person who has witnessed old forms and understands old traditions'. Biswambhar Kataki asked the Jayantia envoys about this charge and they said,—'Yes, we are to blame for not being able to act up to the promises we made before'. The Kataki reported this to the Barbarua who asked the Majindar to read the letter. The bag containing the letter was taken off and the superscription examined, when it transpired that the letter was addressed to the Kuoigayan Mahamantri Dangaria by the general of the Jayantia Raja. 333.

Offence of the Jayantia Kataki.

The Majindar instead of reading the letter reported the matter to the Barbarua who asked a messenger to inform Ramchandra Kataki,—'This letter is evidently addressed to the Mahamantri

Buragohain Dangaria. Why has he brought this letter in such an irregular way?' Ramchandra then said,—'No, the letter is addressed to the Barbarua', whereon the Barbarua showed the address to the Kataki. Having seen this, Ramchandra Kataki admitted the irregularity, saying,—'Yes, this letter was meant for the Mahamantri Buragohain Dangaria; through mistake we delivered it here. The Barbarua's letter is in our camp, and we shall send it to-morrow with Jaydeo Kataki. Please return the present letter'. The letter was not returned, and the Barbarua said,—'Well, Biswambhar Kataki, you should arraign Ramchandra Kataki and tell him.—'His Raja Ram Singha following the old terms of friendship desires the progressive growth of fresh relations of mutual goodwill. How can friendship be on the increase in the company of such men? Oh, the Raja seeks the friendship of sovereigns by associating with men who do not know where and to whom they are to deliver one's letters. Now I understand, it is on account of these associates of the Raja that our Kataki Bara came back without being accorded the customary reception and honour at his court'. Being thus accused Ramchandra said,—'We are Brahmans, we do not know the friendship and procedures of Rajas and chiefs. The Katakis here are properly trained and tutored from ancient times, but we are not so trained. So we are to blame'. Thus saying they apportioned the blame to themselves.

This was reported to the Barbarua who said,—'Tell Kataki Ramchandra that in view of the unapproved manner in which he has acted he deserves severe punishment. As he is a Brahman we have let him off with mere abuses which are surely his due. So for the present he should await at his camp'. He was then offered flowers and sandal-paste and allowed to go. Biswambhar Kataki having accused Ramchandra as above sent him to the camp. Ramchandra said,—'Please return this letter to-morrow; the letter addressed to the Barbarua is in our hands and we shall deliver it to-morrow'. They then retired to their camp. The Barbarua returned the letter on the following day, and brought from the camp the letter addressed to himself by deputing Jaydeo Kataki. The letter was examined, but it was also found defective, and the matter was reported to His Majesty. The Swargadeo ordered Ramchandra Kataki to be sent back and turned out of the frontier outpost with his letters and presents. As commanded by the King, Biswambhar Kataki took him out of his camp, and made him over to Jay Bara for expelling him beyond the choki or Jagi outpost. The Bara led him off. On the way he prayed for permission to remain at the choki instead of being sent back to his own country; he further gave assurance that he would despatch men to the Raja and submit letters and articles in the customary fashion. To this prayer the King replied,—'All right, as they have implored, let a Bara belonging to the Barbarua's service escort him to the choki and keep him there'. The Barbarua then deputed Jay Bara as escort who kept the Jayantia embassy at Jagi-choki under proper guard. 334.

Kusai, the hero.

The Parvatia Aikuanrideo, consort of King Gaurinath Singha, had adopted Keteki as her *ligiri* or handmaiden. She was a daughter of Ramnath who was a *doloi* or clan-chief in the territories of the Panchrajias. He was a Chutia by caste. A son was begotten of her through Bahjengani, the Dulia-Barua of the Khangia clan. The ex-queen treated this boy with affection as if he was her own son. During the reign of Kamaleswar Singha, the ex-queen attached the boy to the Lahan *khel* after having informed the Swargadeo of her desire. The boy was called 'Birabar Kusai', or Kusai the great hero. This order was communicated to the Duara Barua by the Majindar Barua in court. 335.

The officials of Kamaleswar Singha's reign.

The persons named below were the officers and ministers of the reign of Swargadeo Kamaleswar Singha :—

Buragohain Dangaria of the Kuoigayan family, Prime Minister;

Dola-sharia Barua, brother of the above;

Marangi-khowa, nephew of the Premier;

Rajneog Phukan, son of the Premier's uncle;

Pani-phukan, distantly related to the Premier as grandfather;

Bacha Rajkhowa;

Nam-Dayangia Rajkhowa;

Captain Gohain of the Mou-gohain family;

Bhitarual Phukan of the Dilihial family;

Chetia-patar Barua of the Jabakial family;

Gharphalia Barua;

Nyaya-sodha Phukan of Rangpur, a member of the Langkekia family;
Dekaphukan of the Kuoigayan family;
Barpatra Dangaria of the Kenduguria family;
Naobaicha Phukan;
Bargohain Dangaria, a nephew of the Solal Gohain of the Madurial family;
Gharphalia Barua;
Chetia-patar Barua of the Doijania family;
Solal Gohain of the Barukial family, with his *khel* at Panguadhara;
Barbarua, a member of the Kharikatia branch of the Duara family; he was previously Bhitarual Phukan; before that he was Nyaya-sodha Phukan;
Tarua Dihingia Rajkhowa, in charge of *mul* of the Hahcharias;
Doabajia Rajkhowa;
Barphukan, a member of the Edabaria branch of the Sandikai family;
Nyaya-sodha Phukan of the Betiania branch;
Opar-Dayangia Rajkhowa;
Majiu-Dayangia Rajkhowa;
Dulia-Barua of the Naphukia branch;
Ghiladharia Rajkhowa;
Raidangia Phukan;
Na-phukan of the Dihingia family;
Pani-Dihingia Rajkhowa;
Dhekial Phukan of the Lahan family;
Sologuria Rajkhowa;
Chetia Phukan;
Dihingia Phukan, a Miri-Sandikai by caste;
Nibukial Rajkhowa, a Kukura-chowa by caste;
Dekaphukan, a member of the Buragohain family;
Gandhia Barua;
Khargharia Phukan of the Lanmakharu clan;
Senchowa Barua;
Pani-Abhaypuria Rajkhowa;
Tipamia Phukan, of the Chetia-patar *khel*;
Dihingia Phukan of Gauhati;
Choladhara Phukan of the Chiring family;

Chiring Phukan;
Naosalia Phukan;
Ghora-Barua of the Bakatial family;
Sologuria Rajkhowa of the same family;
Kathkatia Barua;
Saru-Abhaypuria Rajkhowa of the family of the Barphukan of the Patar clan;
Tipamia Rajkhowa of the Moran-Barua family;
Dola-sharia Barua of the Kamantan family;
Chaodang Barua, a Chaodang by caste;
Chaodang Barua, a Phisi by caste;
Raidangia Barua, a Sonowal Kachari by caste;
Majiu-melia Bhandari Barua, brother of the above;
Tamuli Phukan of the Brahman Kakati family;
Jalbhari Phukan, brother of the above;
Malia Barua, son of the same;
Khangia Phukan, nephew of the same;
Parvatia Phukan, nephew of the same;
Barbhandari Barua, son of Sulpani;
Bhandari Barua, grandson of the Doloi, a Brahman by caste;
Khangia Barua of Dewargaon;
Gabharu-melia Barua, a *bez* or physician;
Purani-melia Barua of the family of Rasendra;
Kalichangar Melar Barua;
Gajpuria Rajkhowa, a Pakhimaria by caste;
Dikhoumukhia Rajkhowa, a Tangchu by caste;
Na-melia Barua, a Gayan by caste;
Khanikar Barua, a Barahi by caste;
Changrun Phukan, Okanimaria Chetia by caste;
Tipamia Barua, a Hendu-Solal by caste;
Majindar Barua, a Ganak by caste;
Gajpuria Barua, brother of the above;
Dekaphukan of the Gauhati establishment, a Lukhurakhun by caste. 336.

The King's visit to Rangpur.

On Tuesday, the fourteenth of Sravan, 1728 *saka*, the King proceeded to Rangpur starting from his quarters at Dichoi. The King went out of his residence on that day and boarded a boat on the river Bhogdoi; he went through the rapids in the marshes at Kalipathar; and through Sukatipota at the breach of Chitamani-gar and Mitang; he alighted from the boat at Gaurisagar, travelled by land and reached Rangpur. Quarters were erected for the residence of the King near the Barchora. The Swargadeo halted at the camp, and went round the town of Rangpur on the next day. He visited Rangnathar Doul, the Bardoul, Majudoul and the Devighar of Jaysagar, where he offered his worship; from there he proceeded by boat to Kalugaon where he hunted buffaloes after which he returned to his camp in the evening. He also visited the temples at Rudrasagar, Gaurisagar and Sibsagar. The King went out one day to Kuoigaon to hunt buffaloes at Chakala-pathar. He also hunted buffaloes at Bhatiapar. Sepoys were posted to guard his gate. The King was accompanied by the Buragohain Dangaria, the Barpatra Dangaria, the Barbarua of the Duara family, the Bhitarual Phukan, as well as others consisting of Chamuas, Baruas, Phukans, Katakis, Kakatis, Dolois, Deodhais and Bailungs. Another set of officers were left behind at Dichoi. After amusing himself by hunting buffaloes and deer for twelve days, the King returned to the Dichoi camp by boat through Ailamukh and the deep marshes. 337.

Abetha Chaliha punished.

In the same month of Sravan, one Abetha, a Khangia Kakati of the Kakati-Chaliha family, went out of his quarters early in the morning, entered the Dola-ghar or palanquin-stall and sat for a time on the *kekora-dola* or sedan belonging to the queen-mother. The watchman having seen him at this position seized his person and reported the matter to the King, who commanded him to be bound down with iron chains, and asked the Duara Barbarua to try the accused. The Barbarua framed charges against the accused and tried him in the court. He pleaded,—'What shall I say? What I have done is beyond the limits of the four evils,—temptation, illusion, desire and wrath. It was mere ill-luck that made me act in this way'. His ears and nose were lopped off, and his eyes extracted, after which he was sent to his residence. 338.

The Bargohain's dismissal.

On the fifth of Kartik of the same year, the King ordered the deposal of the Bargohain Dangaria of the Chataialia family on account of his blindness, and the function was to take place at his own quarters. The Majindar Barua instructed the Bahbaria Kataki Biswambhar in the court in the presence of the Duara Barbarua. Mitha, a

Kukura-chowa Bara, was also deputed to bring back the *Dola* and the *Arwan*. The Kataki went to the spot, brought out the Gohain to the Tamuli-chora or ante-chamber, seated him on a mat and dismissed him. He took a perquisite of rupees one hundred. The Kukura-chowa Bara accepted money from the four Hajarikias for bringing the *Dola* and the *Arwan*. On the same day the grandson of Laithepena Bargohain of the Madurial family, who had been dismissed from the office of the Chetia-patar Barua, was now appointed Bargohain at the inner portico of the Barchora towards the east. The Majindar Barua announced the command of the King by standing and gave him a cloth to sit, where he received the usual counsel. The officer then occupied his allotted seat. The Barpatra Dangaria, the Barbarua and the Phukans attended the ceremony on that occasion. The new Bargohain Dangaria offered rupees one hundred for distribution as presents. The money was distributed by the Barbarua to all the persons concerned. The Katakis obtained rupees twenty-four, and the court Pandits rupees twelve, and so forth, according to their rank and position. 339.

Return of Dhireswar Kataki.

After this, in the month of Kartik, Dhireswar Kataki of the Bahbaria family returned from the Kachari country with letters and presents. No letter was sent with him by the Kachari Raja, to the address of the Barbarua. Only two letters were sent, one addressed to the Buragohain Dangaria and the other to the King. The Kachari Raja gave the following presents to Dhireswar Kataki,—*gamkharus* or bangles made of gold, earrings; a cloak and turban of ordinary cotton, waist-band, a pair of *barkapor* or double sheet, and for his expenses forty rupees and a tola of gold. Kinaram the Tekela-Bara was given a pair of silver bangles, gold earrings, a cloak and a turban, a waist-band, one double sheet of fine texture, and rupees twenty for his expenses as well as half a tola of gold. The two Majalia Katakis were given bangles, earrings, *dhutis* and single sheets; the Bartekela was also awarded presents in the same manner; the three received for their expenses thirty rupees and half a tola of gold. The Chokial Baras received single sheets, turbans, and earrings, and rupees twenty for expenses. 340.

In the meantime the Dihingia Phukan of the Lanmakharu family, who was attached to the establishment at Gauhati, was living in inimical terms with the Barphukan. The Phukan adopted a female hawker selling pulses as his wife. Having heard this the King deputed a Kataki to bring the Phukan, who was then dismissed and sent to his residence on account of this offence. His brother who was serving as Bartamuli was appointed Dihingia Phukan and despatched to Gauhati. 341.

A new Dihingia Phukan.

After this, on the fifth of Aghran, 1728 *saka*, the Swargadeo conferred with the three Dangarias, the Barbarua and the Phukans and commanded the occupation of Sadiya in the east and restoration of peace and order in the country after subduing the Khamtis, the Singphous and the Moamarias. In order to proceed with the expedition the Duara Deka-Barbarua, at the instance of the King raised a fleet, taking one, two or three big boats, according to the position and resources of the persons concerned, from the three Dangarias, the Baruas, the Phukans, the Meldagia Baruas and Phukans, the religious heads including the abbots of Auniati and Dakhinpat Satras. The following were then despatched to the war,—the Marangi-khowa who was a member of the Buragohain's family, Captain Bacha Rajkhowa, the Na-phukan of the Dihingia family, the Opar-Dayangia Rajkhowa and Majiu-Dayangia Rajkhowa of the Sandikai family, the Saru-Abhaypuria Rajkhowa of the Khim-patar's family, the Pani-Abhaypuria Rajkhowa of the Lanmakharu family, Hao Bara of Meragarh. The above commanders accompanied by Kanris, shieldsmen, five companies of sepoys, Katakis, Kakatis, Dolois, Deodhais, Bailungs and Dolasharia Baras, proceeded to the mouth of the Pachala-khowa river and encamped on the sands. On the sixteenth day of Aghon, the Mahamantri Buragohain Dangaria of the Kuoigayan family proceeded to the same spot and having halted there for a couple of days issued the necessary instructions. He divided the army into three detachments and despatched them by the river, by the North Bank as well as the South Bank. The Prime Minister then came back and joined the King. The Bacha Rajkhowa and Hao Bara proceeded by the North Bank; the Marangi-khowa by the South Bank; Captain Na-phukan by the river Lohit. Having sailed up in this way the northern division joined Captain Na-phukan at the extremity of the rocky river-banks. The two armies now proceeded up the river and having reached the vicinity of Sadiya

Expedition to the Eastern Frontier.

encamped in a body facing the Khamantis. The Marangi-khowa also crossed the Dibru river and halted with his army. The Naphukan was appointed commander-in-chief of the entire force. The Senapati Phukan acting jointly with Captain Bacha Rajkhowa procured the submission of the Abors and the Miris and brought them over to their camps. The Abors were then despatched towards Kundil. . . . .(Here ends the present manuscript of the chronicle of Srinath Duara Barua with the events of the year 1728 *saka*, or 1806 A.D.[1]) 342.

Purnananda Buragohain's influence.

Kamaleswar Singha was a mere baby when sovereign powers were conferred on him by the Ahom nobles chiefly through the instrumentality of Purnananda Buragohain Dangaria. The King's father Kadam-dighala Gohain held the titular rank of Charing Raja; and his mother Numali Rajmao exercised considerable influence in the deliberations of the state. On account of the depleted finances of the government the ceremony of coronation at the Singarighar, which usually cost four lacs of rupees, was postponed till the return of better days. The King was, however, endowed with the Ahom name Suhengpha. The King being a mere child the actual reins of government were wielded by Purnananda Buragohain. He strengthened his hold upon the King and the government by marrying Kamaleswar's sister Majiu Aideo to his son Lari Gohain and by appointing his nearest relatives to positions of trust and responsibility. All officials high or low were appointed on his nomination, and no one could spend a single rupee from the royal exchequer without the Premier's express permission. Purnananda exercised such unbounded influence in the state that the period is still designated as the 'Days of Buragohain Dangaria'. His motives were

---

[1] The old Assamese chronicle *Tungkhungia Buranji* constituting paragraphs 1 to 342, pp. 1–197 of this book, ends abruptly in the events of the year 1806 A.D. For the benefit of readers who might not have access to histories of Assam we here append the present supplement narrating the circumstances leading to the termination of Ahom rule in Assam in 1826, and the consequent downfall of the dynasty of Tungkhungia rulers. This portion, paragraphs 343 to 377, has been compiled by the translator from existing materials, published and unpublished. The dates have been mentioned here according to the Christian era in place of the *Sāka* era used in the old chronicle.—*S. K. B.*

misunderstood; and autocracy, nepotism and usurpation of sovereign power were not infrequently attributed to him. 343.

Remodelling of the Ahom army.

The Buragohain despatched an embassy, consisting of Baloram Khangia Phukan, Bhudhar Chaliha Changkakati, Madhuram Bara, Govindaram Sarma Khound and Tanusyam Sarma Khound under the leadership of his son the Dhekial Phukan to the Governor-General of British India and requested the latter to supply a quota of well-trained sepoys and a quantity of arms and weapons. The Ahom envoys made over to the Governor-General 2,000 gold mohurs and 10,000 silver rupees as presents from the Ahom government to substantiate the request. The supplies solicited by Purnananda Buragohain were readily granted; and with their help the Ahom army was organised on up-to-date lines. The army was divided into eighteen companies of one hundred soldiers each. One Chandrā Gohain, a relation of Purnananda, was appointed Captain, and he was subsequently raised to the rank of a Major and then a Colonel. The commander had under him a gradation of Subedars and Jamadars. Detachments of the new force were garrisoned at Gauhati, Jorhat, Sadiya and Mahang. 344.

Proposal to convert Assam into a feudatory state.

The Ahom viceroy of Lower Assam, Kalia-bhomora Barphukan, was a farsighted statesman and a capable general. He had suppressed the insurrection of the *Dundias* and of the Kamrup potentate Haradatta Chaudhuri of Jikeri. King Kamaleswar Singha rewarded the Barphukan's gallantry by conferring on him the title of *Pratap-ballabh*, together with the lands of Haradatta which had been confiscated to the state. Pratapballabh Barphukan realised that the association of the East India Company was the only possible remedy for counteracting the grave situation into which his country had been plunged. He submitted formal proposals to the Prime Minister requesting him to negotiate with the East India Company to extend to Assam the protection of the Company's arms. Purnananda had firm faith in his own powers, and thought that he would be able to restore his country to peace and orderly government without the intervention of any exterior power. The Barphukan's proposals were shelved as being pessimistic and premature. 345.

Purnananda Buragohain partly succeeded in his peace efforts. Through his sleepless vigilance Jorhat was made immune from

Moamaria depredations, and he instituted all possible measures to stamp out the germs of anarchy and disorder. The Kacharis living on the banks of the Dhansiri river flouted the authority of the Ahom government. They rose in a body and suddenly attacked our soldiers from the rear. In the open encounter that ensued the Kacharis were repulsed. The insurrection of the Khamtis was also tactfully subdued. 346.

Peace and order restored.

The conspiracy of Panimua reveals the weaker points in the dictatorship of Purnananda Buragohain. Panimua was a member of the Ratikhowa sect, or the fraternity of night-worshippers whose creed sanctioned participation in indiscriminate food and in bacchanalian revelry. He misrepresented the actions of the Prime Minister and collected a number of followers with the avowed object of killing the Buragohain and the King. The conspirators armed themselves with an old rusted cannon which they mounted in the shrubberies in front of the Buragohain's compound. The Premier used to go out with an armed retinue of 240 men. They saw smoke coming out of the bushes and came upon the light-hearted conspirators in a fit of drunkenness. Panimua with reeling steps divulged the object of the junto who were immediately arrested and imprisoned. Panimua committed more mischiefs from within the prison bars than what he had done from without. Whoever had incurred his displeasure or wrath in the past was mentioned by him as his accomplice; and Purnananda ordered Srinath Barbarua, the chief justice, to inflict the death sentence on every such man. This indiscriminate execution would have gone on indefinitely but for the timely intervention and warning of Sibnath Dolakasharia Barua, the brother of Purnananda Bura gohain. Panimua and his immediate accomplices were executed. This took place in the year 1803 A.D. 347.

Panimua's conspiracy.

The Kacharis made common cause with the Matak rebels and burnt down peaceful villages on the banks of the Kapili river. Haripad Dekaphukan conducted the operations against the insurgents from his headquarters at Narikalguri and Chang-choki. The insurrection was suppressed but the rebels appeared again at Bebejia and Khagarijan. They were aided by the Lalungs and the local militia. The Bacha

Moamaria and Kachari disturbances in Nowgong.

Rajkhowa marched against the rebels, and halted at a fort erected at Birah-Bebejia. The rebels burnt down the villages Pathari, Potani-sijia and Bheleuguri. The Dekaphukan who had been absent from the scene of war now joined the royalist force. The Ahom army then marched to Tetelikhana and afterwards to Dabaka, from whence they proceeded to a fort on the bank of the Jamuna river. In the meantime the Mataks had advanced from Barthal to the village Demera. A quarrel then ensued between the Mataks and the Kacharis, precipitated by the refusal of the latter to join the ranks of the Mataks. The Dekaphukan seized this opportunity, and escorted the Kacharis to Birah-Bebejia near the Kalang river where they were properly established. This was followed by an unexpected encounter with a separate wing of the combined forces at the mouth of the Kalang river where the rebels were repulsed with heavy casualties. The Dekaphukan and his lieutenants, the Bacha Rajkhowa and Captain Gohain, then returned with their army to Jorhat. The Kachari wars came to an end in 1805 A.D. and peace reigned in the kingdom for the years 1805 to 1807, except some minor inroads of the Nagas which were readily suppressed, and four Naga Chautangs or headmen came to Barhat with tributes and offered their allegiance to the Ahom monarch. 348.

Works of public utility.

The period of stability and peace allowed the King and his minister to turn their attention towards the fulfilling of the civic and religious obligations of the state. Temples were erected at Chatrakar and Kamakhya at Gauhati with the usual endowments of lands and paiks for their perpetual maintenance. Jorhat having now assumed the position of a full-fledged metropolis several approach-roads were constructed connecting the city with the interior villages. New buildings were erected at Jorhat. Operations for catching elephants were instituted in a village at a distance of six miles east of Jorhat. One hundred and twenty elephants were captured and the village was thenceforth known as Hatigarh. The King and the Buragohain were patrons of letters, and Srikanta Suryya-bipra translated under their auspices, the *Lanka-kanda* of the *Ramayana* into beautiful Assamese verse—a fact unfortunately symbolising the last phase of Ahom supremacy. 349.

In January 1811, there broke out a severe epidemic of small-pox in Jorhat and the neighbouring villages. The people were seized with a dire panic, and they refrained from visiting the houses of their friends, relatives and neighbours. The young King Kamaleswar Singha died of this disease. He was only sixteen years old at the time of his death. 350.

Death of Kamaleswar Singha.

CHAPTER XI.

SWARGADEO CHANDRAKANTA SINGHA.

First time, 1811–1818 A.D.

Accession.

Kamaleswar Singha was succeeded by his brother Chandrakanta Singha who was then only fourteen years old being born in 1797 A.D. His father Kadamdighala Charing Raja had died in 1799, and Chandrakanta held the rank of Charing Raja before he ascended the throne. Purnananda Buragohain continued to act as the *de facto* ruler of the country. Though some section of his contemporaries misjudged his motives, sober history has acclaimed him as an astute politician, a farsighted statesman and a selfless patriot, 'protecting the people like a mother-bird guarding the nestlings under her wings'. The Prime Minister exercised the strictest vigilance in the management of the state finance, and the expensive Singarighar ceremony was withheld as in the case of Kamaleswar Singha. The Ahom priests conferred on Chandrakanta Singha the title of Sudingpha. 351.

Conspiracy against Purnananda Buragohain.

Chandrakanta Singha had a companion named Satram, the son of a royal poultry-keeper. Satram was of the same age as the King, but he was unrivalled in his precocity and cunning. The King was granted his expenses from the royal treasury in a restricted manner owing to the impoverished condition of the state. Satram, subsequently raised to the rank of Charingia Phukan, realised that as long as Purnananda exercised absolute control over state affairs and specially over the royal exchequer his association and intimacy with the monarch would be of little advantage to him. He misinterpreted Purnananda's motives and actions and gradually poisoned the ears of the young King. His campaign of calumniation was extended to other quarters as well. Badanchandra, the Ahom viceroy at Gauhati, was made to believe that Purnananda was his arch-enemy, and that the Premier was planning and maturing schemes at the headquarters to effect the undoing of the Barphukan. Badanchandra's daughter Pijou Gabharu, who had been married to Oreshanath Dhekial Phukan, a son of the Prime Minister, was also made a party to this belief. Satram with several other miscreants launched a regular conspiracy to kill the Prime Minister which was detected and the conspirators duly punished. This was in June 1814. Chandrakanta's own attitude towards the Premier, greatly influenced by the misrepresentations of his unscrupulous associates, was not a friendly one, though he dared not speak out his mind as he owed his succession to Purnananda and it would be difficult for him to win over the nobility and the army against the interests of the powerful Prime Minister. The young King flouted Purnananda's opposition to his marriage with Padmavati, the daughter of a *Bhakat* or disciple of the Bengena-atia Satra, and thus violated the time-honoured custom according to which royal partners had to be selected from the principal Ahom families. 352.

Badanchandra's flight to Burma.

Badanchandra's mind being poisoned against Purnananda through the machinations of Satram he had ceased to send to the Prime Minister his customary greetings and epistles. Purnananda deputed three trusted Brahman officials, the Tamuli Phukan, the Khangia Phukan and the Jalbhari Phukan, on a mission of peace to Badanchandra, to remove any misunderstanding which might have arisen between the Premier and the viceroy, and re-establish their mutual good-will and friendship.[1] The Barphukan's agents at the metropolis despatched a swift courier to Badanchandra attributing hostile motives to the deputation, and they also contrived the simultaneous despatch of a confirmatory epistle from Pijou Gabharu. The Barphukan readily believed in his friends' warning, and escaped from the viceregal headquarters at midnight

[1] Several authorities affirm that a Brahman official named Maheswar Parvatia Phukan of the Rasendra family was deputed by the Premier to arrest Badanchandra and bring him up to Jorhat as a prisoner.

on September 26, 1815, before the messengers of the Prime Minister could deliver their conciliatory overtures. Badanchandra proceeded to Calcutta, interviewed the British Governor-General and solicited from him a contingent of sepoys to restore, as he alleged, the King Chandrakanta Singha to power and influence which had been usurped by Purnananda. In the official documents of the government of the East India Company Purnananda had been continuously described as a sensible and patriotic statesman and a trusted friend of the British. The Governor-General accordingly refused to accede to Badanchandra's request. The disappointed Barphukan then proceeded to Burma and made similar prayers to the Burmese sovereign Bodawpaya. 353.

Bodawpaya, King of Burma, 1782–1819.

Alaungpaya, a petty landlord, worked his way to the throne of Burma in 1752, and founded a dynasty of his own, known as the Alaungpaya Dynasty, which came to an end with King Thibaw in 1885. Alaungpaya was succeeded by his sons Naungdawgyi 1760–1763, Hsinbyushin 1763–1776, Singu 1776–1782, and Bodawpaya 1782–1819. The reign of King Bodawpaya roughly corresponds with the Prime Ministership of Purnananda Buragohain. One of the first acts of his reign was the moving of the capital in 1783 from Ava to Amarapura on astrological grounds. The older capital Ava, at a distance of six miles from the new one, had been selected in 1765 in preference to Shwebo. In 1823 King Bagyidaw again transferred the capital to Ava. The sons of Alaungpaya effected the territorial expansion of Burma. The Burmese army had penetrated into Siam, Manipur, annexed neighbouring tracts and had even waged wars with the Imperial Majesty of China. So when Bodawpaya ascended the throne in 1782, followed by a most ruthless massacre of his rivals with their wives and servants, Burma had attained the zenith of her power and prestige. Bodawpaya was a capable monarch and a strict disciplinarian. He annexed Arrakan in 1785, despatched several expeditions against China, and schemed to conquer China and India. He was a patron of literature and religion. He collected the inscriptions of Burma as part of a revenue inquest, despatched priests to Bodh-Gaya, received Ceylonese monks with great cordiality and deputed Burmese monks to Ceylon. With better organisation, discipline and introspection he could have become one of the great sovereigns of the world. 354.

First Burmese invasion.

King Bodawpaya considered himself to be an unparalleled and invincible sovereign, and any entreaty made to him was looked upon as a compliment to his omnipotence and majesty. Any scheme of aggrandisement was readily welcomed by the Burman monarch; but his suspicious temperament was responsible for the detention of Badanchandra for full sixteen months at the court of Amarapura before he announced his final decision on the prayers of the fugitive Assamese viceroy. King Bodawpaya ultimately convinced himself that Badanchandra was of noble extraction and that he was a gallant fighter and capable of properly conducting and utilising the aid that might be placed at his disposal. His Assamese consort Rangili Mepaya, sprung from the same Duara family as Badanchandra, played an important part in securing for the fugitive the solicited help from the Burmese monarch. Badanchandra Barphukan, accompanied by this Burman force which was strengthened by reinforcements from the territories through which he passed, appeared on the gates of Assam in March 1817. The Burman army was commanded by Bom Senapati and Kamini Phukan. Ultimatums were despatched to the Ahom court from the Barphukan's encampment at Meleng in which the Burmese avowed their intention to place on the throne one Garbhe Sing Raja whom they described as the son of Gaurinath Singha, born during that monarch's flight from the capital which was obviously a *ruse de guerre*. Purnananda had in the meantime breathed his last and the feeble opposition offered to the invaders at Ghiladhari was easily repulsed. 355.

Murder of Badanchandra.

Badanchandra triumphantly entered the capital Jorhat, interviewed Chandrakanta and offered to run the affairs of the state in his capacity as Mantri-Phukan. Ruchinath Buragohain, son and successor of Purnananda, had fled down to Gauhati leaving the young King to the mercy of Badanchandra and his Burman allies. The King had no alternative but to acquiesce in Badanchandra's proposal. Friendly overtures were also made to Chandrakanta from the Burmese camp. Chandrakanta offered Hemo or Bhamo Aideo, sister of Jogeswar Singha, as a present to the Burmese harem, and the Burmans peacefully retired to their kingdom. Badanchandra now in possession of the supreme executive power wreaked vengeance upon his old enemies. He robbed the house of Purnananda Buragohain and confiscated his belongings to the state. His own uncle Srinath Barbarua, a supporter of the policy of the deceased Buragohain, was dismissed from office. The Queen-mother Numali Rajmao, however, found in Badanchandra a poor substitute of the great statesman Purnananda Buragohain to whom she was personally attached for raising her two sons to the throne. She intrigued with Dhani Barbarua and Nirbhaynarayan Bargohain to destroy the Barphukan. Rupsing Subedar and Rahman Khan Jamadar[1] were appointed to carry out their purpose into execution. The two assassins approached the Barphukan one morning when he was rubbing his hands with clay after performing his ablutions on the riverside. When questioned as to the object of their visit, the two sepoys replied that it was customary for servants to come to pay respects to their masters and to persons of authority and eminence. Thus disarmed of all suspicion the Barphukan continued busy in the water when Rupsing dealt him a cut over the neck with his sabre which felled him to the ground. The Jamadar followed up the stroke and the minister breathed his last imprecating curses on the King, his country and the assassins. 356.

Chandrakanta deposed.

Chandrakanta's peace with the Burmans, his support of Badanchandra and his refusal to go down to Gauhati at the approach of the Burman army, had raised the suspicion of Ruchinath Buragohain as being mainly responsible for the attempts made previously against his father Purnananda followed by the visit of the Burman troops. Ruchinath took up the cause of Brajanath Gohain, son of Bijoy Barmura, grandson of Ratneswar Saru-gohain, and great-grandson of Rajeswar Singha. Brajanath who had shared with his father Barmura Gohain the vicissitudes of a wanderer's life among the mountain fastnesses of Cachar and Manipur had been aspiring for the throne since 1809 when he visited Calcutta soliciting assistance to accomplish his ambition. Being now assured of the support of Ruchinath Buragohain he repeated his overtures to the British Governor-General, but having failed in his mission

---

[1] Rupsing was hitherto regarded as the only hero in the episode of Badanchandra's murder. Col. White writing in 1834, sixteen years after the occurrence, mentions an associate of Rupsing Subedar, named Rahman Khan, which has been confirmed by Maniram Dewan writing in 1838.

he returned to Gauhati where he dressed up a native sepoy with the full regimentals of a Firinghee Captain as a make-believe to win more recruits to his side. Ruchinath and his party then proceeded up to Jorhat. Chandrakanta fled to Rangpur, and the resistance offered by Luku Dekaphukan, on his behalf, was easily repulsed. The victors succeeded in bringing over the royal troops to their interests. They then triumphantly entered Jorhat on February 17, 1818. On assurance of allegiance and fealty Chandrakanta was led to Jorhat where he was deprived of power and banished to Taratali, an unhealthy place. Ruchinath and his followers had hesitated to place Brajanath on the throne as he had been previously disqualified for the succession by the mutilation of one of his ears. They had already sent for Brajanath's son Purandar, then only ten years old, who had been left behind at Silmari in Bengal. Purandar arrived in time and was acclaimed as sovereign, and a few days after Biswanath Marangikhowa Gohain effected the slicing off of Chandrakanta's right ear. Brajanath had already struck coins in his name in anticipation of his succession, which bear the dates 1739 and curiously enough 1840 *sākas*; and after the installation of his young son on the throne he exercised the virtual powers of a sovereign in his capacity as Juvaraj. 357.

CHAPTER XII.

SWARGADEO PURANDAR SINGHA.

Independent King, 1818–1819 A.D.

Bodawpaya's Assamese consorts.

The Assamese consorts of King Bodawpaya exercised considerable influence in shaping the policy of their royal partner permanently affecting the destiny of their motherland. Bodawpaya had 122 children and 208 grandchildren and his seraglio was a crowded and magnificent one. Two Assamese ladies graced his harem. The first was Rangili,[1] sister of the father of Baram Barua of the

---

[1] For further information about Rangili and Hemo Aideo, see Srijut Benudhar Sarma's article published in the *Banhi*, Vol. XV, pp. 492–6, and Rai Bahadur Anandachandra Agarwala's account of the Assamese fugitives in Burma, *Usha*, Vol. I, pp. 131–5, as well as Prof. S. K. Bhuyan's edition of *Barphukanar Git* and *Asamar Padya-Buranji*.

famous Ahom Duara family. The Singphous in concert with the Moran rebels had imported troops from Burma and ravaged a number of villages in the eastern part of Assam. To placate the Singphou leader Bichanong, Purnananda Buragohain had presented to him Rangili, together with numerous slaves and attendants. Bichanong in his turn palmed off Rangili to King Bodawpaya with the object of strengthening his friendship with the Burmese monarch. Attended by a proper retinue Rangili arrived at the Burmese capital on June 17, 1797. Captain Cox gives in his diary a vivid description of the preparations made to receive this new recruit to the Burman harem. June 26 was fixed as the date of her formal entrance into the royal palace. The shops were gaily decorated, the roads were swept by armies of sweepers, cannon were mounted at regular intervals, and the procession started towards the palace amidst unprecedented pomp and splendour. Queen Rangili became a favourite of the King, and though she was described in the Singphou despatches as an Assamese princess, her fair rivals soon came to know of her non-royal origin, and made capital out of this fact, and so when Badanchandra of the Duara family made his appearance at the Burmese capital in 1815, she described him as her kinsman, and the success of Badanchandra at Bodawpaya's court was mainly due to Rangili's anxiety to impress her royal partner and his other queens with the nobility of her descent and relationship. Bodawpaya's second Assamese consort was Hemo Aideo. She was the sister of Jogeswar Singha, and at the suggestion of Badanchandra after his return to Assam with the Burman force, Chandrakanta had presented her to King Bodawpaya describing her as his own daughter. The Burmese King allotted for her maintenance a few villages near Bhamo, mainly inhabited by Assamese fugitives. She had great influence with the Burmese monarch, and she was partly responsible for the second Burmese expedition to Assam, the object of which was to reinstate Chandrakanta on the throne and avenge the murder of the Barphukan. 358.

Second Burmese invasion.

The news of Chandrakanta's deposal and the murder of Badanchandra reached the Burmese court in due time. The Burmese monarch interpreted the subversion of his allies as gross impertinence on the part of Purandar Singha and his supporters. He despatched a fresh army under Kiamingi Bargohain, also known as Alungmingi.

One Gogoi-Senapati was sent at the head of the Ahom force to encounter the invaders. A battle ensued at Phulpanichiga near the Janji river on February 17, 1819, where the Burman army gained a decisive victory. The triumphant Burmans now searched for Chandrakanta, led him from his retreat and properly installed him on the throne. Purandar Singha and his adherents left the capital and fled down to Bengal. Not having met the real culprits responsible for the humiliation of Chandrakanta, the Burmese committed atrocities upon all people who were suspected of having sympathy for Purandar Singha or Ruchinath Buragohain. One Momai Barua, an Assamese noble who had risen to eminence in the court of Burma, had guided the Burmans during their second invasion of Assam. He interceded on behalf of the hapless Assamese subjects and procured from the Burmese general an order for the stay of the atrocities. Like Rangili, Hemo Aideo became an important figure in the seraglio of the Burmese monarch. It is believed that it was she who urged upon her royal paramour the urgency of despatching an expeditionary force to Assam to avenge the humiliation to which her brother Chandrakanta had been subjected in the hands of Ruchinath Buragohain. 359.

CHAPTER XIII.

SWARGADEO CHANDRAKANTA SINGHA.

Second time, 1819–1821 A.D.

Bagyidaw, King of Burma, 1819–1837.

King Bodawpaya had died in the meantime, and he was succeeded by his grandson Bagyidaw. The new monarch was a finished gentleman having charming and dignified manners. But living in the midst of sycophants he failed at times to measure accurately his strength or that of his adversaries. With absolute ignorance of international affairs King Bagyidaw attributed to himself omnipotence and invincibility ; in his opinion, which was confirmed by Mingimaha Bandula, the English were mere traders and they could be easily subdued by his Assamese levies, and his redoubtable Burman commanders might rest in peace behind the shadow of the Golden Throne. Bandula appeared to him a veritable Afrasiyab and his war-strategy was superior to that of the greatest English general. The success of the British in India was attributed to the incompetency of the Hindus ; but the Burmans were not Hindus, and consequently the British army would experience different results when they would have to deal with the stalwart Burmans. The Burman Majesty proposed to replenish his impoverished coffers caused by a future war with the British by the plunder of Calcutta ; and the surplus provisions and ammunitions would enable him to undertake an expedition against Siam. The Burmans had conquered the Chins, the Singphous, the Manipuris and the Assamese ; and after such a series of triumphs their victory over the British was a foregone conclusion. After the conquest of Calcutta King Bagyidaw proposed to march to England, the occupation of which would be signalised by the installation of his son as viceroy of all the British dominions. King Bagyidaw was nurtured in such beliefs which were strengthened by the continued victories of the Burmese in Assam. Having too great confidence in the prowess of himself and his commanders King Bagyidaw failed to realise the primary fact that though his armies succeeded in their contest with the tribes of the neighbouring countries, more or less sprung from kindred origins, their present enemy the British were of different extraction and mettle, whose war-methods and strategy the Burmese monarch nor his flatterers ever cared to fathom and effectively counteract. Their chief resort was violence and barbarism which were ineffective before subtler organisations. The Burmese policy towards the British was one of wanton aggressiveness untempered by political exigency and foresight. The Burmese atrocities in Assam which had been held in check by the iron hand of King Bodawpaya now relapsed into prominence during the reign of his weak-kneed grandson. 360.

Third Burmese invasion.

The Burmese general returned to Amarapura leaving express directions to his commanders to refrain from molesting the Assamese subjects. Momai Barua was left behind in Assam along with two other commanders, Sajati Phukan and Mingimaha Tilowa Bajuphaya. Having suspected a possible manœuvre on the part of Ruchinath Buragohain and Brajanath to reinstate Purandar Singha on the throne Momai Barua marched at the head of a large Burman force towards Nowgong. Taking advantage of Momai's absence the two Burmese commanders killed a number of Ahom officials and nobles on allegations of secret sympathy for Purandar Singha. Chandrakanta did not approve of these high-handed actions of his Burmese friends and proposed to shake off their cowering predominance once for all. Taking advantage of the return of the Burmese commanders to their country Chandrakanta despatched Patalang Barbarua to erect a line of fortifications near Dighalighat or Jaypur which lay in the route of the Burmese march to Assam. Chandrakanta adopted other measures to undo the effects of the Burmese ravages. Chandrakanta's efforts to rehabilitate himself reached the ears of the Burmese monarch and a fresh army was despatched to Assam under the two old experienced commanders Mingimaha Tilowa Baju and Sajati Phukan on the pretext of handing over some presents to Chandrakanta. The Burman force approached the borders of Assam in March 1821, and witnessed the preparations made at Jaypur. Patalang Barbarua was killed without any provocation and his wife Majiu Aideo who happened to be the sister of Chandrakanta was outraged in an inconceivably inhuman manner. The soldiers stationed at Jaypur deserted the garrison and all hope of thwarting the march of the Burmans into Assam was now dashed to pieces. Chandrakanta apprehended the bursting of a terrible storm. Seeing no hope of success with the Burmans he left the capital and fled down to Gauhati. He had however despatched a force under Kalibar Buragohain to encounter the invaders ; but the panic-stricken and dastardly Ahom soldiers were easily vanquished by the Burmese army. 361.

Burmans become masters of Assam.

The Burmans now triumphantly entered the capital. Chandrakanta received repeated invitations from the Burmese general to come up to Jorhat and accept the presents which had been sent to him by the Burmese monarch. Chandrakanta read through the secret motives behind the offer of friendship ; he fled further down and took shelter in Bengal. The Burmese general Tilowa Baju marched towards Gauhati and found himself the unopposed master of the Brahmaputra Valley. 362.

CHAPTER XIV.

SWARGADEO JOGESWAR SINGHA.

Burmese rule in Assam, 1821–1825 A.D.

Jogeswar Singha, a puppet king.

The news of the Burmese triumphs in Assam was duly transmitted to Amarapura. The Burmese monarch issued orders to his army in Assam to place on the throne Jogeswar Singha, the brother of Hemo Mepaya, his Assamese consort inherited from his grandfather Bodawpaya along with the succession. The appointment of Jogeswar Singha, which took place in November 1821, had evidently a double advantage; it would enhance the prestige of the Assamese queen of the King of Burma, and would also placate the Assamese subjects who would naturally appreciate a native ruler being set up in their country. Jogeswar Singha had no vestige of any sovereign power; and the Burmese general was all in all in Assam. 363.

Chandrakanta's patriotic *coupés*.

Chandrakanta utilised his residence in Bengal by collecting an army of 2,000 men, mostly Sikhs and Hindusthanis, for the repulsion of the Burman invaders. He marched up and successfully encountered the Burman army at Hadirachoki and Gauhati. He proceeded further up and pitched his tent at Mah-garh. Mingimaha Bandula the redoubtable general had now joined the Burmese forces in Assam. He led the Burmese van in the battle of Mah-garh where Chandrakanta is reported to have displayed unusual vigour and courage. But his half-hearted mercenaries could not stand the dash and fury of the Burmans, who were now confirmed in the undisputed possession of the land. The battle of Mah-garh took place on Baisakh 6, 1744 *saka*, April 19, 1822 A.D. Chandrakanta fled to Goalpara but returned some time after to the capital of Assam where he was given a pension by the Burmese, but his position was nothing better than that of a state-prisoner. Mingimaha Bandula was ordered back to Burma to attend to more pressing needs at home.[1] 364.

---

[1] Bandula, also called Maung Yit, 'wielded an almost magical influence over his men. His mere presence inspired confidence and was worth a corps...... At the outbreak of the First Burmese War Bandula commanded

Burmese reign of terror.

The last attempt to repulse the Burmese was made by Hao Sagar-Bara of North Lakshimpur with his Baskatia soldiers but without any success. The Burmese made some attempt to establish a systematic government in Assam; but as it was based on motives of exploitation it had no far-reaching effect in securing peace and order in the country. The Burmese fortune-hunters knew very well that their occupation of Assam was bound to be abortive and short-lived and so they made the best use of their stay by the gratification of their animal appetites. Virgins were deflowered before their parents and wives before their husbands; infants served as throw-sticks to drop down mangoes from trees; all property and belongings had to be surrendered unconditionally and spontaneously on pain of mutilation or death; and rights and records of property were thrown into wells and rivers to efface any titles thereto. The sword and all other instruments of lust were used without any scruple or restraint. The Burmans avowed that 'their oppressions were committed out of set policy, and the Burmese prided themselves on it, saying though at home they were a mild people, when invading foreign countries they deliberately gave way to all their passions, plundering and murdering without control so that foreigners should learn not to provoke them'.[1] 365.

CHAPTER XV.

BRITISH OCCUPATION OF ASSAM.

Anglo-Burmese relations.

The British relations with Burma were far from satisfactory. The oak forests of England were depleted by the protracted naval warfare with France, and the British had to build their merchant ships with Burma teak. The French were surveying the possibility of attacking the English through Burma. Besides, the con-

---

the Burmese army in Arrakan which contemplated the invasion of Bengal, and caused no small anxiety in Calcutta'.—Major C. M. Enriquez, in *Journal of the Burma Research Society*, Vol. XI, Part 3.

1 G. E. Harvey's *History of Burma*, pp. 298-299, to which I am also indebted for the facts of Burmese history.

solidation of Burmese hold in Arrakan was itself a menace to the safety of the British in India. These problems necessitated the despatch of British embassies to Burma. Captain Symes was sent in 1795, Captain Cox in 1797, Captain Symes again in 1802, and Captain Canning in 1803, 1809 and 1811. The English envoys were treated with scant courtesy. They were subjected to humiliation, delay and caprice, which, though tolerated by the myrmidons of an oriental autocrat, were appalling to the business-like instincts of the westerners. The ambassadors were despatched by the Governor-General of India, and the Burmese monarch insisted on the despatch of accredited representatives of his peer His Britannic Majesty who alone would be entitled to the consideration of the Golden Throne. 366.

British proposal to dislodge Burmans from Assam.

In 1821 the Burmese forces strengthened their hold in Manipur and Assam. Purandar Singha and Chandrakanta Singha both fled to British territories, and the Burmese ruled over the land with Jogeswar Singha as their nominee on the throne. The two Assamese royal fugitives in their turn organised, though separately, counter-measures against the Burmese from their safe retreat in Bengal with the connivance of British officials who regarded their attitude as morally justifiable as the sole object of the activities of the two Ahom princes was to put an end to the barbarities committed upon the innocent civil population of Assam. This was alleged by the Burmese as an act of gross misdemeanour on the part of the British, and ultimatums were despatched demanding the extradition of Chandrakanta and Purandar Singha. The Burmese had received further provocation from the British in the opposition offered by the latter in their intrigues in Manipur, Cachar and Jayantia. Mingimaha Nand Kroden, commander-in-chief of the Burmese forces in Assam, sent repeated warnings to David Scott,[1] Agent to the

[1] On November 14, 1823, David Scott was appointed Agent to the Governor-General on the North-East Frontier in addition to his post as Civil Commissioner of Rungpoor, on a consolidated pay of Rs. 52,000 per year, the terms of his appointment being,—'He should exercise a general control and superintendence over our political relations and intercourse with the petty states in that quarter, including Sikkhim, Bootan, Tibet, Cooch Behar, Bijnee, Assam, Cachar, Manipur and Jyntia, and other independent states'.—Governor-General's minute to the Board.

Governor-General on the North-East Frontier, against British counteraction of Burmese designs. The island of Shapuree on the estuary of the Naaf river had long been under the British, being administered by the Collector of Chittagong. In September 1823, the Burmese had forcibly taken possession of the island after massacring the British garrison stationed there ; and the attempt made by the British to re-occupy Shapuree met with little success. The Government of India realised that an open rupture with Burma was imminent. The Burmese maintained a powerful flotilla at Gauhati, and unless they were dislodged from their commanding position they could at any time sail down the river Brahmaputra and attack the British territories which commenced down from Goalpara. It was therefore proposed by David Scott that British troops should advance to Gauhati and occupy the country between Gauhati and Goalpara as a measure of defensive policy against the Burmese. 'The object of the expedition into Assam would be to operate a diversion and to expel the Burmese from the commanding position which they occupied at the upper part of the Brahmaputra.'[1] Boats, men, and provisions were collected at Goalpara, and a depôt was formed at Dacca for field equipments. 367.

The First Burmese War.

However provoking might be the activities of the Burmans they had not yet aggressively entered into British territories in Assam. In January 1824, they crossed the Cachar frontier and fired the first shot at Bikrampur near Badarpur in Cachar. Major Newton completely defeated the Burmese force in the battle that followed. On the completion of the preparations for the advance of British troops from Goalpara, the Governor-General made a formal declaration of war against Burma on March 5, 1824. The circumstances leading to the war, as narrated in the declaration, can be summarised as follows : The relations of peace and friendship between the Hon'ble East India Company and the State of Ava have been strained by the latter's acts of provocation and aggression, placing the two countries on the brink of hostilities averted only by the moderation and forbearance of the British power. The Burmans elated by their conquest of Assam have

---

1 Secretary G. W. Swinton's letter to Captain Davidson, February 20, 1824.

offered studied insult, menace and defiance to the British power. The Burmans have laid a false claim to the island of Shapuree, their official communications have been singularly boastful, assuming and insolent. The Burman interference in Cachar, Manipur and Jayantia have been unwarranted. The officers and crew of the Company's armed vessel 'Sophia' have been released but no apology or explanation of their detention has been offered. For their wanton violation of the relations of friendship, the Governor-General in Council has ordered the advance of the force assembled at Goalpara into the territory of Assam to dislodge the enemy from their commanding position which they occupy at the head of the Brahmaputra; but is ready even yet to listen to pacific overtures on the part of His Burmese Majesty. 368.

Assam passes into British hands.

A week after the declaration of war the British troops under the command of Lieutenant-Colonel Macmorine moved from Goalpara and arrived at Gauhati unopposed on March 28, 1824. The Burmans retired to Maramukh in Upper Assam. The Burmese, encouraged by the long haltage of the British army at Gauhati, marched back to Kaliabar, from where they were repulsed. The Burmese then retired to Rangaligarh, and Colonel Richards established his headquarters at Kaliabar. On the failure of supplies during the rains Colonel Richards's force was compelled to return to Gauhati. The Burmese re-occupied Kaliabar, Raha and Nowgong, and this time they perpetrated their atrocities with redoubled cruelty. The people of Nowgong fled to the Surma Valley, and some to the British territory in Goalpara. Dabaka and the Kapili Valley were practically depopulated. In October 1824, the British resumed their operations against the Burmese. The enemy were repulsed from their strongholds in Kaliabar, Raha, Nowgong and Maramukh. The Burmese retreated to Jorhat, but dissensions arose amongst their commanders whereupon they fell back upon the old capital Rangpur. Colonel Richards and Lieutenant Brooke succeeded by the end of January 1825 in repulsing the Burmese from Rangpur, and they extorted an undertaking from their generals Sham Phukan and Nebaru Phukan that they would renounce all hostilities against the British and would peacefully return to Burma. In June 1825, the Burmese leagued with the Singphous, but Captain Neufville suppressed the hostilities and procured the release of six thousand

Assamese captives who had been carried off by the Singphous and their Burman allies. Colonel Innes effected the expulsion of the Burmese from Cachar, and Captain Pemberton similarly ousted them from Manipur. The Burmese had also met with reverses in the war waged in Burma. Captain Marryatt, the famous English novelist, had taken part in the naval engagements near Rangoon. The Burmese were now cleared out of Assam, and by Article II of the Treaty of Yandaboo, enacted on February 24, 1826, it was agreed that 'His Majesty the King of Ava renounces all claims, and will abstain from all future interferences with the principality of Assam, and its dependencies, and also with the contiguous petty states of Cachar and Jynteea'. 369.

End of Ahom authority in Assam.

The Treaty of Yandaboo marked the termination of Ahom rule in Assam. David Scott with his characteristic judgment and sobriety devoted his entire energy towards the restoration of peace and orderly government to a country which had been devastated by the depredations of the Burmese preceded by internecine feuds and dissensions. The British Government did not first contemplate the permanent annexation of any part of Assam; but it was also realised that any eventual withdrawal of the British army would be invariably followed by the recurrence of the internal disturbances to which the country had succumbed. After seven years of correspondence with the British headquarters at Calcutta on the subject of handing over a part of the country to an Assamese prince and retaining the other part under direct British control, it was decided to appoint Purandar Singha as a protected prince in charge of Upper Assam on a stipulated tribute of Rs. 50,000. This proposal originally initiated by David Scott was given effect to in April 1833 by his successor Mr. T. C. Robertson, as Scott had died in 1831 at Cherrapunji as a result of strenuous work in a very inclement climate. Purandar Singha began well, but within three years he defaulted in his payments. Captain Jenkins, Mr. Robertson's successor in the Commissionership of Assam, locally investigated into the administration of Purandar Singha and found it a hot-bed of corruption and misfeasance. Purandar Singha having thus proved a failure, his country was placed in September 1838 under direct British control. With the deposal of Purandar Singha and the annexation of Upper Assam to the territories of the East India Company all vestiges of Ahom authority in Assam came to an end after a practically uninterrupted sway of 610 years, 1228 to 1838 A.D. 370.

The Tungkhungia Dynasty.

With the downfall of the Ahoms in Assam the Tungkhungia Dynasty also came to an end. They governed the country for 145 years, 1681 to 1826, and five years more if we take into consideration Purandar Singha's administration of Upper Assam as a feudatory prince, 1833 to 1838. Little more than a hundred years have elapsed since the Tungkhungia rulers resigned their sceptre of authority and the passage of a century has not been able to efface their names and their actions from the recollections of the Assamese people. Titles conferred by the Tungkhungia sovereigns on their officers and nobles are used by the descendants of the latter with zeal and pride ; and land-grants and endowments issued under their seal and authority are still enjoyed by the beneficiaries, and almost in all cases the conditions of the grants as imposed by the original donors are rigidly carried out as far as present-day circumstances permit. The temples, edifices and roads erected by them are still fulfilling the functions for which they were made. During all these decades of epoch-making changes, the stories of their exploits and misfortunes have been deeply rooted in the memory of men on account of the wide circulation which they have gained in the country. In popular traditions the name Tungkhungia is associated with imperiousness and majesty. The vainglorious gasconades of a braggart are still snubbed with the retort,—'Oh, look at him, His Highness has sprung from the Tungkhungia race!' 371.

Purandar Singha's descendants.

After the resumption of his territories Purandar Singha continued to live at Jorhat. In October 1838 a pension of Rs. 1,000 per month was granted to him but he declined to accept it as he hoped for the eventual restitution of his state as a result of his petition to the Governor-General. He died at Jorhat on October 1, 1846. He had married a daughter of Purnananda Buragohain, and Kameswar Singha was born of this union. In 1847 Kameswar Singha was permitted by the Government to use the title of Raja, and he died five years after on June 10, 1852, leaving behind three widows, Rani Lakhipriya, Padmahari Kuanri and Madhavi Maju-Kuanri, as well as a concubine named Rupavati Khatania. Kandarpeswar Singha, Kameswar's son through Lakhipriya, was born in 1840. In 1848 the title of Charing Raja was conferred on Kandarpeswar. During the Sepoy Mutiny Kandarpeswar Singha was suspected of disloyal manœuvres. He was placed under arrest as well as his agent Maniram Dewan Barbhandar Barua who was then in Calcutta petitioning the Governor-General for the restoration of the government of a part of the country to Kandarpeswar as Maniram had previously done on behalf of Ghanakanta Singha Juvaraj. As a result of the trial the Charing Raja was sent to Alipur and then to Burdwan to be detained there as a state-prisoner. Maniram was executed on February 26, 1858. Kandarpeswar was afterwards released and granted a pension and he died at Gauhati. His two sons, Kumudeswar and Nareswar, through his wife Rani Kamalapriya, had died during their father's lifetime, and his daughter Troilokyeswari Aideo survived her father. 372.

Chandrakanta Singha's descendants.

The unfortunate monarch Chandrakanta Singha was granted a pension of Rs. 500 per month and certain Khats or estates in Upper Assam of the annual value of Rs. 408-14-0. He lived first at Kaliabar and later on at Gauhati amidst the splendour which could be commanded by a fainéant prince. Through his wife Padmavati Kuanri he had two sons and one daughter, Ghanakanta Singha Juvaraj, Hemakanta Singha Gohain and Devajani Aideo. Rani Madamvika was the mother of Lambodar Gohain. Chandrakanta's third wife Nirmilia Kuanri was issueless. He had also a number of concubines mostly recruited from Hajo. Chandrakanta visited Calcutta in 1837 and submitted a memorial to the Governor-General for the restoration of his kingdom. He died in 1839 soon after his return to Gauhati. Hemakanta Gohain, who had been enjoying a pension of Rs. 100, had died on July 3, 1857, leaving two widows, Basundhari and Chandrakala, the first a sister of the Buragohain, and the second a daughter of Bapuram Barphukan. Devajani Aideo was married to Chakradhar Gohain, grandson of Bailung Bargohain. Ghanakanta Juvaraj died at Gauhati on September 10, 1858, leaving behind his widow Padmarekha, and a young son Kesavkanta then aged ten years. Rani Padmarekha applied to Colonel Jenkins, Commissioner of Assam, for the grant of the Sraddha expenses. Colonel Jenkins sanctioned a sum of Rs. 1,500, justifying his action by saying that all the royal property of the Rajas was carried off by Purandar Singha's branch of the family, and that Chandrakanta's branch only obtained their personal jewels. Kesavkanta continued to live at Gauhati where he died in 1894 leaving behind his widow Rani Mahendri and her two step-daughters. Rani Mahendri died at Gauhati in 1923, and the two daughters of Juvaraj Kesavkanta, Mrs. Lauhityakumari Bargohain and Mrs. Prafullabala Chaudhuri are still living. Pensions to the members of the Ahom royal families have ceased with the death of Rani Mahendri Devi. 373.

Jogeswar Singha's descendants.

Jogeswar Singha had died at Jogighopa in 1825. He was descended from Jambar Gohain Charing Raja, the younger uterine brother of Gadadhar Singha. His sister Hemo Aideo became the consort of King Bodawpaya of Burma. He had one more sister Taravati Aideo, and three brothers, Mantan Charing Raja, Bihuram Tipam Raja and Dhaniram Gohain. Bihuram, also known as Biswanath, accompanied his sister Hemo Aideo to Burma, and became the governor of Mogaung and ultimately a chief minister of the Burmese monarch. Dhaniram also sought refuge in Burma together with his mother. In May 1838 Bihuram deputed his nephew Singman Gohain to the British authorities in Upper Assam with the message that he was prepared to return to his nativeland with the 40,000 Assamese fugitives then residing in Burma. Hemo Aideo was accompanied by a large retinue consisting of ladies and attendants. Her fair companions, or Aideos as they are called in Assamese, were established in a village to the north-west of Mandalay, and the place is still known as Ayadaw or the City of Aideos. In the Burmese records the two brothers of Jogeswar Singha who went to Burma with their sister figure as Tabangacha and Malomin, the Burmese forms of Tangkeswar and Malo which are very common Assamese names. Tabangacha had five sons, Maung Gyi, Maung Mitha, Maung Lat, Maung Gale and Maung Son, all of whom rose to prominence and power. Of his three daughters Madaya Mepaya became the consort of King Mindon, 1853–78. Malomin ordinarily resided at the capital with his mother and sister. Tangkeswar and Malo were no other than Bihuram and Dhaniram, and it is not unusual for members of the Assamese gentry to have a plurality of names. The descendants of the Assamese fugitives in Burma can still be seen in Mogaung, Mahaung, Ywathit, Kyaingale Lwisun and Nankaiktaw. Jogeswar Singha left a son named Dambarudhar

Singha Juvaraj, and a daughter named Padmavati. Dambarudhar's descendants are still living at Holongapar. 374.

Pensions to Ahom nobles.

The Ahom princes and nobles whose fortunes were undermined by the change of government were granted pensions and allowances in cash, as well as lands and *likchows* for their maintenance.[1] In some cases the expenses of their pilgrimages, Sraddhas and other ceremonies were met by the new government. The following are some of the lords and ladies who solicited or obtained aid from the British Government: Krishnaram and Tilakchandra, descendants of Jogeswar Singha; Baga Gohain Charing Raja who lived under the protection of Chandrakanta Singha; Trilochan Dekaphukan, son of Purnananda Buragohain; Manjur Gohain, Srimat Gohain, Durga Gohain, Nareswar Gohain, Namrupia Gohain and Narayan Gohain, all descendants of the royal family; Khargeswar Charing Raja, brother of Chandrakanta; Narahari Rajkhowa who died on October 15, 1836; Jajna Charingia Barua; Chakradhar Gohain, grandson of Bailung Bargohain and son-in-law of Chandrakanta Singha; and Pado-kowanr Sing Gohain; Thakur Gohain, grandson of Rajeswar Singha; Rupahi Aideo was granted in 1852 a pension of Rs. 600 per year; Devajani Aideo, daughter of Chandrakanta Singha and wife of Chakradhar Gohain, a pension of Rs. 600 per year in 1846; Narayani Aideo, daughter of Jayanti Aideo who was the only child of King Gaurinath Singha: Jayanti was married to Dambarudhar Choladhara Phukan and she died at Calcutta: Narayani had lived with Janardan Barbarua till her marriage with Dhenudhar Changrung Phukan: Narayani was granted a pension in 1848 of Rs. 240 per year; Taravati Aideo, sister of Jogeswar Singha, Rs. 120 per year from 1850; Sarupahi Aideo, Rs. 120 per year from 1852; Madhavi Maju-kuanri, the second consort of Raja Kameswar Singha; Padmahari Kuanri, grand-daughter of the Barbarua and wife of Kameswar Singha; Rupavati Khatania, concubine of Kameswar Singha; Binandini, aunt of Chandrakanta Singha being the sister of his mother Numali Rajmao, Rs. 240 per year from 1841; Keteki Gabharu, wife of Narahari Rajkhowa, brother of Chandrakanta Singha's Parvatia Queen Padmavati, Rs. 96 per year from 1848; Rani Madamvika, widow

---

[1] 'In 1853 the pensions payable to various Ahom noble families still exceeded Rs. 12,000 a month.'—Gait's *History of Assam*, 2nd ed., p. 308-*n*.

of Chandrakanta Singha and mother of Lambodar Singha, Rs. 480 per year from 1839; Rupanta Aideo, Chandrakanta's niece and wife of Bhakatram Gohain, Rs. 48 per year; Rani Padmarekha, widow of Ghanakanta Singha Juvaraj; Basundhari and Chandrakala, widows of Hemakanta Gohain; Rani Lakhipriya, widow of Kameswar Singha and mother of Kandarpeswar Singha; Rani Kamalapriya, widow of Kandarpeswar Singha; Maharani Chandrakala, the Parvatia Queen of Maharaja Purandar Singha, she was a Manipuri princess; Kumudini Aideo, daughter of Nareswar Gohain, the third son of Bhubaneswar Tipam Raja; Banduli Barkuanri, widow of Kamaleswar Singha, 1840; Padmavati, daughter of Jogeswar Singha; Radhakanti, widow of Kaliabhomora Barphukan; Rupeswari Aideo and Malati Phukanani and Saru Aideo; Annapurna, daughter of Pado-kowanr Sing; Koorwa Aideo, sister of Chandrakanta Singha and wife of Lambodar Barphukan, head of the Civil Panchayat in Upper Assam; and Luturi Aideo, niece of Purandar Singha. 375.

Grants of paiks.

In 1828 Captain Neufville, in charge of the administration of Upper Assam, made allotments of *likchows* or servitors on the following: Bhagi Bargohain, 10 *likchows*; Khorasole Barpatra-gohain, 10; Pijali Barpatra-gohain, 10; Dandeswar Barpatra-gohain, 10; Ani Barpatra-gohain, 2; Dhanjoy Bargohain, 20; Burha Bargohain, 10; Solal Petal Bargohain, 10; Janardan Barbarua, 10; Khamti Barbarua, 10; Radhanath Barbarua, 10; Bailung Barua, 16; a Bidhipathak Brahman, 3; Ghanasyam Muktiar, 4; Jajna Sarma Charingia Barua, 4; Bapuram Khangia Phukan, 4; Lokenath Jalbhari Phukan, 4; Durgaram Barkakati, 2; Prabhakar Pandit, 2; Chandrakantar Namrupia Gohain, 10; Ugrasen Gohain Rajkumar, 4; Bailung Bargohain's son, 2; Mukalimuria Gosain, 4; Lambodar Daroga, 10; Sangalu Kataki, 5; Bhagia Hazarika, 10; Hoki Gohain, 10; and Pijou Dihingia Phukan, 10; mother of Jogeswar Singha, 40; Majiu Aideo, sister of Chandrakanta Singha, 10; and the widow of Kamaleswar Singha, 4 *likchows*. 376.

Majiu Aideo.

Majiu Aideo who had played an important part in history lived at Gauhati with her younger brother Chandrakanta. She had been first married in November 1805 to Lari Gohain, a son of the Prime Minister Purnananda Buragohain; and her marriage symbolising the union of the Kuoigayan Buragohain family with the house of

Tungkhung was celebrated with great pomp and grandeur. She quarrelled with her husband, parted with him and became the wife of Oreshanath Dhekial Phukan, another son of Purnananda. Pijou Gabharu, daughter of Badanchandra, had thus a powerful rival in this new wife of her husband. Majiu Aideo was a cunning and capable woman, and her royal brother Chandrakanta conferred on her the management of the Naosalia *Khel* or the guild of boat-builders—the first instance of a lady being formally entrusted with such responsibilities of state. It was believed in certain quarters that the letter of warning to Badanchandra, purported to have been despatched by Pijou Gabharu, was in reality the handiwork of Majiu Aideo, who intended thereby to place her rival in her husband's disfavour, presumably for the offence of divulging the Phukan's official secrets. The letter contained the official seal of the Dhekial Phukan, and Badanchandra entertained no suspicion regarding its authenticity. As a result of the transference of the allegiance and support of Ruchinath Buragohain and his brothers from Chandrakanta to Purandar, Majiu Aideo was wrested back from the Buragohain family, and afterwards married to Patalang Barbarua, the builder of the fort of Jaypur. Majiu Aideo proceeded to Jaypur, perhaps to help her husband in the affairs of the Dighalighat dockyard with her experience gained as the superintendent of the boat-builders. After Patalang's murder by the Burmese she was subjected to very severe assaults in the hands of the lustful invaders. She escaped to Jorhat, and related to Chandrakanta all that had happened at Jaypur. It was she who pointed out to Chandrakanta the secret motive lying behind the invitation to receive the presents which the Burmans had brought for him from the court of Amarapura. She shared the subsequent vicissitudes of Chandrakanta and after 1826 she lived for some time in Nowgong on a pension from the British Government at the rate of Rs. 600 per year, and the grant of 10 *likchows*, and then joined her brother at Gauhati. Besides her pension, she was also entrusted by the new Administration with the management of a *khel* in Naduar in order to contribute to her comfort and respectability. But the complaints preferred by the people of her oppression caused her removal from the charge. In 1853 when

Judge A. J. Moffatt Mills visited Assam she was still in the enjoyment of her pension from the British Government.[1] 377.

[1] The facts about Majiu Aideo have been collected from *Tungkhungia Buranji,* paragraph 321 *ante*; Gunabhiram Barua's *Assam Buranji,* 4th edition, p. 178-*n.*; and *Asamar Padya-Buranji,* pp. 163–5, 294; and Colonel White's Manuscript Notes. Two sons of Purnananda became her successive husbands, but their names are conflicting in the different sources. Besides Lari Gohain and Oreshanath, Biswanath Marangi-Khowa Gohain and Jaganath Naosalia Phukan are also mentioned in this connection.

APPENDIX I.

GENEALOGICAL TABLES OF THE TUNGKHUNGIA DYNASTY.

A. GENERAL TABLE SHOWING THE KINGS OF THE DYNASTY.

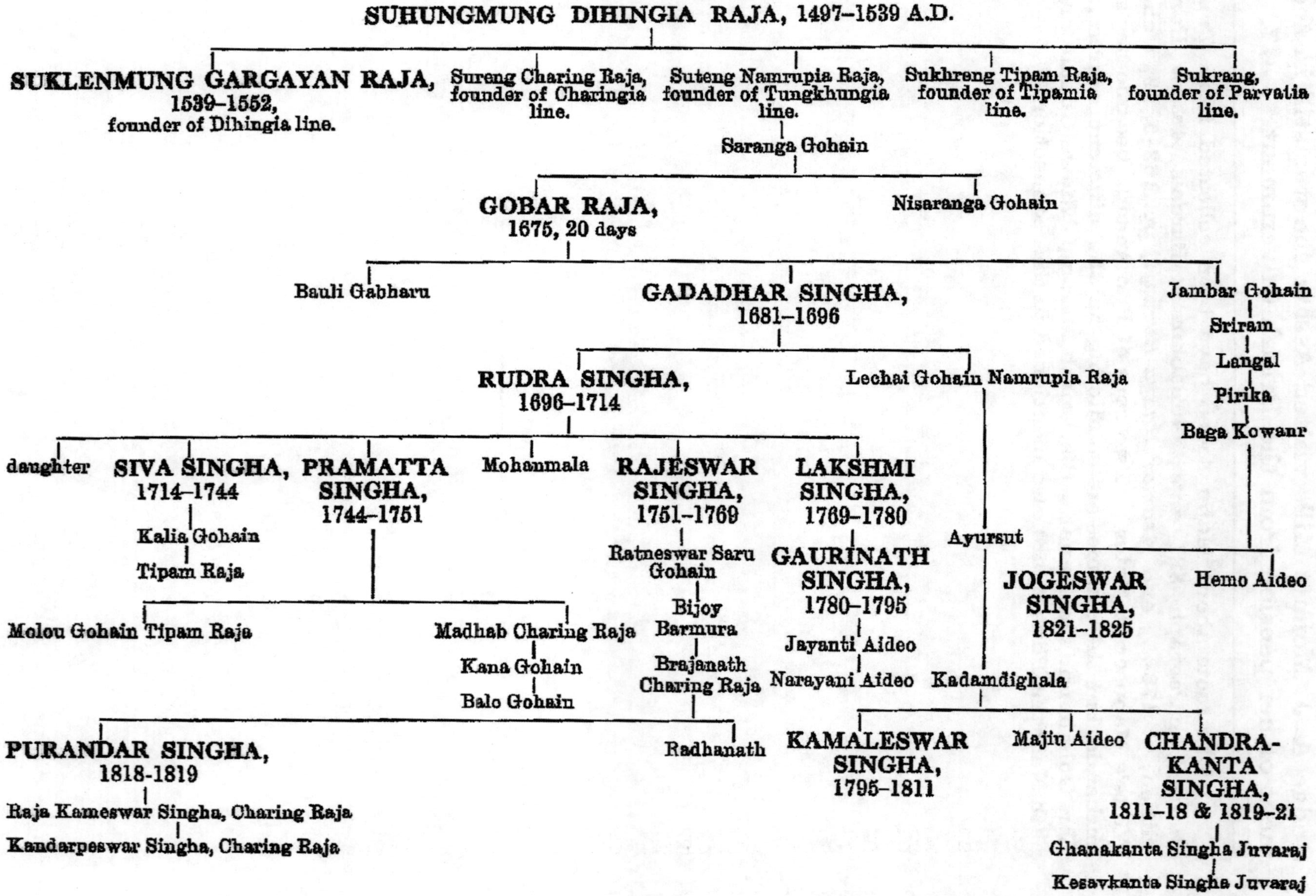

B. DETAILED TABLE OF KING RAJESWAR SINGHA'S LINE.

RAJESWAR SINGHA, 1751–1769 A.D.

- Kandura
- Charu Singha, Charing Raja
  - Cherela Gohain
    - Giridhar
      - Lambodar
        - Chandrhans
- Ratneswar, Tipam Raja
  - Bijoy Barmura
    - Brajanath Charing Raja
      - PURANDAR SINGHA
        - Kameswar Singha
          - Kandarpeswar Singha
            - Nareswar
            - Kumudeswar
            - Troilokyeswari Aideo
          - Saru Gohain
      - Radhanath
        - Naranarayan Majumelia
          - Kumar Chandanarayan *
            - Dandeswar*
            - Nagendra *
          - Gunanarayan
          - Padmanarayan
    - Bhubaneswar Tipam Raja
      - son
      - son
      - Nareswar
        - Manjur
        - Durga
        - Akara
        - Kumudini Aideo
    - Indunath Sarumelia
      - Srimat Gohain
        - Siddheswar
          - Nilapadmi Aideo *
          - Deveswar, B.L.
          - Sureswar, M.Sc.*
          - Padmavati Aideo *
          - Kumudeswar *
        - Ramakanta
          - Krishna
        - Kamal
        - Nareswar
        - Padmeswar *
          - Jibeswar *
      - Hemakanta, *alias* Numali Gohain
        - Nilakanta *
          - Three sons *
    - Apa Gohain
      - Iswar Gohain
        - Rosheswar
- Patkowanr

C. DETAILED TABLE OF JAMBAR GOHAIN'S LINE.

GOBAR RAJA,
January 1675, 20 days.

- Bauli Gabharu
- **GADADHAR SINGHA**
- Jambar Gohain Charing Raja
  - Sriram
    - Langal
      - Pirika
        - Bagakowanr Tipam Raja
          - Taravati Aideo
          - Sarupahi Aideo
          - **JOGESWAR SINGHA**
            - Dambarudhar Singha Juvaraj
              - Krishnaram
                - Umar Sing
                  - Durga*
                  - Siva*
                  - Rajeswar*
                  - Chandra*
                - Kumar Sing
                  - Jaychand
              - Usha Aideo
              - daughter
              - Tilak
                - Ram*
              - Amra Aideo
              - Prabha Aideo
            - Padmavati Aideo
          - Mantan Charing Raja
          - Bihuram, *alias* Biswanath Tipam Raja
            - Maung Gyi
            - Maung Mitha
            - Maung Lat
            - Maung Gale
            - Maung Son
            - Madaya Mepaya, Queen of King Mindon of Burma.
          - Hemo Aideo
          - Dhaniram Gohain
        - Bhagi Gohain
        - Bhog Gohain
      - Padmanath

* Names with asterisks denote living persons.

D. DETAILED TABLE OF LECHAI GOHAIN NAMRUPIA RAJA'S LINE.

- **KING GADADHAR SINGHA**
  - **RUDRA SINGHA**
  - Lechai Gohain Namrupia Raja
    - Ekadah
    - Balia
      - Bhatar Gohain
        - Phaguna
    - Bayursut
      - Basanta
        - Kinaram
          - Kerkan
            - Kelkeli
              - Krishnaram
                - Heramba
                  - Tamradhwaj
    - Ayursut
      - Kadamdighala
        - **KAMALESWAR SINGHA**
        - Majiu Aideo
        - **CHANDRAKANTA SINGHA**
          - Ghanakanta Singha Juvaraj
            - Kesavkanta Singha Juvaraj
              - Mrs. Lauhityakumari Bargohain*
              - Mrs. Prafullabala Chaudhuri*
          - Hemakanta
          - Devajani Aideo
      - Khora Gohain
      - Kalia
      - Dhupal
      - Sakhi Gohain
        - Bhakatram, *alias* Sardar Gohain
          - Ugrasen
            - Bhadrasen
              - Devadatta*
                - son*
                - Sarbananda, B.A., S.D.C.*
              - Rai Sahib Lilasen Gohain*
              - Lakshmi Gohain
              - Pani Gohain*

* Names with asterisks denote living persons.

APPENDIX II.

BIBLIOGRAPHY.

History of Assam : Tungkhungia Period, 1681–1826 A.D.

1. Wade, Dr. John Peter. *An Account of Assam*, compiled during 1794–1800. Edited by Srijut Benudhar Sarma, Sibsagar, Assam. 1st impression, 1927. The original manuscript is in the India Office Library, London.
2. Wade, Dr. John Peter. *Geographical Sketch of Assam*, compiled during 1796–1802. Edited by Prof. S. K. Bhuyan from the original manuscript in the India Office Library, and published in *The Assam Review* as a serial in Vols. I and II, December 1928 to August 1929, under the title *Assam in the Eighteenth Century*.
3. Wade, Dr. John Peter. *Memoir of the Reign of Gowrinath Singha*, King of Assam, 1780–95. Compiled in 1796. Untraced. Vide *Note* below.
4. Wilson, Horace Hayman. *Documents Illustrative of the Burmese War*. 1827.
5. Dhekial Phukan, Haliram. *Āsām Deser Itihās*, or a history of Assam in Bengali, published in 1829. Reviewed by Prof. S. K. Bhuyan in the Journal of the Bangiya Sahitya-Parishat, B.S. 1333, No. 1.
6. Pemberton, Captain C. B. *Report on the Eastern Frontier of British India*, 1835.
7. Buchanan-Hamilton, Dr. Francis. *Description of Assam*, 1809, inserted in Montgomery Martin's *Eastern India*, 1838, Vol. III, with an account of the commerce of Assam.
8. Robinson, William. *A Descriptive Account of Assam*, published in 1841.
9. Tamuli-Phukan, Kasinath. *Assam Buranji*. Published in 1844 by the American Baptist Mission Press, Sibsagar. Reprinted in 1906.
10. Aitchison, Sir C. U. *A Collection of Treaties, Engagements and Sunnuds relating to India and the Neighbouring Countries*, Vol. I, first published in 1862, contains the Treaties with Assam Kings and Chiefs. Reprinted.
11. Barua, Rai Bahadur Gunabhiram. *Assam Buranji*. 1st edition, 1875; 4th edition, 1900.
12. Johnstone, Major-General Sir James. *Captain Welsh's Expedition to Assam, 1792–94*. Published by the Government of Assam. 1st edition, 1877; 2nd edition, 1912.

13. MACKENZIE, SIR ALEXANDER. *History of the Relations of the Government with the Hill Tribes of the North-East of Bengal*, 1884.

14. GAIT, SIR EDWARD. *A History of Assam*. 1st edition, 1906; 2nd edition, 1926, published by Thacker Spink and Co., Calcutta and Simla.

15. BOTHAM, A. W. *Catalogue of the Provincial Coin Cabinet of Assam*. Published by the Government of Assam. 1st edition, 1911; 2nd edition, 1930.

16. SHAKESPEARE, LIEUTENANT-COLONEL L. W. *History of Upper Assam, Upper Burma, and the North-East Frontier*. 1914.

17. GOSWAMI, HEMCHANDRA. *Purani Assam Buranji*. Published by the Kamarupa Anusandhan Samiti. 1st edition, 1922.

18. BHUYAN, PROF. S. K. *Ahomar Din*, or an account of the Ahom system of administration. 1st edition, 1918.

19. BHUYAN, PROF. S. K. *Barphukanar Git*, or the ballad of Badanchandra Barphukan who brought over the Burmese to Assam. 1st edition, 1924. Reviewed in *J.R.A.S.* for October 1925.

20. BHUYAN, PROF. S. K. *History of the Reign of Rajeswar Singha, 1751–1769 A.D.* Published as a serial in the *Banhi*, Vols. XV and XVI, April 1925 to June 1926, *sākas* 1847-48.

21. BHUYAN, PROF. S. K. *An Assamese Nur Jahan*, or life of Queen Phuleswari Devi, consort regnant of King Siva Singha, 1714–44. Reviewed in *J.R.A.S.* for July 1927. 1st edition, 1926.

22. BHUYAN, PROF. S. K. *Early British Relations with Assam*. 1st edition, 1928. Published by the Government of Assam.

23. BHUYAN, PROF. S. K. *Assam Buranji*, or a history of Ahom rule in Assam, by Harakanta Barua Sadar-amin. Published by the Government of Assam in the Department of Historical and Antiquarian Studies. 1st edition, 1930.

24. BHUYAN, PROF. S. K. *Kamrupar Buranji*. Published by the D.H.A.S. 1st edition, 1930.

25. BHUYAN, PROF. S. K. *Asamar Padya-Buranji*, or a metrical chronicle of Assam, consisting of two separate books, by Dutiram Hajarika and Bisweswar Vaidyadhipa. Published by the D.H.A.S. 1st edition, 1932.

26. BHUYAN, PROF. S. K. *Deodhai Asam Buranji*, with several shorter chronicles of Assam. Published by the D.H.A.S. 1st edition, 1932.

27. BHUYAN, PROF. S. K. *Tungkhungia Buranji*, or a chronicle of the Tungkhungia Kings of Assam, Assamese version. History of Assam from 1681 to 1806 A.D. Published by the D.H.A.S. 1st edition, 1932.

28. BHUYAN, PROF. S. K. *Tungkhungia Buranji*, English translation of No. 27, with a supplement bringing down the history to the end of Ahom rule in 1826, Genealogical Tables,

Bibliography, Glossary, and Index. Published by the Oxford University Press for the D.H.A.S. 1st edition, 1933.

29. HARVEY, G. E. *History of Burma*. Longmans. 1925.

30. BARUA, RAI SAHIB GOLAPCHANDRA. *Ahom Buranji*, English translation of an Ahom chronicle with the original Ahom text. Published by the Government of Assam. 1st edition, 1930.

NOTE.—Of the above books Nos. 9, 11, 17–20 and 23–27 are in Assamese. Nos. 17 and 23–27 have introductions both in English and Assamese; and No. 25, viz., *Asamar Padya-Buranji*, has, besides, a detailed synopsis in English.

OTHER BOOKS AND ARTICLES.—In the above bibliography I have mentioned only the general books on the history of Ahom rule in Assam with special reference to that of the Kings of the Tungkhungia dynasty. The D.H.A.S. has collected a large number of contemporary manuscript chronicles or buranjis, a list of which has been inserted in its Bulletins, Nos. I and II. There are, besides, numerous articles and papers published from time to time in English and Assamese journals written, among others, by the following: Captain J. B. Neufville, Lieutenant Wilcox, Captain S. O. Hannay, William Robinson, Major-General Francis Jenkins, Maniram Dewan, J. M. Foster, Rai Bahadur Gunabhiram Barua, Srijut Ratneswar Mahanta, Sir Edward Gait, Lieutenant-Colonel P. R. T. Gurdon, Srijut Hemchandra Goswami, Srijut Sonaram Choudhuri, Srijut Hiteswar Barbarua, Srijut Benudhar Sarma, Srijut Suryyakumar Bhuyan and Srijut Khetradhar Bargohain. A full bibliography is under compilation by the D.H.A.S. A complete list of books and articles dealing with the history of British beginnings in Assam has been inserted in 'Early British Relations with Assam', pp. 57–65.

DR. WADE'S 'MEMOIR OF THE REIGN OF GOWRINATH SINGHA'.—Dr. Wade's monograph on Gaurināth Singha has been included in the present bibliography though it has not seen the light of day, with the hope that someone living in Europe will resume its search in the numerous libraries and archives. All our efforts to trace this book have failed. The book would be a precious document as Dr. Wade came into personal contact with King Gaurinath Singha during Captain Welsh's expedition to Assam which lasted from November 1792 to July 1794, as he was the Assistant Surgeon attached to the detachment. Dr. Wade wrote about this book in his dedicatory epistle addressed to Lt.-Col. Kirkpatrick, prefixed to his *Account of Assam*,—'The curious and interesting circumstances relating to Assam are exhibited, at some length, in the continuation of the history, containing the reign of the late Monarch Surgedeo Gowrinath Singha. I have compiled the memoir of his reign from authentic documents, and despatched the book to Europe for publication in April 1796, with the approbation of Lord Teignmouth; but I have not as yet received any account of it, and not having retained a copy I am deprived of the pleasure of sending it to you'.—Kishenganj

Bengal, March 20, 1800. He repeated his regret in a similar dedication in his *Geographical Sketch of Assam*, dated July 4, 1802,—'I regret the Europe Press has not yet enabled me to offer you a copy of the history of Maharaja Gowrinath Singha Surgedeo, late monarch of Assam'. Wade died at Calcutta on October 14, 1802. Full information about Wade's historical works has been embodied in my paper *An Early Historian of the East India Company*, read at the Gwalior Session of the Indian Historical Records Commission, 1929, subsequently published in its proceedings, and also in *Bengal : Past and Present* for January to March, 1930, pp. 32-42.

A few stray leaves embodying a portion of Wade's history of Gaurinath Singha were found in the India Office manuscript of his *Geographical Sketch of Assam*. They refer to the contest between the Moamaria rebels and the Manipuri allies of the Ahoms led by the old Raja Jai Singha in person and his son Juvaraj Madhuchandra, and can be read with advantage as an elaboration of paragraphs 231-2 of the present book *Tungkhungia Buranji*. The account, though fragmentary, offers us evidence of Wade's style and treatment, and is important in the light of the subsequent history of Assam. The piece is reproduced below :—

Jai Singha against the Moamarias.—The Moamarias had received accurate intelligence of the designs and route of the Rajah's army. On either side of the road a luxuriant vegetation of several years had covered the country with lofty grass and reeds impenetrable to the eye of the travellers. The Moamarias had lined the vicinity of the road with cannon which had been conveyed from Rungpoor, and not improbably from Zoorhath. The young Prince, by design or accident, passed unmolested, entered Gurgown where he defeated a body of Moamarias, repaired to Rungpoor, forced his way into the fortress, and massacred the Moamarias of every age and sex. But his triumph and cruelty were checked by the news which he received from his enemies that the concealed batteries had been opened on his father's army, and that a great number of his men had perished. The victorious Prince returned and experienced a similar fate. One hundred of his party fell a sacrifice to the well-directed fire of the Moamaria cannon, and in this unfortunate occasion the Rajah lost seven hundred of his bravest warriors. He was now perfectly convinced of the Gohaign's perfidy, and after passing one night in his entrenchments near Zoorhath during which the Moamarias approached and exulted in his defeat, he led the remains of his army by the nearest route over the hills to the southward of the capital into the country of Cossary, uttering his execrations on the treacherous Gohaign as the secret author of the depression of his people.

Jai Singha at the Kachari capital.—The unfortunate Prince experienced a more hospitable reception from the people of Cospoor in the vicinity of which he established his residence, for the King of Burma had taken possession of his country and his capital, either previous to his arrival in Assam or during his absence in that country. Since the connection of Swargadeo with the British Government, if we may credit report, the Boora-Gohaign has frequently solicited the alliance and forces of Krishna-Sundreh, the Cossari Rajah, in order to prevent the restoration of tranquillity through the British influence, supposed to be inimical to his personal independence. He might wish to deter, though he would not dare to oppose the Government of Bengal, in their timely exertions to re-establish order throughout this ill-fated country. Krishna-Sundreh, however, has hitherto rejected his equally vain and interested offers, and is satisfied to rule this little colony of his emigrant subjects in the peaceful security of Cossari.

Wade's prophetic remarks.—Before we take our final leave of the Moamarias we may venture to prophesy that the mere name of the British Government will, at any time, prove sufficient to repress the overt resistance of the Boora-Gohaign or the Moamarias, although every kind of secret counteraction may be expected from those who derive advantage from the destruction and desolation of the country. The miserable band of cowardly and undisciplined peasants amounting perhaps to six or seven hundred men, armed with awkward weapons which they dare not and cannot use, the small body of unwilling and unpaid burkenduzes not exceeding the number of sixty or seventy Bengal subjects which form his mighty army, would scarcely venture to oppose a single company of sepoys armed with the name of Swargadeo. It is necessary to distinguish between the man and his title. Gowrinath is a tyrant they fear; but every rank of subjects holds the race and the lawful authority of Swargadeo in a degree of veneration, scarcely to be paralleled in history. The Boora-Gohaign himself affects to rule his districts in the name of Swargadeo, and we may freely believe that the meanest peasant would be gratified by Swargadeo's restoration to his throne and capital if he were promised a permanent protection against the tyranny of Gowrinath and his ministers. In a former part of this narrative we have observed the extreme dislike of the people of Bossa-Doyungh to the Boora-Gohaign. The character of the man authorises us to believe that his government cannot be more popular among the inhabitants who reside nearer his person.[1] If he might dare to oppose, he must assuredly experience a general defection of all, except his personal adherents and connections. But we cannot possibly suppose the Gohaign to be destitute of common sense or...........*unfinished*.

---

[1] Look at this picture and that. The saner opinion about Purnananda Buragohain Dangaria depicted him as 'an able minister whose administration was productive of much comfort to the people. He endeavoured to repair the damages which the country had sustained in point of population, raised a body of soldiers dressed in the English uniform and employed a large number of sephahees of Upper Hindoostan.'—Lt.-Col. Adam White's Manuscript Notes, 1834.

APPENDIX III.

GLOSSARY OF VERNACULAR TERMS.

[NOTE.—The Glossary explains the vernacular terms occurring in the body of the text. Many words have been explained along with the translation and those necessitating fuller treatment have been reserved for the Glossary. A large mass of information on the machinery of the Ahom government, and the religious, social and political institutions of the age has been compressed in the Glossary; and the explanations and notes inserted therein will help the reader in going through other Buranjis or old Assamese chronicles, and even histories and treatises on Assam written on new lines. The figures refer to the numbers of the paragraphs where the words occur.—*S. K. B.*]

Āchāryya, paragraph 168, a teacher of the Vedas, and of rituals and morals; secondarily, any teacher, preceptor or religious guide.

Adhikār, 279, 286, the head of an Assamese Vaisnava Satra or monastery.

Āghon, Āghran, Agrahāyan, the eighth month of the Hindu year, generally corresponding to November 16 to December 15.

Āhin, Āswin, the sixth month of the Hindu year, generally corresponding to September 16 to October 15.

Āhom ethā, 325, a very tenacious glue used in pasting up the sticks of wicker baskets and boxes to make them water-tight.

Āhom-jarā, 301, an ornamental receptacle or casket of superior metal used for holding precious or sacred articles, generally kept by the bed-side of princes and nobles.

Ankiā Nāt, 309, 329, a dramatic piece written on the lines of the dramas of Sankardev and Madhabdev which had been distinguished by the use of *Ankas* or painted scenes. A post-Sankarian drama could be called an Ankiā *Nāt* or drama even though it does not use painted scenes. An Assamese Ankiā Nāt is distinct from the type of Sanskrit drama called Anka or Utsritikānka.

Āo-bar, 68, 79, 169, literally the banian tree auguring the longevity of a monarch, the planting of which constituted a distinct ceremony during the coronation days.

Aparājitā, 324, a species of flowering creeper bearing dark-blue blossoms.

Arghā, 249, a small vessel, generally of copper, but also of gold and silver according to the position of the worshipper, in which water is offered to an image or deity.

Ārwān, 169, 316, 339, the Āhom mace or insignia of authority which could be used only by the King, the Burāgohāin, the Bargohāin and the Barpātra-gohāin, and the three frontier wardens, viz. Sadiyā-khowā, Marangi-khowā and Solal Gohāins. It was circular in shape and made of wicker-work covered with an embroidered cotton or silk case. Some distinction was maintained between the Ārwān of a monarch and that of his Gohāins. The Ahom royal colour was white.

Āshār, Āhār, the third month of the Hindu year, generally corresponding to June 16 to July 15.

Asokāshtami day, 180, the eighth day of the light half of the month of Chaitra, when bathing in the Brahmaputra river is enjoined.

Ātlas, 308, Indian satin occasionally wrought with threads of gold and silver.

Bahāg, Baisākh, Baisākha, the first month of the Hindu year, generally corresponding to April 14 to May 15.

Bahatiā, 266, a tenant of a land-owner who was bound to render personal service to his overlord, his services being permanently attached to and thus transferable with the land.

Bahuā, 182, a buffoon, a clown, a jester, who commonly appears in a serious dramatic performance to supply comic relief. He may also amuse audiences with humorous skits independently.

Bāilung, 79, 138, 191, 201,...., an Ahom priest mainly engaged in astrological calculations. The Bailungs claim descent from Pujāk-ji.

Bairāgi, Barāgi, 227, 237, 238, an itinerant sannyasi; a member of a religious sect having no fixed habitation; an Assamese *khel* founded by King Rudra Singha, the members of which were deputed to other parts of India to study local customs, dresses, etc., as well as political movements and designs.

Bākhām, 79, an Āhom word meaning the recital of benedictory verses on an auspicious occasion, also the name of an Ahom god.

Bāmuniā Mahanta, 129, the head of a Satra founded on the principles of the Brahman Vaisnava leader Dāmodardev and his immediate apostles.

Bānaprasthi, 282, a hermit or anchorite in the third stage of life having passed through the stages of a student and a householder and abandoned his house and family for an ascetic life in the woods.

Bānat, 319, 323, a fine kind of woollen fulled cloth; broadcloth.

Bangāl, 14, 16, 17,...., a term applied by the Assamese to a stranger, an outsider, a foreigner or an alien; any non-Assamese.

Bar-āideo, 169, the eldest daughter of an Ahom king.

Barā, 71, 85, 108,...., an officer of the Ahom government entrusted with the command and supervision of twenty paiks, also known as *Kuriā Barā*.

Bāra-aniā, 301, a cotton yarn of very fine texture.

Barāhi, 336, an aboriginal tribe of Assam, a branch of the Kacharis, whose political authority in Upper Assam was supplanted by the Ahoms. The Barāhis generally served as cooks and physicians in the royal household.

Baratiās, 126, literally, adherents or observers of a *brata* or religious vow; usually applied to Moāmariā insurgents who had promised before their spiritual leader to avenge the insults and wrongs perpetrated on their community, the actual wording of their vow being,—'I shall kill or I shall die, and thereby repay my debt to my Guru'.

Barbaruā, 33, 35, ..., the Āhom officer who was the head of the executive wielding control over all judicial, revenue and even military functions.

Barchetiā, 60, 68, the officer in charge of a unit of Chetias who were Ahoms of high standing in society.

Barchorā, 67, 92,...., the council-chamber of the Ahom king, where the sovereign used to preside over state deliberations in the company of his ministers and officers.

Bar-Deodhāi, 24, the head of the Deodhāis or Ahom priests.

Bardhāk, 34, 79, 108, the great state drum; one of the numerous fixed symbols of Ahom royalty, supposed to be handed over by Indra to his grandsons Khunlung and Khunlāi. It is prohibited from being beaten except on the day of the sovereign's inauguration.

Barduār, 38, 46, 85, ..., the principal gate of the royal enclosure containing the palace and the secretariat; the name of a vassal state in Kamrup.

Bāreghariā Mahantas, 329, heads of the twenty-four monasteries founded on the principles of Sankardev and Madhabdev, under the inspiration of their grandsons and apostles, Purushottam Thākur and Chaturbhuj Thākur. There are two sets of Bāreghariā Mahantas, viz. Bar-bārejaniās and Saru-bārejaniās.

Bargohāin, 33, 35, 43, ..., one of the three cabinet ministers. The descendants of Thāo-mung-kānangan Bargohāin, who was Sukaphā's assistant in the conquest of Assam, enjoyed the office of Bargohāin. As a matter of convention the Bargohāin was regarded in early days as being mainly concerned with war affairs. The title Bargohāin is also applied to the commander-in-chief of the army of a neighbouring tribe, e.g. Bargohāin Rājā of Jayantā, Alungmingi Bargohāin of Burma. The Ahom Bargohāin's political jurisdiction extended as a matter of convention over the area from the south of the Dikhou river to Kaliābar where his clansmen were expected to live and settle. A relative of the Bargohāin lived at Kaliābar as Solal Gohāin.

Barkāpor, 308, 340, a large coarsely-woven, heavy cloth, worn double, serving the purpose of a wrapper or a shawl for wear in the winter. Size varies from $15 \times 2\frac{1}{2}$ ft. to $27 \times 4\frac{1}{2}$ ft.

Barkuanri, 69, 72, 155, the consort of an Ahom monarch, whose children were entitled for succession. Either the Parvatia Kuanri or the Raidangia Kuanri could be raised to the rank of a Barkuanri. The Barkuanri was an inseparable partner of the monarch in the ceremonies connected with his enthronement.

Barmel, 176, 183, a state meeting attended by the king and his full quota of officers.

Barnāosal, 21, the principal royal dockyard situated at Rangpur ; others being Sākbāri Nāosal at Gargāon, Sarāibāri Nāosal at Mājuli, Negheri Nāosal at Dergāon, Dighalighāt Nāosal at Jaypur.

Barpāni Rājā, 281, literally, the Rājā of Barpāni or the land of large waters ; this title was uniformly applied to the Barphukan or Ahom viceroy of Gauhāti by frontier tribesmen to whom the Brahmaputra offered a marvellous contrast to their petty hill streams.

Barpātra-gohāin Dāngariā, 27, 33, 35, ..., one of the three cabinet ministers. The office was created in the reign of the Dihingia Raja, A.D. 1497–1539, and first conferred on the prince Kancheng. A member of the Barpātra's family was generally appointed as Marangi-khowā Gohāin to control the relations with the Nāgās, Kacharis and Mikirs.

Barphukan, 32, 33, 35, ..., the Ahom viceroy posted at Gauhāti ; entrusted with the civil and military administration of the area from Kaliābar to Mānāhā.

Bar-rajā, 69, 316, title applied to King Siva Singha's three queens, Phuleswari, Ambikā and Sarbeswari, who actually wielded sovereign authority during the period of their husband's disability on astrological grounds.

Barsāheb, 237, 241, 244, title uniformly applied in the Assamese documents of the eighteenth and early nineteenth centuries to the Governor-Generals of British India.

Barsātolā, 188, 190, the head of the Sātolas, or officers appointed by the Adhikār of Dihing Satra for collecting tithes from his disciples.

Bartāmuli, 341, head of the Tāmulis or attendants appointed to look after the supply of betel-nuts ; his duties extended to other spheres as well.

Bartekelā, 26, 297, 308, ..., head of the Tekelās or emissaries of the king and his officers.

Baruā, 40, 50, 54, ..., an officer of the Ahom government of a high rank, being the head of a department or *khel* or *mel* which had no Phukan, or the deputy or second officer of a department which was presided over by a Phukan. The title of Baruā found among the inhabitants of Chittagong is of different origin, and does not imply that its holder is an Assamese.

Bāruati, 136, 139, 319, a shieldsman.

Baruk, Buruk, 17, 290, 304, a petty officer generally entrusted as a courier, errand-man or punisher.

Baswāl, 301, 'A cloth worn over the waist-cloth by officers of the Assam Rājā extending from the waist to the knee and tied to the waist with a cloth girdle'.—*Hema-Kosha*.

Batā, 79, 91, 95, ..., 'A tray with a foot, lower than a *sarāi*, on which betel-nuts are kept for use, or offerings are made to the gods or anything is presented to a respectable person'.—*Hema-Kosha.* It is made of wood, gold or silver, but generally of *Kānh* or bell-metal.

Bāt-bar, 169, a banian tree planted on road-side for shelter and shade to passers-by, constituting a distinct ceremony during the coronation days.

Bebejiā, 41, 348, an Ahom subject whose name does not appear in the records as belonging to any definite unit or *khel*; the Bebejiās were, from time to time, grouped under new units which were named Bebejiā khels, or distributed among the existing units to fill up vacancies or raise their strength.

Bez, 108, 114, 336, a Vaidya or physician ; also used in the sense of a barber in the district of Kāmrup on account of the practice of a crude form of surgery by barbers.

Bhābuki, 325, an earthen pot with a lid.

Bhāda, Bhādra, the fifth month of the Hindu year generally corresponding to August 16 to September 15.

Bhāgavat, 69, one of the eighteen Purānas, in twelve cantos, dealing with the glorification of Sri-Krishna, a cardinal book of Vaisnavism.

Bhāgavati, Bhāgati, 69, a reader and interpreter of the Bhāgavat Purān, attached to a Satra.

Bhāi-rajā, 85, literally a brother king, a term applied by the Shan chieftains to the Āhom Rājā and *vice-versa*, to designate their mutual relationship on the assumption of their common origin.

Bhakat, 191, a disciple resident in a monastery or a Satra having specific functions to render to the institution or to the Adhikār.

Bhandāri, 119, 125, a store-keeper ; an officer in charge of a royal *bhandār* or store ; variant *Bharāli.*

Bhāwanā, 94, 180, a dramatic performance conducted on indigenous Assamese lines with Sutradhār, Gāyans and Bāyans, and almost universally with a Bahuā.

Bhismāshtami day, 167, the eighth day of the bright half of the moon in the month of Māgh when there is a festival sacred to Bhisma, the great Kaurava warrior.

Bhitaruāl Phukan, 56, 67, 73, ..., the Āhom commander in charge of the household troops keeping guard over the royal palace and its precincts.

Bhuni, 308, a dhuti.

Biali-mel, 316, Āhom royal banquet held at night, which presumably served as a political dinner.

Bihu, 183, the last day of Aswin, Poush and Chaitra, which are regarded as festive occasions by the Assamese people of all denominations, marked by interchange of presents and offering of refreshments. The three Bihus are respectively called Kāti Bihu, Māgh Bihu and Bahāg Bihu.

Bijayā-Dasami day, 90, 315, the tenth day of the white moon immediately following the three days of Sāradia Durgā Pujā. This day is marked by the immersion of the Durgā image in tanks, pools or rivers.

Brāhmaniā Gosāin, 146, *see* Bāmuniā Mahanta.

Burāgohāin, 32, 33, 35, ..., one of the three cabinet ministers or Dāngarias. The first Burāgohāin Thāo-mung-kling-lung-mang-rāi assisted the first Āhom prince Sukāphā in planting his supremacy in Assam : and his descendants by right of joint conquest enjoyed the office of Burāgohāin till the termination of Āhom rule. The Burāgohāin was regarded, as a matter of convention, the seniormost member of the cabinet, and his relatives were appointed as frontier wardens at Sadiyā and Kājali. The Burāgohāin was supposed to be the lord over the area extending from the north of the Dikhou river to Sadiyā, and his clansmen usually settled in this area.

Burā-pāchani, 35, 43, head of the pāchanis or attendants of a superior order.

Burkendāz, 222, an armed retainer ; up-country stalwarts and fortune-hunters who constantly pillaged Assamese villages during the eighteenth and early nineteenth centuries.

Chābukdharā, 110, a man in charge of the whip and other instruments of punishment.

Chaitra, Chait, the twelfth month of the Hindu year generally corresponding to March 16 to April 13.

Chaklang, 93, 321, a marriage in the prescribed Āhom form. Vide *Deodhai Asam Buranji*, Introduction, pp. xiv-xv and pp. 134–137.

Chāl-ghugurās, 311, tinkling bells forming part of the decorations of an elephant.

Chamuā, an Āhom subject of a higher status than the Kāri Pāiks. The Chamuās were holders of offices, or were employed as goldsmiths and artizans, and were ordinarily exempted from manual service. They were also called *Apāikān Chamuās.*

Chandra-chilimi, 315, a species of horse generally brown in colour.

Chāngmāi, 302, a cook ; an Āhom *khel*, the members of which served ordinarily as cooks.

Chāngtaliā Hāri, 63, a Hāri or scavenger who worked under the platforms in the residences of Āhom princes and nobles.

Chāodāng, 336, an Āhom clan, the members of which were appointed to inflict punishments on criminals including sentences of death.

Chāringiā Mel, 83, the estate of the Chāring Rājā consisting of the lands, officers, pāiks, etc.

Chāring Rājā, 2, 3, 35, ..., an Āhom title conferred on the nearest male relative of the reigning king. It is equivalent to a dukedom, and in course of time the title was conferred on the heir-presumptive to the throne.

Chatāi-chorā, 79, a court chamber where cane mats were spread (?).

Chekani, 131, a slender bamboo birch or stick.

Cheleng, 296, 297, ..., a sheet of cloth used as a wrapper, worn single, usual size being 9 ft. by 3 ft.

Chengdeo, 79, the tutelary image of the Āhom kings ; its possession implied uninterrupted prosperity and power. It is believed to be 'a jewel set in a cylinder'. Purandar Singha is reported to have sold it at Calcutta during his period of flight. Also called *Chum-cheng*, meaning a precious stone. Some similarity was established between the Āhom Chengdeo and the Hindu Sālagrām.

Choki, 194, Chouki, a frontier outpost, or entrance to a town, duly fortified and garrisoned.

Choladharā Phukan, 177, the officer in charge of the store containing the regalia, consisting of the royal cloaks or *cholas*. This Phukan had also the portfolio of commerce and international affairs.

Chota-bardār, 234, a bearer or a messenger holding a junior rank.

Chota Sāheb, 240, 243, a European officer who is junior in command or authority in military or civil functions.

Dā-dharā Barā, 37, 38, 175, ..., the Barā in charge of twenty soldiers or guards armed with *dāos* or swords.

Dafalā-Bahatiās, 182, 183, Assamese subjects inhabiting the villages on the outskirts of the Dufla hills, whose services were made over to the Dafalās as blackmail. They were first assigned by Gadadhar Singha and formed into a district clan consisting of Āhoms. They gradually adopted the manners, customs and costumes of the Dafalas and could not be readily distinguished from their masters.

Dakshinkul, the part of Assam lying on the south bank of the river Brahmaputra.

Danda, 28, 29, 33, ..., a division of time equivalent to twenty-four minutes. A day of twenty-four hours is divided into sixty dandas.

Dāngariā, 31, 33, ..., a title applied to the three cabinet ministers, the Burāgohāin, the Bargohāin and the Barpātra-gohāin. Its use was strictly confined to these three, though now it is applied to any man of respectability. From *Dāngar*, large or great. The title *Dāngrika*, meaning a *Mahāmātya* or chief minister, appears in old South-India inscriptions.

Dānsāgar, 167, a Srāddha ceremony in which sixteen sets of sixteen articles are given away in charity. Dānsāgar Srāddha is the grandest of all post-funeral religious rites.

Dāo, 38, 42, 75, ..., a cutting instrument, shorter than a sword, with crooked or straight ends, with sharp edge on one or both sides, hafts generally made of wood.

Dekā-Barbaruā, 60, 89, 94, ..., the heir-presumptive to the office of the Barbaruā.

Dekā-gosāin, 49, 228, a Gosāin or pontiff who is nominated for succession to the office of Adhikār, more usually called Dekā-Adhikār ; a senior pontiff of a Satra having chances of succession to the Dekā-Adhikārship or Adhikārship. The Deka-gosāin may be the Dekā-Adhikār, or a Gosāin junior in rank to the Dekā-Adhikār.

Dekāphukan, 14, 36, 73, ..., the title originated from a king's appointment of a favourite of his to the command of six thousand chosen youths or Dekās. There were two holders of this title, one at Rangpur and the other at Gauhati : the latter exercised jurisdiction over Nowgong.

Deodhāi, 54, 79, 181, ..., literally the nurse of the gods : an Āhom priest who offered worship to the deities of the Āhom pantheon in strictly orthodox form. The gods worshipped were Phu-rā-tā-rā, Lengdon, Kāokhām, Lengbin, Lengdin, Phāi, etc. The Deodhāis claim descent from Lāokhri, the Āhom Vrihaspati. Charaideo was the Jerusalem of the Āhoms, and the important worships were performed at the shrine there.

Deuries, 69, 289, Brahman priests attached to a temple or a Satra with specific duties ; the priestly caste of the Chutiās and of several animistic tribes of Assam.

Devatra, Devottar, 81, the tenure applied to lands granted rent-free for the support of a temple.

Dhekiā, 111, a species of edible fern.

Dhuti, 261, a waist-cloth ; a single unsewn piece worn round the waist by men ; also called *Churiā* and *Bhuni*.

Dingā-kheh, 282, Chinese or Manipuri silk (?).

Dolā, 117, 316, 339, the Assamese litter, sedan or palanquin, having no wooden cover, and containing only an oval-shaped hollow boat-like seat with a curved or straight ridge-pole.

Dolā-kāshariās, 37, 38, 110, ..., attendants who walked on either side of a *dolā* as guards to an occupant of distinction.

Dolā-shariā, 211, 272, attendants who walked at some distance of the *dolā* either in the rear or in the van.

Dolāshariā-chorā, 315, 329, the open hall in front of the stalls for the dolās.

Dolois, 181, 270, 290, ..., an astrologer of the Daivajna caste attached to the establishment of a king or an officer ; the superintendent of a temple : a headman of the Jayantiā and Khāsi tribes, etc.

Dopdar 14, 140, 196, ..., the council-chamber, *Darbar-mandir*, and loosely the secretariat of the Barphukan of Gauhāti. From Dufter, *Arabic-Hindi*, an office, and Dufterdār, a minister of great power and importance.

Dowāls, 95, 96, ..., the levy of workers and soldiers for civil and military purposes, consisting of every second man in a unit or *got* of four and sometimes three pāiks or subjects.

Dualiās, 41, same as *Dowāls* : refers also to the officers in command of a *Dowāl* levy : now applied to a junior in rank, as Dualiā Lāt or Lieutenant-Governor.

Dukhariā, 325, an ear-ornament (?).

Duliā, 198, the bearer of a *dolā* or sedan.

Durgotsav, 240, 246, 281, the Sākta festival connected with the worship of Durgā or the goddess of power, generally held in September or October.

Dwārakā, 280, 282, a kind of cloth manufactured at Dwārakā, the city of Sri-Krishna. Dwārakā cloths were imported to Assam from Bhutān (?).

Ekādasi, 44, the eleventh day of a lunar fortnight dark or bright, a day particularly sacred to Vishnu, when fasting is practised by many Hindus, specially widows.

Gābharu, 72, the daughters, daughters-in-law, sisters and nieces of Āhom kings and the wives of his principal nobles : now applied to grown-up girls before their marriage.

Gāmkhārus, 340, bracelets worn by men.

Ganak, 88, 153, 179, ..., a man of the Daivajna caste. *Ganak* literally means a calculator, and hence a man who calculates the future with the help of astrological or astronomical data.

Gandhiā-bhandār, 170, the record-store or archives of the Āhom sovereigns, where diplomatic letters, treaties, records of titles, manuscripts, etc., were preserved, and the contents protected from pests by the fumigation of *Gandhak* or sulphur.

Gāonburhā, 131, 133, the headman of an Assamese village ; a collector of tithes on behalf of the Māyāmarā Satra.

Gāyan, 188, 336, a man appointed to lead or participate in the recital or singing of hymns or devotional songs to the accompaniment of music.

Gelān, 280, 281, a Tibetan or Bhutanese monk or priest.

Gharphaliās, 180, 203, 207, ..., members of a *khel* first formed by Rudra Singha by selecting the robust men of each family. He thus raised an army of 40,000 men.

Ghorā-Baruā, 138, 144, the superintendent of ostlers, the officer in charge of royal ponies, stables and fodder, etc.

Ghorā-chowās, 56, royal jockeys or horse-riders. They were employed as cavalry fighters, and as messengers on horseback during war and peace, from *Ghorā-chowār* or *Ghorā-āchowār*.

Ghorāsāl, 174, royal stable.

Gohāin, 42, 43, 56, ..., a title applied only to the Burāgohāin, Bargohāin and Barpātra-gohāin Dāngariās and the wardens of the frontier, during the period of their office, and the sons of kings and other princes of the Āhom blood royal.

Gomcheng, 280, a fine and glossy variety of Chinese silk or brocade spotted and flowered with figures.

Gosāin, 49, 154, 171, ..., a generic title applied to persons and objects of reverence : a religious instructor ; the head of a Satra ; a sacred image ; a god.

Guru, 247, a preceptor.

Hābiāl Baruā, 124, the Barua or the Āhom officer in charge of forests and forest revenues.

Hāchati, 88, 95, a small piece of cloth used for holding betel-nuts, betel-leaves, lime-pot, knife, etc. : it is generally of muga silk, but occasionally of cotton.

Hājarikā, Hājarikiā, 31, 32, 54, 85, ..., an officer in charge of one thousand men, employed in civil or military operations ; a chiliarch.

Hāris, 63, 251, scavengers.

Hāti-Baruā, 73, 167, 221, ..., superintendent of elephants.

Hati-chungi, a member of a unit of subjects employed in catching and training wild elephants. They had to supply their quota of elephants to the government in due time and order.

Hātimur, 147, 271, a unit of retainers allotted to the Burāgohāin, Bargohāin and Barpātra-gohāin, usually consisting of one thousand men. Each of the first two Gohāins had five *Hātimurs*, while the Barpātra had ten.

Hātisāl, 35, 44, 88, ..., the stable or pilkhānā for elephants : used also as prison.

Hengdān, 110, a straight sword, used by the Shan people ; the royal sabre, an indispensable item of an Ahom king's insignias.

Hilaidāris, 56, musketeers, constituted as a distinct *khel*.

Holi, 57, 60, 62, the Phalgutsav festival, 'a sort of carnival held in honour of Krishna and the milkmaids, in which passers-by are chaffed and pelted with red powder, or drenched with yellow liquids from squirts'.—*Hobson-Jobson*.

Holong-ghar, 33, 45, 60, ..., the house made of Holong wood used in the coronation of an Āhom king. The monarch accompanied by his queen 'sits on a stage made of bamboos, under which is placed one of each species of animal that can be procured, such as a man, an elephant, a horse, a cow, a deer, a hog, a fowl, a duck, a snake, an insect, a fish, etc. The water from nine tirthos or holy places, is poured over the king and the queen, and falls on the animals'.—Martin's *Eastern India*, Vol. III, p. 611.

Jeth, Jaistha, the second month of the Hindu year, generally corresponding to May 16 to June 15.

Jakhariā, 35, an Āhom subject whose duty was to collect or assist in the manufacture of saltpetre for state purposes.

Jālbhāri Phukan, 331, 336, 353, the Phukan in charge of the men working with royal nets for catching fish, deer, tiger, buffaloes, birds, etc.

Jāngphāi, 325, amber.

Jāpi, 92, 246, 260, ... a hat made of wicker-work.

Jarā-patā, 325, a piece intersewn with laces, or having embroidered stripes (?).

Jinkāps, 280, 281, Bhutanese priests or nobles.

Jugi, 58, a mendicant or Sannyasi devoted to the practice of Yoga : a man of Jugi caste whose profession is weaving and extraction of yarn.

Juvarāj, 165, 167, 230, a crown-prince ; an heir-apparent, appointed during a king's lifetime to succeed him on the throne.

Kāka, 111, 325, a species of bamboos generally found on hills, with joints at long intervals.

Kākati, 181, 290, 304, ..., a writer, a scribe, a surveyor, or an accountant. There were several families of Kākatis employed on state duties,—Gargayān, Nāmtiāl, Duarā, Chalihā, Bangāl, Gajpuriā, Tukariā, Abhoypuriā, Sologuriā, Tiro, Manipuriā and Baniā.

Kārchipi, 165, a kind of cloth having embroidery of gold thread, with various kinds of flowers and natural objects portrayed both in the border and in the body of the cloth.

Kāris, 38, 85, 136, ..., the lowest order of Assamese subjects who had to render personal service to the state, so called because they went to war as archers or bow-men, with *Kārs* or arrows.

Kāti, Kārtik, the seventh month of the Hindu year, generally corresponding to October 16 to November 15.

Katakis, 60, 90, 116, ... Envoys of the Āhom government, deputed within the province and to foreign courts. The Katakis were first Āhoms, but were afterwards Brahmans as well from the reign of Pratap Singha, A.D. 1603–1641. There were several families of Brahman Katakis,—Kaliā, Kaupatiā, Khalahiāl, Sitaliāl, Chandi, Bāhbariā, Bokā, Uriyā, Nirah, Pātra-kalāi, Dilihiāl, Ratna-kandali, Mādhab-kandali, Sāgar-kandali, Bar-kandali, Chota-kandali, Birinā, Chaturbhuj, Gadādhar, Ekādah, Thānkuri, Barguru, Haramiāl. The Āhom Kataki families were,—Chiring, Chengeli, Nagā, Bakatiāl, Baghguāl, Rāmu and Lailengiā.

Kalak, 79, an ornament (?).

Kathā-sodhā Phukan, 73, the Phukan whose duty was to put questions in the court on behalf of the king. Perhaps a nickname of a person, and not a title.

Kāth Majindār, 220, a Majindār of the Kāth or Kāyastha caste.

Kāwai, 53, a kind of fish, an anabas.

Keru, 297, an ear-ornament.

Khadāban, 301, a handy receptacle for water (?).

Khārghar, 207; the royal arsenal or emporium of ammunitions, gun-powder, guns and ordnances.

Khārghariās, 227, 313, men employed under the Khārghāriā Phukan.
Khātaniār, 263, an accredited representative of an Adhikār or Mahanta: a favourite, a medium.
Khāt, 225, an estate consisting of lands and retainers.
Khel, 147, 149, ..., a division or unit of Assamese subjects having to perform specific services to the state, presided over by a Phukan or a Baruā, and commanded by the usual gradation of officers, viz. Rājkhowās, Hājarikās, Saikiās, Barās, etc.; an association or fraternity of men having some common social object.
Khulu, 282, a kind of blanket (?).
Khunbāo, 44, a Naga chieftain or headman.
Kilmij, 280, 282, a kind of cloth of scarlet or crimson colour (?).
Kingkhāp, 311, gold brocade, damasked silk, originally imported from China.
Koch, 35, a Hindu caste into which all converts to Hinduism from the different animistic tribes are admitted on conversion. They rank as a regular Sudra caste.
Kocha, 282, a muslin of a close fine texture, as mentioned in *Ain-i-Akbari* (?).
Koshā, 249, a small boat-shaped vessel for holding sacramental water for offering to gods at a Hindu worship; used along with *Arghā*.
Kowanr-Hilaidāris, a unit of Āhom musketeers consisting of princes first created by Khora Raja, 1552–1603. The King selected the handsome youths of the land, gave them a feast and affiliated them to his own family. These newly made princes were provided with gold-mounted guns, and formed into a distinct regiment employed mainly in the protection of the Raja's palace and enclosures, the capital and its environs. There were two divisions,—Bājuā Hilaidāri-kowanrs and Bhitaruāl Hilaidāri-kowanrs.
Kuchi, 282, a kind of cloth (?).
Kukurā-chowā, 336, a royal poultry-keeper. His duties included the determination of fowls or *Kāi-cheng-mungs* as to their fitness for purposes of divination by Āhom priests.
Kunmin, 57, 79, the indigenous costume of the Āhoms, consisting of a turban and a long coat, while *Kun-khā* denotes the *baswāl* and the *tangāli*.
Lālim, 271, the name of a Hātimur or unit of one thousand retainers forming part of the paik allotment to the Burāgohāin.
Lāljang, 301, a kind of cloth (?).
Langar, 331, an anchor.
Lānkuri, 44, a god of the Āhom pantheon: also a god worshipped by several animistic tribes of Assam, parallel to Mahādeva.
Lari-Gohāin, 71, 78, ..., the eldest son of, or heir-presumptive to the office of the Burāgohāin, Bargohāin or Barpātra-gohāin.
Laskar, 283, 303, 306, a soldier or a camp-follower: a headman of the Kacharis.
Lathā, 331, a kind of musk-deer.
Lekhāru, 280, a writer, a scribe, an accountant.
Lemā, 280, 281, a Buddhist priest of Bhutan or Tibet; a Lama.
Ligirā, 147, a male attendant or servant employed in the household of a prince or a noble; feminine, *Ligiri*.
Lo, 29, iron.
Lon-sāl, 58, an emporium or repository of salt.
Maglu, Magalu, Maglou, 89, 93, 107, ..., a term uniformly applied in old Assamese records to the people and country of Manipur: also *Mekhili*.
Māgha, the tenth month of the Hindu year, generally corresponding to January 16 to February 15.
Māgur, 53, a kind of fish.
Mahājan, 34, 50, 52, a religious preacher: the head of a Satra; a trader, a money-lender.
Māh-bhandār, 127, a store or emporium of pulses.
Majaliā, 308, 314, of the intermediate rank.
Majindār, 28, 71, 149, ..., an accountant, a secretary, also *Majumdār*.
Majindār Baruā, 153, 159, ..., an officer with functions resembling those of a king's Private Secretary. He announced royal orders, despatched envoys

to foreign courts, drafted diplomatic epistles, and generally served as an intermediary between the king and his principal officers and nobles.

Matak, 277, an old division of Upper Assam roughly comprising the whole of the Lakhimpur district on the south bank ; also applied to the people of this area. The origin of this name is controversial. Some say Matak means a sturdy, robust man, with meagre human qualities : while others maintain that the Mataks were so called as in their religious attitude, influenced by their spiritual leader the Māyāmarā Satrādhikār, they were all of one opinion, *ek mat* or *mat ek*.

Medhi, 50, 59, ..., the head of a Satra ; an officer appointed by a Satrādhikār (except Dihing and Māyāmarā Mahantas) to collect tithes.

Mehengā, 85, a raised dish with a tripod, used by princes and nobles, also called Māihang ; an altar of plantain trees and bamboos for the performance of Āhom worship by Deodhāis, and also a receptacle of bamboo for offerings in such worship.

Mel, 83, 96, ..., an estate consisting of lands and paiks, duly administered by officers of the government, for the maintenance of the king's children, wives and other near relatives : a conference, meeting or trial ; a royal banquet.

Meldagiā Baruā, 342, a Barua serving in one of the various *mels*, viz. Khangiā, Rāidangiā, Parvatiā, Purani-mel, Na-mel, Māhi-mel, Enāighariā, Gābharu-mel, Kalicheng, Chāringiā, Tipamiā, Nāmrupiā, Āmguriā, Sarumeliā, Mājumeliā.

Meldagiās, 96, men forming part of the paik allotment of the various *mels*.

Mit-dāo, 88, a straight *dao*, used by some hill tribes, e.g. Duflas, Khāmtis, etc. *Mit*=dāo.

Moāmariās, 59, 119, 128, ..., disciples of the Moāmarā or Māyāmarā Satra, who rose in arms against the Āhom government.

Morāns, 109, 111, 112, ..., one of the original tribes who lived in Assam before the advent of the Ahoms ; they were disciples of the Māyāmarā Satra, took up arms against the Āhom government to avenge insults and humiliations.

Mul, 96, 110, 145, ..., a levy of men consisting of the first man of every *got* or unit of four or three paiks.

Nāg, 34, a sacred pillar planted in the centre of a newly excavated tank.

Nāmdāng, 282, a kind of cloth (?).

Nāmghar, 200, 210, literally a house of prayer, a hall of congregation for the Hindu residents of a village where Bhāwanās or dramatic performances of the older fashion and other religious and even secular functions are held.

Nāobaichā Phukan, 22, 35, ..., the Phukan in charge of boatmen.

Nāo-sāl, 219, a dockyard : a repository of boats. See *Barnāosāl*.

Narā-pirā, 97, 319, a raised wooden seat, in vogue among the Naras, from whom the Assamese possibly got the pattern.

Nat, 69, a Hindu caste devoted to music and dancing.

Nupurs, 311, small tinkling bells.

Nyāya-sodhā Phukan, 144, 148, literally, the enquirer of truth, the officer of the Āhom government who presided over judicial matters ; chief justice.

Ojā-ligirā, 302, the head of the servants in attendance upon a king.

Ostāz, 86, 94, an expert artificer : a teacher of any of the arts and crafts ; a superintendent of any branch of engineering.

Outengā, 111, dilennia.

Pāchani, 190, 250, an attendant of a higher order.

Pāik, 85, 113, an enrolled adult subject of the Āhom government having specific duties to render to the state.

Pakighar, 167, a masonry building built of brick or stone.

Pālighar, 170, guard-house in the immediate vicinity of the royal palace, a waiting house for officers having duties at the court or the royal enclosures.

Panchami tithi, 1, the fifth day of either the light half or dark half of a lunar month.

Pandit, 44, 59, 333, a scholar, a man learned in the scriptures, philosophy, literature or religion.

Pāni-duār, 190, 194, a sluice-gate : the gate or door opening towards a stream or canal.

Pāni-phukan, literally the Water-phukan, the Āhom officer exercising judicial, revenue and military jurisdiction over the North Bank of Kamrup. He served under the Barphukan with headquarters at Aswakrānta in North Gauhati.

Parvatiā Kuanri, 38, 70, 153, ..., one of the principal queens of an Āhom monarch, whose sons were entitled to succession. Kuranganayani, wife of Rajeswar Singha was the first Parvatiā Kuanri, so called as she was the daughter of the Manipur Raja, whose kingdom lay in the midst of *Parvats* or hills.

Parvatiā Phukan, 54, 202, ..., the officer in charge of the estate allotted to the Parvatia Queen for her maintenance.

Pāsouj, 92, or Khol, a kind of drum of a longish shape generally used in Assam for religious and semi-religious functions.

Patding, 301, a kind of cloth (?).

Pātghar, 83, 126, ..., literally, a throne or timber house; the house with timber platform where the first ceremony connected with the coronation of a king is performed. 'The Raja and his queen first enter the Pātghor, where some water is poured on them from a shell called Dokhyinaborto Songkho, the mouth of which is turned the way contrary to that of the shell, which is usually sounded by the Hindus, in order to attract a little notice from the Gods.'—Martin's *Eastern India*, Vol. III, p. 611. The term is also applied to the Singarighar where the king formally sits on the *Pāt* or throne.

Patukā, 297, 300, ..., spotted cloth for headwear ; a waist-band (?).

Phāgun, Phālgun, the eleventh month of the Hindu year, generally corresponding to February 16 to March 15.

Phāku-yātrā, 60, see *Holi*.

Phālgutsav, 240, 246, ..., see *Holi*.

Phukan, 31, 32, 33, ..., the head or superintendent of a *khel* or a *mel*, whose strength ranged up to 6,000 men, according to the importance of the unit. A word of Āhom origin. Some departments or units had only a Baruā, and no Phukan at the head.

Phul-baruā, 33, 60, the superintendent of the royal flower gardens.

Piprangā, 282, a blanket of reddish-brown colour resembling the skin of some ants (?).

Prahar, 66, 136, ..., one-eighth part of a day ; one prahar is equal to three hours.

Puh, Push, Poush, the ninth month of the Hindu year, generally corresponding to December 16 to January 15.

Puraniā Bhakat, 198, an appellation of the disciples of the Māyāmarā Satra, so called because its founder Aniruddha Dev preferred to walk by an old approach-road to the house of his host Gopaldev, in preference to the new road constructed by the latter for the use of his guest.

Purani-mel, 198, literally the old *mel*, a name applied to the estate for the maintenance of the Purani-melia queen, who was third in rank among the royal consorts, the first two being the Rāidangiā Kuanri and Parvatiā Kuanri.

Puthi, 59, a manuscript : loosely applied to any book, printed or handwritten.

Rāidangiā Phukan, 147, 336, the officer in charge of the Rāidangiā mel or estate allotted for the maintenance of the chief queen of an Āhom sovereign.

Rajkhowā, 31, 38, 60, ..., an officer having jurisdiction over a prescribed area or unit of paiks, in command of three thousand men. 'The Rajkhowas attend the court of justice, and are employed as umpires to settle disputes, and to superintend any public work for the king.'—Martin's *Eastern India*, Vol. III, p. 614.

Rājmantri, 331, ... or Prime Minister : a title applied to the head of the council of the three Gohāins. The Rājmantri enjoyed the services of an additional allotment of paiks, viz. one thousand men of Jākāichuk.

Rāj-māo, 180, ..., queen-mother.

Rāsa, 264, the dance or sport practised by Krishna and the Gopis.

Sabāh, 68, a congregation of people for religious or semi-religious purposes, marked by the chanting of hymns and singing of chapters of the scriptures.

Sāgar-Barā, 183, 287, a title applied to the administrator of the Mājuli area in Upper Assam ; literally means an Ocean-Bara, on account of the numerous character of the streams of Majuli and its constant exposure to floods and inundations.

Sahariās, 143, 198, men belonging to a district, or ecclesiastical unit organised for the realization of tithes, a city or a group of villagers ; in Darrang it meant an officer employed on administrative and revenue work.

Saikiā, a commander of one hundred paiks.

Sāka, 45, the Hindu era founded in 78 A.D. by Kāniksha Sakāditya, also known as Sālivāhan.

Sakā-Sākini, 45, a female demon attendant on Durga ; the name applied to a flood in Assam in A.D. 1691, for its ravaging character.

Sālagrām, 69, a black stone which contains a fossil ammonite and is chiefly found near the village Sāla-grāma on the river Gandaki ; this stone is sacred to and is worshipped by the Vaishnavas and supposed to be pervaded by the presence of Vishnu.

Sankrānti, 133, the passage of the sun to a new sign or position : the last day of a Hindu month.

Sarāi, 79, 279, 290, ..., a platter or tray mounted on a rounded and tapering pedestal, usually higher than a *batā*, a receptacle for offering articles to persons and objects of reverence, generally made of wood or brass. In matters of precedence the Sarāi stands higher than the Batā.

Sāri, 291, a single sheet of cloth constituting the main item of dress of a woman in some parts of India, specially Bengal. It is wrapped round the body and then thrown over the head.

Saru-mel, the estate for the maintenance of the Sarumelia Raja.

Sāstra, 95, a scripture : any book of religion or reverence.

Sātin, 301, a closely-woven silk with a lustrous and unbroken surface, sometimes figured.

Satra, 41, 49, 50, ..., an Assamese Vaishnava monastery, consisting of the Adhikār, barracks for his Bhakats, a small image of Vishnu or of one of his incarnations, the *Bhāgavat* or any allied scripture, a wooden throne-like dais, chāmar, canopy, a big circular drum or dabā, and a nāmghar.

Satranj, 282, a carpet or floor-cover of coarse texture.

Sāwan, **Srāvan**, the fourth month of the Hindu year, generally corresponding to July 16 to August 15.

Senāpati, 110, the commander of an army.

Simalu, 106, a silk-cotton tree, lofty and thorny with red flowers, *Salmalia Malabarica.*

Singari-ghar, a house of Singari wood where the formal enthronement of an Āhom king takes place. There he receives the homage of his nobles, officials, subjects, and feudatory chiefs, accompanied by the exchange of ceremonial presents. A king who has not performed the ceremony of ascending the Singari-ghar was called a Suleng Raja, and was not regarded as a full-fledged sovereign.

Srāddha, 68, 78, ..., a ceremony in honour and for the benefit of dead relatives observed with great strictness at various fixed periods, constituting an act of reverential homage to dead relatives.

Sudra, 59, a man of the fourth of the four original classes or castes among the Hindus.

Swargadeo, 32, 40, 60, ..., literally the God of heaven, a title adopted by and applied uniformly to the Āhom sovereigns of Assam ; a shortened form of Swarga-narayan-dev, the progenitor of the family of the Ahom monarchs, who was born of Indra, through a mortal mother. The title is also attributed to the fact that the first princes Khunlung and Khunlai, grandsons of Indra, came down from heaven to rule this earth in 568 A.D. This heaven of the Ahoms is possibly China, and the Ahom word for heaven is *Chin*. In contemporary Mogul documents the Ahom kings appeared as Swargi-raja or Swarga-maharaja. Swargadeo is a title of Brahmanical origin, the Ahom equivalent being Chāophā, *Chāo*, a god or king and *Pha*, heaven.

Talachā, 311, a sheet of cloth spread over a mattress or a quilt.

Tāmol-katā, 289, a personal attendant of a noble whose chief function was to maintain a constant supply of betel-nut, but it extended to other duties as well.

Tāmuli-chorā, 339, an ante-chamber, prior to the general hall of audience.

Tāmuli-ligirā, 154, 218, a ligira of a higher rank in attendance upon the king. He supplied betel-nut to the king in a golden *batā*.

Tāmuli Phukan, 159, 190, ..., the superintendent of the royal parks or orchards.

Tangāli, 301, a cloth belt, a girdle, a waist-band, used by males only, usual size 4 yds. × 6 inches, having the two ends embroidered with ornaments of silk or gold wire, or red cotton thread.

Tāngani, 185, a definite area, or a number of villages grouped together for administrative purposes ; a piece of a sugarcane.

Tāobān, 279, a vase or receptacle for water (?).

Tekelā, 35, 88, ..., an emissary or a messenger attached to the staff of an Ahom officer despatched for the execution of public duties. In Kamrup such a man was called a Sārā, and in Bengal a *Piādā* or a *Peon*.

Temi, 102, a lime-pot.

Tengchol, 308, a scarf (?).

Thān, 280, 282, ..., a long piece of cloth.

Thākuriā, 48, 69, pertaining to a Satra founded by Sankardev's successors Purushottam Thakur and Chaturbhuj Thakur ; a revenue officer in Kamrup with some amount of administrative and judicial authority.

Til-kusa, 41, sesamum seeds and blades of the sacred grass, *poa cynosuroides*, constituting the essential ingredients of a Hindu worship.

Tithi, 82, a lunar day : anniversary of an early Vaishnava reformer, e.g. Sankardev, Madhabdev, Damodardev, Gopaldev, etc.

Toka gumuni, 282, a species of cow mainly imported from Bhutan (?).

Tokon, 120, a thick stick, a club.

Ukil, 152, 303, an envoy, a representative of a foreign court.

Uttarkol, 267, the country lying on the north bank of the Brahmaputra.

INDEX.

[NOTE.—The figures against the entries refer to the paragraph numbers, and *not to the page numbers*; and this somewhat novel system has been adopted to obviate alterations in future editions of the book. The Index has been made complete and exhaustive; and every proper name, whether it be the name of a person, place, office or institution, has been inserted here to present a full pageantry of the times of the Tungkhungias. Future compilers of encyclopædias and national biographies will find in this Index a ready-made nucleus for expansion and elaboration; and the possession of accurate information on each one of the entries in the Glossary and the Index will provide a suitable stimulus to students of Assam history.—*S. K. B.*]

THE END.

Government of Assam.

Department of Historical and Antiquarian Studies.

Honorary Provincial Director :
MR. A. H. W. BENTINCK, C.I.E, I.C.S., M.A. (Oxon.).

Honorary Assistant Directors :

MR. J. P. MILLS, I.C.S., M.A. (Oxon.), for the Surma Valley Division.

PROF. S. K. BHUYAN, M.A., B.L., for the Brahmaputra Valley Division.

"The Assamese are justly proud of their national literature. In no department have they been more successful than in a branch of study in which India, as a rule, is curiously deficient. The historical works, or *Buranjis*, as they are styled by the Assamese, are numerous and voluminous. According to the custom of the country, a knowledge of the *Buranjis* was an indispensable qualification to an Assamese gentleman."—*Sir George Abraham Grierson, Linguistic Survey of India.*

"The Department of Historical and Antiquarian Studies is doing very valuable work in publishing the Buranjis and similar old records and in stimulating the interest of the people of Assam in the past history of their country."—*Sir Edward Gait,* June 26, 1933.

PUBLICATIONS FOR SALE.

The Department has published several old Assamese historical masterpieces, edited on most up-to-date lines by Professor S. K. Bhuyan. Each book is furnished with Preface and Introduction in English and Assamese; an exhaustive Table of Contents; and Marginalia against every paragraph; and *Asamar Padya-Buranji* has, besides, an elaborate Synopsis in English. Publication No. 6, viz., *Tungkhungia Buranji : A History of Assam, 1681–1826 A.D.*, is the first English translation of an Assamese chronicle.

1. **Assam Buranji.**—A History of Assam, from the commencement of Ahom rule to the British occupation of Assam in 1826, being an enlarged version of the chronicle of Kasinath Ṭamuli Phukan, by the late Srijut Harakanta Sarma-Barua Chaudhuri Sadar-Amin, pp. xxii + 152. Preface in English, pp. i to v; preface in Assamese, pp. vii to xiii. Prescribed as a text-book in Assamese Vernacular for the Intermediate Examinations in Arts and Science of the Calcutta University. Cloth bound, with gilt letters on front and spine, price Rs. 2-8 per copy; and paper bound, Re. 1 per copy.

2. **Kamrupar Buranji.**—A History of Kamarupa, from the earliest times to the cessation of hostilities with the Moguls in 1682 A.D. The book contains a detailed contemporary account of the conflicts with the Moguls, and of the early relations of the Moguls with Assam and Cooch Behar, with 18 contemporary epistles between the Ahom and Mogul courts. The appendices to the book contain valuable accounts of Kamarupa compiled from the manuscript records of Buchanan-Hamilton, etc. With a contemporary portrait of Nawab Mir Jumla. Preface in English, pp. i to vi; Preface in Assamese, pp. vii to xii. Pp. xvii + 152. Prescribed as a text-book in Assamese Vernacular for the B.A. Examination of the Calcutta University. Cloth bound, with gilt letters on front and spine, price Rs. 2-8 per copy; and paper bound, Re. 1 per copy.

3. **Deodhai Asam Buranji.**—A History of Assam, from the earliest times to the accession of Jayadhwaj Singha in 1648 A.D., written in conformity with Ahom traditions, being the translation of an old Ahom Buranji ; with a number of shorter chronicles,—*Bahgaria Buragohain's Buranji*, compiled by Atan Buragohain Rajmantri Dangaria, Prime Minister of Assam, A.D. 1662 to 1679 ; *Datiyalia Buranji* or an account of the Ahom relations with neighbouring chieftains ; accounts of the ceremonies of Ahom marriages, hawk-flights and burials ; an account of the official functions of Daivajnas or astrologers ; early history and traditions about the Koches, Kacharis, Jayantias, Chutias, Naras ; conflicts between the Nara and Mantara ; the first Ahom sovereign Swarganarayan, and the Mikirs ; with a complete list of Ahom Kings and a table for converting *Laknis* or years of the Shan Aijepi calendar to their corresponding Hindu *Sakas*. Text with marginalia, pp. 1 to 222 ; Preface and Introduction in English, pp. iii to liv, Introduction in Assamese, pp. lv to lxx. Cloth bound, price Rs. 3 per copy.

4. **Asamar Padya-Buranji.**—A Metrical Chronicle of Assam, comprising, *1st*, Dutiram Hazarika's *Kali-bharat Buranji*, or a History of Assam from the accession of Sulikpha Ratnadhwaj Singha Lora Raja in 1679 to the transfer of the territories of the Honourable East India Company in 1858 ; and *2nd*, Bisweswar Vaidyadhipa's *Belimarar Buranji*, from Captain Welsh's expedition to Assam in 1792 to the victory of the Burman forces at Khagarijan or Nowgong in 1819. Assamese text with marginalia, pp. 1 to 278 ; Synopsis in English, pp. 279 to 308 ; Preface and Introduction in English, pp. iii to xvi ; Introduction in Assamese, pp. xxix to lv. Cloth bound, price Rs. 3 per copy.

5. **Tungkhungia Buranji.**—Assamese Version. A Chronicle of the Ahom Kings of Assam of the Tungkhungia Dynasty, being the chronicle of Srinath Duara Barbarua with prefatory chapters collated by the editor. From the accession of Gadadhar Singha to the eleventh year of the reign of Kamaleswar Singha, 1681 to 1806 ; with an account of the period of disruption, 1671 to 1681. Contains valuable accounts of the reigns of Gadadhar Singha, Rudra Singha, Siva Singha, Pramatta Singha, Rajeswar Singha, Lakshmi Singha, Gaurinath Singha and Kamaleswar Singha. Assamese text with marginalia, pp. 1 to 186 ; Preface and Introduction in English, pp. iii to xxvii ; Introduction in Assamese, pp xxxv to xlvii. With four-coloured contemporary portraits of King Siva Singha and his Queen regnant Maharani Amvika Devi. Cloth bound, price Rs. 2-8 per copy.

6. **Tungkhungia Buranji.**—A HISTORY OF ASSAM, 1681 TO 1826 A.D. English translation of the above by Prof. S. K. Bhuyan, with supplement bringing down the history to the end of Ahom rule in 1826. With Introduction, Genealogical Tables, Bibliography, Glossary and Index. Published by the Oxford University Press for the Government of Assam in the Department of Historical and Antiquarian Studies. Pp. xxxii+262. Cloth bound, Rs. 10 per copy.*

7. **Bulletin No. I.**—Report on the Work of the Department with a Hand-list of Manuscripts and Transcripts, with a Foreword by His Excellency Sir Laurie Hammond, Governor of Assam, 1927-1932. Pp. 48. Price Re. 1 per copy.

8. **Bulletin No. II.**—*In the Press.*

The above books can be had of : Srijut Basudev Misra, B.A., Assistant, D.H.A.S. Office, Gauhati, Assam, India.

---

* *Tungkhungia Buranji : A History of Assam, 1681–1826 A.D.*, can be had of the publishers,—Oxford University Press, India and England.